Democracy and Lawlessness

Hans Petter Graver

Democracy and Lawlessness

The Penitentiary Laws and Civil Disobedience in Norway 1928-1931

Springer

Hans Petter Graver
Department of Private Law
University of Oslo
Oslo, Norway

ISBN 978-3-031-69054-9 ISBN 978-3-031-69055-6 (eBook)
https://doi.org/10.1007/978-3-031-69055-6

Translation from the Norwegian language edition: "Tukthuslovene Sivil ulydighet og trusselen mot rettsstaten" by Hans Petter Graver, © Dreyers forlag 2024. Published by Dreyers forlag. All Rights Reserved.

This Springer imprint is published by the registered company Springer Nature Switzerland AG
The registered company address is: Gewerbestrasse 11, 6330 Cham, Switzerland

Contents

Chapter 1
Grandfather

1.1 The Paradox: A Law Abiding Criminal

Grandfather was a convicted man. Still, he was a man of honor. Not only was he a man of honor, but he was also an auditor. First as municipal auditor in the city of Rjukan, then as head of audit in the Norwegian Confederation of Trade Unions, LO. An auditor enforces the law. An auditor must be of impeccable character, reliable and accurate. He was also a member of the Tinn municipal council and the conciliation board for tax complaints. He had the trust and was one of the pillars of his community.

Grandfather was proud of many things, his children, grandchildren and much more. He had been on the Norwegian aid committee for Spain and organized support for the Spanish people during the civil war against Franco. During the second world war, he continued in his position in the nazified LO and was the liaison to the illegal Trade Union Committee, which coordinated the resistance work in the trade union movement. An important task was to protect LO and the confederations against the National Socialist rulers supplying themselves from the union coffers. He protested when the nazified leadership wanted to use LO's money to support *Nasjonal Samling* (NS, Quisling's Party) and their activities. NS started tapping the Shipping Association instead, perhaps they met less resistance there.

But one of the things he was proud of puzzled me. He was proud he had a criminal record. On 9 August 1928, Tinn District Court sentenced him to pay a fine of NOK 50. This corresponds to approximately NOK 2000 today (200 Euro). Good money for a father with a wife and 3 children to support in a time of economic hardship and wage cuts. He was born in 1893, so there was no question of any youthful sin. As an adult, he had committed a crime for which he had been punished, and he was proud of it.

For me as a young law student, this seemed strange. Not only was he proud, but he told of it to a youth at the start of a legal career. What kind of respect for law and

H. P. Graver, *Democracy and Lawlessness*,
https://doi.org/10.1007/978-3-031-69055-6_1

justice would this instill in the future jurist? My grandfather was a person I looked up to.

"There was no true justice. It was class-domination by biased law," said grandfather. At that time, it was the Marxist-Leninists who talked about class oppression, class judges and student-worker unity. They went around the reading rooms and canteens at the university and collected money for striking workers at *Norsk Hammerverk*, *Norsk Champignon* and *Vinmonopolet* and talked about armed revolution and support for *Khmer Rouge* in Kampuchea. But grandfather had little sympathy with them, moreover, no one was at this time subjected to punishment, neither the striking workers themselves nor the sympathizing students. Had grandfather been like the Marxist-Leninists in his youth? I couldn't get that to add up.

1.2 Partial Courts and Class Rule?

Nor did my grandfather's statement about biased law agree with what I learned as a young law student. I knew of course about the revolutionary line of the Labor Party and its connection with the Russian Revolution in the early 1920s. I also knew that prominent Labor Party politicians and communists, such as our later Prime Ministers Einar Gerhardsen and Oscar Torp, the labor leader Martin Tranmæl and a number of others, had been sentenced to prison terms in the great military strike case (see Rt. 1924 p. 861) for having encouraged conscripts to refuse to perform military service.

A case against the communists Kyrre Grepp, Olav Thorsen and Rudolf Nilsen was central to the syllabus. The three were accused of having introduced communist propaganda from Russia. As there was no law which expressly forbade this, the prosecution had brought charges under a law which regulated the importation of various types of goods. The law was given to regulate the importation of goods during the First World War to secure supplies to the country and protect the country's economy under the conditions that prevailed during the First World War. The Supreme Court acquitted the accused.

Strong accusations about class justice and about courts being an instrument of the capitalist ruling class have over time been directed at the judicial apparatus. These accusations assert that the courts are not independent and neutral. Generally, such claims lack substance in the history of Norwegian law, although there are certain notable exceptions (Ringvej 2005). Our highest court was fairly balanced in dealing with opposing viewpoints in the class struggle, writes Erling Sandmo, author of the major work on the history of the Supreme Court of Norway in the twentieth century, refuting claims that the court was an instrument of class domination (Sandmo 2005, p. 246).

In May 1928, over 4000 construction workers went on strike to protest an arbitration award that reduced wages and collective agreements by between 12 and 21 percent. 1928 was a dark year for the Norwegian labor movement. Unemployment was high, the workers' organizations were divided, and the workers had had to endure several years of declining wages. The authorities had already stopped strikes with forced arbitration for several years, and so this time too.

The striking workers received wide-spread sympathy and support. Since the strike was illegal, the trade unions could not support them financially or in any other way. A new law made them liable to pay damages to the employers if they did not do everything within their means to prevent and contest illegal actions. The unions therefore had to publicly distance themselves from the strike. As the striking workers were not formally unemployed, they received no support from the welfare services, and there was great hardship. The government even issued an order to the local governments not to support the striking workers or their families. But support groups were organized, and money was collected for strikers and their families, even though this was a criminal offence under the new laws. The support came from all over the country, including the small industrial town of Rjukan, up in the mountains of southern Norway. The town is famous for its innovative production of fertilizer from thin air, with the aid of hydro-electric power.

We let professor and Rjukan historian Helge Dahl narrate the events (Dahl 1984, p. 163):

> On 12 June 1928, *Rjukan Arbeiderparti og Samorganisaison* (The Labor Party and the local coordination body between the party and the trade unions) organized a mass meeting with speeches by Kristian Hansen (chairman of *Rjukan Arbeiderparti*) and Jakob Friis (editor of *Rjukan Arbeiderblad*, the local newspaper of the labor movement). The meeting joined the protest that had been raised around the country against the two laws (Arbitration Act and Penal Code § 222 II), expressed its warmest sympathy for the construction workers' action and recommended the trade unions to give the strikers all possible support. Furthermore, the meeting decided to start a fundraising. 1,100 people contributed and were named in the *Rjukan Arbeiderblad*. Shortly afterwards, the police cracked down and fined 100 people. The next day they fined another 100.

According to *Arbeider-Avisa*, a socialist newspaper, this was the worst job the police had experienced, "because everywhere they are met with sneer and laughter".[1] The encounters had repercussions in the courts when those fined refused to accept the fines.

Dahl continues: "In August, Dalastøl (Knut Dalastøl, business manager of *Rjukan Arbeiderblad*) and municipal auditor Torjus Graver stood before the district court in Tinn. One had contributed 3 kroner, the other 2. The court was administered by magistrate Egil Elster, the prosecutor was police chief Berg, and the defense lawyer Emil Stang, the well-known Labor Party politician. Lay judges were not summoned as the prosecutor claimed that it was difficult to obtain lay judges who would not allow political consideration to come into play."

The Criminal Procedure Act had been amended in 1927, with a rule that lay judges should only be summoned in misdemeanor cases "if the court deems it necessary". The judge could therefore refrain from summoning lay persons. Dalastøl and Grandfather each represented their group of fined, those who had been fined NOK 100 and those who had been fined NOK 50. The magistrate wanted these two

[1] Arbeider-Avisa Tuesday 3 July 1928.

as test cases before the rest, in groups of 5 and 5, were to be summoned until all 200 who had received fines had received their judgment.

Further, according to Dahl: "The two defendants used the opportunity to agitate against the arbitration law and even lectured the court on Ricardo's iron law of wages. The preliminary injunction was upheld for both, and they were also ordered to pay NOK 10 each in legal costs. They appealed the verdict all the way to the Supreme Court."

This is how Helge Dahl describes it. David Ricardo was one of the nineteenth century's most influential economists. He had a great influence on, among others, Karl Marx. His "iron law" stated that wages in an unregulated capitalist market would always remain at the level of subsistence and would not rise higher.

After the verdict, a protest meeting was held in the community house, where lawyer Emil Stang, who had represented the accused, and editor Friis of the *Rjukan Arbeiderblad* spoke to a full house. The meeting adopted the following resolution:

> Workers at Rjukan, gathered for a meeting in a number of around 400, strongly object to Magistrate Elster's arbitrary behavior during the trial against two of the workers' trustees. First, the magistrate refused to let the workers have their case dealt with according to a democratic legal principle, as he failed to summon lay judges. But apart from this, the verdict that has been handed down is a mockery of the perception of justice of the entire working population of Rjukan.[2]

"Friis wrote an outraged editorial as a comment on the judgement," continues Helge Dahl. "Among other things, he pointed out that the enragement over the unfair sentences was probably going to be felt in the workplace. The workers' awareness of the law meant nothing to the small group of people in power who owned the factories and the law and the villas, and thus also the chief of police and the magistrate."

The meeting threatened with strike if any of the convicted were to be sent to prison. Of course, they would not pay voluntarily. *Telemark Arbeiderblad* gave the following comment: "Considering that legal proceedings are pending against 300 of the approximately 1000 contributors, the resentment that the first judgment triggered will undoubtedly grow over time and could entail the most serious consequences."[3]

Could this be the whole story? Did they try to punish people for having given a few kroner in support to people who otherwise were going to starve? A fundraiser had been held, and many people had made contributions. Why in particular did grandfather and one other person end up in court, had they done something that does not appear in the story, which could justify prosecution and punishment?

---

[2]Telemark Arbeiderblad Saturday 11 August 1928.

[3]Telemark Arbeiderblad Saturday 11 August 1928.

1.3 In Search of an Answer

Trying to find an answer to this led me to the history of the penitentiary laws. In connection with the description of these laws professor of constitutional law and legal philosophy Frede Castberg wrote that the laws contributed to sharpening the revolutionary attitude in large parts of the labor movement and that "within large parts of the labor movement, however, the hope and belief on a revolution was a reality" (Castberg 1974, p. 77). He quoted the young Einar Gerhardsen, later prime minister, who had said that all legal avenues are closed to proper working people who are starving and freezing. "They have the choice between going under or following the only path that remains: Through the law to the prisons. Follow it!".

Gerhardsen, Tranmæl and the others were political agitators with ties to the international workers' movement. But grandfather? He was a farmer's son from simple circumstances in the rural county Telemark, from a deeply religious background, who had secured an education and a respectable position as municipal auditor.

Today nobody talks about class struggle in Norway, and law and the legal order is generally in high trust and accepted as neutral. But we do not have to go far before we find conflicts and battles over the legal institutions. Those in power in highly polarized societies such as Hungary and Poland use the law to enforce their policies and attack the courts. If we travel back in time, we find episodes in our own history where the court and the courts were an arena for political struggle. It was to the penitentiary laws that I had to go to learn about the use of the court as a partisan instrument in the social struggle in Norway, a struggle which politicized both the law and the courts in a way that we see in countries like Poland and Hungary today. By studying what happened back then, we can learn something about how our own society and legal order react when the autonomy of the law is put under pressure.

It was with the penitentiary laws as a background that later law professor Kristen Andersen wrote in 1932 (Andersen 1932, p. 32):

> It is not at all recommendable that the legislators seek to deprive one party in the conflict of the most important means to assert its interests, without the same authorities at the same time doing anything to strengthen or improve this party's position. This approach does not achieve any solution, but on the contrary an intensification of the conflict.

The story of the Penitentiary Laws is the story of how the legislature, by promoting one party's cause in a strongly polarized society, threatened the autonomy of the legal order. The conservative side set the rule of law at stake to protect employers' interests against an increasingly strong working class and trade union movement. But the judicial system reacted in a way that the conservatives saw as resistance to the laws. It is striking how a legal complex, in the public and in the courtrooms, with participation far into the judiciary, right up to the Supreme Court, engaged against the attack on the law's autonomy. Threats and accusations of illegitimate interference in the functioning of the courts were made in the Norwegian Parliament (Stortinget), in the conservative press, and in municipal councils around the country.

This is a situation we recognize from today's Poland and Trump's USA. The Norwegian rule of law was at a tipping point.

The history of the penitentiary laws is therefore not only part of the history of the labor movement, but also of the history of the Norwegian rule of law, a history of the relationship between law and politics. It is a story about when, in our recent past, the court became part of a polarized struggle between battling social forces. Antagonisms were great across Europe at the time. An absolute and irreconcilable contradiction between social classes' conception of law will sooner or later, "if no reconciliation is achieved, turn into a struggle with physical weapons," wrote the renowned professor of jurisprudence Ragnar Knoph in 1923 (Knoph 1923, pp. 28–29). In many countries it went wrong, and fascist regimes developed to fight the working class. In Norway, this development stopped, the state did not step up the use of force to enforce laws which in their content were both biased and contrary to basic justice. The Penitentiary Laws put both democracy and the rule of law to the test, and the country emerged stronger from it.

This is a story about civil disobedience, and how it can strengthen democracy and the rule of law. The Swedish legal sociologist Håkan Hydén has emphasized that civil disobedience is always a signal that there are conditions in society that the legislators have overlooked or have not considered (Hydén 2022, p. 211). When the law is profoundly unjust, even law-abiding citizens may feel justified in breaking it to convince those in majority of its injustice. This is the text-book example of civil disobedience, as, for example, the famous philosopher John Rawls defines it in his classic work on justice. Just democratic institutions can also occasionally produce unjust results, and majorities in democratic bodies can converge on solutions that turn out to be wrong. In such cases, breaking the law can be both justified and morally praiseworthy, and it can do democracy a service, according to Rawls. Civil disobedience stabilizes and strengthens democracy, he claims. The fight over the penitentiary laws joins the series of examples that prove Rawls right. This is the story that this book tells in the following chapters.

The book is one result of my work on Judges under Stress—the Breaking Point of Judicial Institutions.[4] For several years, I have investigated the methods authoritarian rulers use to force judges to apply oppressive and unjust legislation and how judges respond to such pressure (Graver 2015). Under what conditions is the rule of law brought to its knees? The work has taken me to the fascist and Nazi Europe of the nineteen thirties and forties, the communist regimes of the Cold War and the current pressure on the courts in countries such as Poland and Hungary.

Apart from during the German occupation, Norway has not had an authoritarian regime in modern times. The courts are highly trusted as independent and neutral, and the *Storting* or the government have to little extent challenged them. If one were to find situations in Norwegian history where the independence of the courts and

---

[4]Judges under Stress JuS - the Breaking Point of Judicial Institutions - Department of Private Law (uio.no).

trust in the judges were threatened, I thought that one would have to go to the great class struggle in the period between the First and Second World Wars.

I had a notion that the judicial system at that time, more then than now, was the target of political controversy. A sign of this was that the Labor Party several times put forward proposals to limit judicial review with legislation. In addition, my grandfather, who for a large part of his life worked in the federation of trade unions (LO), told me about oppressive legislation and about courts that applied them biased and uncritically. My grandfather's story is part of this book, as an example of the many who threw themselves into an illegal fight against unjust laws.

I found what I was looking for. In 1927, the Storting passed a set of laws which changed the rules of the game between the employers and the workers, by turning the legal order into a tool for one social class in the fight against the other. Thus, the legislators deviated from the classic rule of law ideals of equality and autonomy of the law. These laws were called the Penitentiary Laws, based on a conception of earlier German law where striking workers were brought to the penitentiaries. The passing of these laws led to a forceful reaction from the labor movement and from people far beyond it, who refused to accept the legitimacy of the laws and who engaged in mass violations of the law. It also led to demands in the trade union movement to take control of the courts. The laws were perceived as the politicization of the law in the service of Capital, which had to be met with politicization from the labor movement. This could have led to the collapse of the rule of law in Norway, with the end of a neutral and independent judiciary.

The penitentiary laws and the fight against them have been extensively reported, both at the time and in later historical works. Even though what I am presenting is well-known, I have not found any corresponding in-depth treatment of the political and legal material. Putting the conflict in a rule of law perspective, as I do, involves a new look at the political history and legal history of the interwar period and gives a deeper understanding of the relationship between law and politics.

In 1927, Supreme Court judge Edvin Alten wrote an opinion about the independence of the courts. Here he commented on the appointment of judges and lay judges. "Any political consideration, any thought of party reward must be banned by those who are responsible for the selection og judges," he wrote. "Not all municipal councils and not all governments can say they are free of having sinned against this requirement."[5] Political appointments and attempts to fill the courts with judges loyal to a particular political party are a negation of the rule og law. I started with a hypothesis that the Labor Party, to sabotage the law, used its power to gain political control over the courts, and that many jurors refused to apply the law by acquitting cases where the law had clearly been violated and the defendant was guilty. Thus, the labor movement succeeded in sabotaging the law by appointing lay judges who were loyal to the movement. This was what the great authority in constitutional law, Professor Frede Castberg, wrote in his book "Law and revolution in Norway" (Castberg 1974, p. 74). When I checked in the proceedings of the Storting, this

---

[5] Dagbladet Saturday 11 June 1927.

was confirmed. It was also the story the conservative party and the farmers' party put forward in their election campaign in 1930. The events therefore seemed well suited to shed light on what happens when there is a political battle over the courts and the judges come under political pressure. My study of the sources proved this to be a false track.

The source material for this book is reports and propositions from the government to the Storting, the debates in the Storting, court rulings, contemporary literature and the press. I have also made use of secondary literature to a certain extent. Thanks to the digitalization of virtually all newspapers by the Norwegian National Library, a vast of material on court cases and debates in local government councils is readily available.

Investigations of the elections in the municipal councils for lay judges in 1928 and 1931 showed that the allegation of political abuse of power was consistently incorrect, while investigations of legal practice confirmed that there were several acquittals. However, these were mostly due to the courts interpreting the laws restrictively in relation to what the parliamentary majority had assumed when they passed the laws, i.e., that it was the professional judges and not the lay judges and members of the jury who were the cause of the acquittals. The labor movement had no role in the appointment of professional judges.

Thus instead, a fascinating story emerged about the effects of civil disobedience against unjust majoritarian decisions within liberal democracy and the workings of a legal complex to defend the court's autonomy against partisan legislation. The book tells this story.

References

Andersen K (1932) Streik og arbeidsboikott efter norsk rett (Strike and labor boycott according to Norwegian law). JW Cappelens forlag, Oslo

Castberg F (1974) Rett og revolusjon i Norge (Law and revolution in Norway). Universitetsforlaget, Oslo

Dahl H (1984) Rjukan, volume 2: from 1920-1980. Tiden, Oslo

Graver HP (2015) Judges against justice on judges when the rule of law is under attack. Springer, Berlin-Heidelberg

Hydén H (2022) Sociology of law as the science of norms. Routledge, Oxon. https://doi.org/10.4324/9781003241928

Knoph R (1923) Rett og rettsbevissthet (Law and legal consciousness). Olaf Norlis forlag, Kristiania

Ringvej M (2005) Høyesteretts unntakstilstand og Marcus Thranes revolusjon (The Supreme Court's state of emergency and Marcus Thrane's revolution). In: Michalsen D (ed) (Unntakstilstand og forfatning Brudd og kontinuitet i konstitusjonell rett). Pax Oslo 2013

Sandmo E (2005) Siste ord Høyesterett i norsk historie 1905-1965 (Last word Supreme Court in Norwegian history 1905-1965). Cappelen, Oslo

Chapter 2
The Years of Great Struggle

2.1 Law and Industrial Action

The first major legislation on labor-capital disputes in Norway was the Labor Disputes Act of 1915. This law brought the law into the conflict between labor and capital. Until then, the relationship between employers and workers was largely a private relationship between the parties. The formation of trade unions was not prohibited but was often opposed by the employers. Attempts by the labor movement to obtain legal protection for the right to organize were repeatedly taken up in the Storting (the Norwegian Parliament) but voted down.

The Labor Disputes Act was not a biased piece of class legislation, and it was not intended to prevent the implementation of the labor movement's demands (Ousland 1975, p. 328). All this changed with the penitentiary laws of 1927. Then the capital-owning class succeeded in turning the law into a weapon against the working class and shifted the class struggle into the legal order. Under such conditions, the law loses its character of neutrality, and its character of being relatively independent of other social and political processes in society is challenged. That is what happened in 1927–1928, in the legislation and in the courts.

The important legislation on mediation, arbitration and the creation of the labor court, the Labor Disputes Act of 1915, was not the result of any hostile thinking towards the workers and their organizations. On the contrary, the law was a codification of the development that the parties had stood for, it was a "society-grown law", as Professor Kristen Andersen wrote in his book on the history of the Labor Disputes Act (Andersen 1965, p. 120).

The Labor Disputes Act established a framework for resolving conflicts between employees and employers. It introduced the distinction between legal disputes and interest disputes, which is still the main distinction in modern collective labor law. Legal disputes concern the validity, understanding or existence of a collective agreement or about claims based on a collective agreement. Interest disputes are

H. P. Graver, *Democracy and Lawlessness*,
https://doi.org/10.1007/978-3-031-69055-6_2

disputes outside collective agreements, such as about having a collective agreement created or revised, about the right to organize, wages or other matters.

The law established the obligation to observe peace in legal disputes. It was forbidden for the parties to use strikes or lockouts in such conflicts, they were to be brought before the Labor Court. For disputes of interest, the Act established certain procedural rules as a requirement for the parties to submit to mediation. But otherwise, the disputes of interest were and are the domain of the struggle between employers and employees.

In the time of this book, the late nineteen twenties and early nineteen thirties, the class conflict invaded the law. As the trade union's power increased, the employers' side searched for means to counter this. The period from 1921 to 1931 has been characterized as "The Years of Great Struggle" marked by major labor conflicts and the introduction of anti-worker legislation (Ousland 1975). It started with a major conflict in 1921 and ended with the largest lockout ever in 1931.

Both on the conservative side and in the labor movement, there was a wing that stood for crushing the other and a wing that stood for cooperation (Seim 1972, pp. 206–207). In the labor movement, the division was between those who sought revolution, the communists, and those who sought to improve workers' conditions through negotiations and legal reforms, the social democrats. From the mid-1920s social democracy was the line of the majority of the Labor Party and the trade union movement, while the Communist Party stood for revolution. Among the conservatives, the distinction was between those who wanted to stifle the labor movement through the criminalization of the labor struggle and those who accepted the trade unions as useful channels for the workers to advance their interests through. Of the right-wing parties, the conservative party and the peasant party were the most uncompromising, while the liberal party supported negotiations and reform of capitalism to promote social aims.

It was a period when the radical part of the employers and the conservative parties, with the support of state, were on the offensive against the trade union movement (Falkum 2008, p. 216). However, the radical wing of the conservatives had a short-lived impact. The decade was characterized by mass unemployment and wage cuts forced by the employers. The supply of "willing to work" during labor disputes was large, which led to great resentment among the organized labor movement. Strike-breakers were considered the worst of the wretched, described as "bloodsuckers" and "more wretched than the father or mother who follows their 16-year-old daughter to the rich horny glutton" (Hansteen et al. 2015). Physical combat was not uncommon and many a strike-breaker was given a real thrashing. On the right, there were fascist-like groups creating disturbances and political violence.

The crises in the period after the First World War weakened the trade unions and increased the level of conflict. Conflict was also increased by the revolutionary ideology inspired by the Communist Party's rise to power in Soviet Russia. The conservatives responded by seeking to employ criminal law in the regulation of industrial action. With this, the conflict between labor and capital challenged the neutrality of the legal order. The criminal law was given a clear bias as it was in practice aimed unilaterally at the workers' use of their means of struggle. The development culminated with changes to the law in 1927, which aimed to put an end to strikes and harassment of strikebreakers, and which were named the Penitentiary Acts. These marked a qualitative change in the legal regulation of the struggle between labor and capital and made the legal system itself an arena of struggle.

Illustrative of how the conflict played out in the legal system is an interview that LO's chief lawyer Trygve Lie gave after the great lockout in 1931, which gives a snapshot of industrial action in the courtrooms.

The headline was: "After the lockout. Heaps of lawsuits in the pipeline."[1] "It has never been as bad as now," said Trygve Lie. "The State Mediator's unclear proposal creates controversy." The great lockout came after the stock market crash in 1929 which plunged the world into an economic crisis. The employers began negotiations in 1931 by demanding a 20 per cent wage cut. The trade unions responded by demanding a reduction in working hours. The employers refused to conduct any real negotiations and went to a systematic lockout, industry by industry. Over 60,000 workers were out of work for over 5 months. The time was characterized by demonstrations, conflicts and battles against strike breakers that the companies brought in to be able to keep their business going with unorganized workers. Unemployment was huge, therefore there were plenty of people willing to take the jobs. One of the most famous conflicts in connection with the lockout was the Menstad battle in the city of Porsgrunn, which had a background in Norsk Hydro's use of strike breakers to get goods transported out of the plant (Johansen 1977). The later notorious Vidkun Quisling was Minister of Defense and sent 5 warships and 2000 troops to Menstad.

After 23–24 weeks of conflict, the parties accepted a proposal from the State Mediator, and the conflict was over. But this was only the beginning of the battles in the courts. Trygve Lie explains that there are legal cases related both to the understanding of the agreements the parties had entered into and to the prosecution of workers after the conflict. "The Penitentiary Act is in operation all over Eastern Norway," tells Lie.[2]

There were 29 cases brought before the labor court. Of criminal cases, Lie mentioned the cases following the Menstad conflict. He also mentioned a criminal case against the Labor Party chairman Oscar Torp for having signed the party's anti-military petition. The editor of the newspaper Ny Dag in the city of Gjøvik was prosecuted for defamation in connection with newspaper articles about the situation of emergency in rural villages. Lie highlights 7 criminal cases for breach of the penitentiary clause of the criminal code. Among other things, former Member of Parliament Edvard Endresen from Lillehammer was charged in connection with demonstrations against the conservative newspapers in Lillehammer during the lockout. One case, which he highlighted as particularly interesting, was an indictment against some conscript soldiers who had refused to carry out blocked work when blasting timber in the Snarum River between Lake Krødern and the Drammen

[1]Interview in 1 May, Saturday 7 November 1931.

[2]Interview in 1 May, Saturday 7 November 1931.

River. He also mentioned a case that the trade union had brought against the municipality of Hole in Ringerike. The council refused to support a worker and his family when he refused to accept work that was blocked by the union. He had previously applied for work at the plant without getting it, but when the plant was hit by a strike, they wanted him. The authorities used hunger to break solidarity between the workers.

Many of these lawsuits resulted from the state using legal repression in response to the labor movement's demands for social change and better conditions. The authorities have always used the law to put down rebellions and radical demands, this was also the case in Norway at the beginning of the twentieth century. But as the workers organized, and the trade union grew strong, the employers mobilized to crush the trade union movement. This they did by using lockouts and by putting in strike breakers, and they also appealed to the law for help. And they got the help they wanted. While the law had largely remained neutral to the struggle between labor and capital, contenting itself with establishing a framework to prevent it from having too great socially destructive consequences, in 1927 the law was put in the service of employers. This meant that the struggle spread into the legal apparatus and threatened the autonomy of law.

The penitentiary laws led to demands in the trade union movement to take political control over the courts through the appointment of lay judges. This led to accusations from the conservatives that the courts ruled politically rather than based on the law. None of the positions recognized or accepted the autonomy of the legal process.

An autonomous, that is independent, legal order is a prerequisite for a society to be governed by the rule of law. In an autonomous legal order, legislation is created by political processes, while it is the legal order itself that decides on the interpretation and the application of the laws. To a certain extent, law is also created within an autonomous legal order, both by the fact that the courts and lawyers must decide on questions that the legislation does not expressly resolve, and by the fact that the laws can be adapted and reshaped in response to the diverse development of society.

This process is independent and self-driving, both through recognition of the separation of powers principle that the state's other authorities must not intervene in the decisions of the courts, and through the fact that judges must act independently and impartially. It is also autonomous be the law being practiced by a separate profession, the lawyers, who have their own separate base of knowledge and their own method for understanding and interpreting the law. The method must satisfy requirements for intersubjectivity and rationality, so both methods and results must be justified as far as possible using recognized arguments and logical inferences.

Another important element of the rule of law is equality. "Our time recognizes (. . .) that society does not have the right to knock the weapons out of the hands of the warring parties without giving them the means to enforce their rightful demands," wrote the chief justice of the Supreme Court Paal Berg in his text-book on labor law in 1930 (Berg 1930, p. 29). The penitentiary laws departed from this. Laws that fundamentally break with the basic elements of the legal order are an attack on the autonomy of the law. The penitentiary laws approached such legislation, both through their one-sided favoring of employer interests, which was a breach with the rest of the system which strived for a certain form of neutrality, and through the criticism the courts were met with in their application of the law. Section 222 II of the Criminal Code "hit with punishment such boycotts of workplaces that were carried out by otherwise legal actions", writes Frede Castberg (Castberg 1974, p. 73). How should such provisions be applied in the rather tough confrontations that could arise between striking workers and strikebreakers?

Appointment of judges based on purely political considerations challenges the independence of the judiciary. This is the case if lay judges and jurors, through membership in an organization or in some other way, are bound or required to rule in a certain way. The penitentiary laws led to demands from trade union members that the labor movement exercise control over the lay judges. When the struggle between the warring classes was brought into the law, both parties challenged law's autonomy.

2.2 Organization and Strike

"Norwegian law has always recognized the right of association. It has never been considered illegal or unlawful for workers to join in trade unions for the protection of common interests. According to Norwegian law, trade unions have had the same legal capacity as all other associations. And it has not been illegal or unlawful for the unions to use the work stoppage as a means of coercion against the employers in the fight for working conditions." This Paal Berg wrote in his book labor law (Berg 1930, p. 27). Berg was formerly a politician for the liberal party and chairman of the Labor Court. When he wrote this, he had just taken up his post as a president of the Supreme Court, the country's foremost and most prestigious legal position.

The battle over the penitentiary laws formed the background when the law-professor Jon Skeie, a liberal and one of the great names of Norwegian jurisprudence, wrote in 1931: "It should not be necessary nowadays to highlight or further justify, that it is also of the greatest importance for society as a whole to avoid everything that creates bitterness and increases class antagonisms." (Skeie 1931, p. 519).

Despite the great conflict between labor and capital that emerged with the industrialization of society, the courts, led by the Supreme Court, had taken a relatively neutral position in the struggle. Strikes were a legal means of struggle, and with them also blockades and boycotts to ensure the strike's effectiveness. The Supreme Court was "very careful in setting up legal barriers to the use of these means of warfare", wrote Kristen Andersen (Andersen 1932, p. 41). The Supreme Court was, in the political battles fought between the social classes, "a liberal court that fulfilled its function", which saw it as its "task to contribute to the fact that the political battles are fought in a fair and just manner," according to Erling Sandmo in his great work on the history of the Supreme Court in the twentieth century (Sandmo 2005, p. 228).

This was the case until 1927, when the majority of the Storting made the law directly an instrument in the class struggle. The legislation was and was perceived as directly anti-union, as a means of crushing the power of the workers' movement (Hansteen 1927).[3]

The changes to the law in 1927 effectively removed both the possibility for workers to have support of the trade unions and to use strike as a means of struggle. The government was given a broad mandate to impose compulsory arbitration in wage disputes. The authorization in practice became a ban on the use of strikes as a means of fighting for reasonable wages and working conditions. The law made unions financially responsible for the consequences of an illegal strike unless they actively opposed it, thus crippling the trade unions.

In addition, the Act criminalized any activity aimed at preventing strikebreakers from replacing workers on strike, whether the strike was illegal or not. "A strike that cannot even be accompanied by a blockade of the company in question is, however, a highly questionable means of struggle. And strike is not a particularly valuable weapon for the strikers either, when the employer can dismiss them without the risk of losing access to new labor," wrote the later pioneer of Norwegian labor law, Kristen Andersen (Andersen 1932, p. 3). With the changes to the law in 1927, "one party was handed over unarmed to the arbitrariness of the other party," as Paal Berg put it (Berg 1930, p. 29). Admittedly, this comment was not made as a direct comment on the penitentiary laws, but the relevance was clear enough.

Today, Norway does not penalize breach of the duty of peace in industrial relations. The penal provision was repealed in 1956, as the last remnant of the penitentiary laws (Hem 2012, p. 727). Trade unions can still be held liable for damages for an illegal action under Section 9 of the Labor Disputes Act, but only when the union is to blame for the breach. It is also possible for the courts to relax this liability according to § 10 of the Act (Hansteen et.al. 2015 chapter 15). Expressing support for an illegal conflict or to raise funds to support striking workers is not forbidden. Nor is it illegal to harass or intimidate strike breakers or otherwise influence them to stop working, unless this is done with the use of violence or threats of unlawful behavior, see section 251 of the current Criminal Code.

We also have no general law which gives the government the right to decide that wage disputes must be resolved by compulsory arbitration. On the other hand, it is still recognized by law through long practice that the authorities can intervene and stop an otherwise legal strike. However, for this to be legal today, the Storting must adopted legislation for each case. The power to prohibit strikes thus cannot be delegated to the executive, and the freedom to adopt such legislation is limited by the Constitution and international human rights.

Another important difference is the use of the criminal justice system to prevent labor disputes, and that the regulations at the time were also aimed at weakening the workers' right to organize. In addition, the penal provision went far to limit the freedom of expression, by criminalizing any public support for illegal conflicts.

[3] Hansteen (1927) also contains a reprint of the laws in question.

We must keep in mind that the level of conflict between labor and capital was much higher at that time. This also applied to the level of conflict between the left and the right in politics. We are in a time in Europe where the fear of revolution and communism was widespread, a time that led to the rise of fascism and authoritarian rule in many countries of Europe.

2.3 The Penitentiary Laws

The so-called Penitentiary Law was actually three laws. Firstly, new rules in the Labor Disputes Act which extended and tightened criminal liability for participation in and incitement to illegal strikes and which made the trade unions financially responsible for losses the employer suffered as a result of the action. Particularly important was section 4 which determined that "if members of a trade union or employer's association have broken a collective agreement or have been guilty of an illegal work stoppage, the association is liable, unless it proves that it is not itself to blame for or through the means at its disposal, has sought to prevent the breach or continuation of the collective bargaining agreement or the illegal work stoppage." In form, the provision was aimed at both employees and employers, but in reality, it was unilaterally aimed at crushing illegal actions by the workers. The provision prevented union support to workers in conflict, and effectively deprived them of the possibility of acting collectively to further their interests towards the employer.

Furthermore, there was section 40 no. 1 b, which made it a criminal offence for anyone "who encourages to start or continue, support with contributions, or who supports or collects or distributes collected contributions to its implementation (i.e. the illegal work stoppage or illegal work closure) or continuation or who contributes to this." In addition, it was a criminal offense to take part in deciding on an illegal action. This made the expression of public support for an illegal strike in the media or by other means a crime.

Secondly, the addition of a new chapter in the Labor Disputes Act on compulsory arbitration in interest disputes. The temporary law determined in § 1 that "if the King finds that such a dispute as the Act on Labor Disputes § 6 no. 3 mentions, exposes significant public interests to danger, and mediation has been tried in vain, the King may - on the opinion of the State Mediator - decide that the dispute shall be settled by arbitration. (...) When the King has decided that a dispute is to be settled by arbitration, the King can also prohibit any implementation or continuation of work stoppages on the occasion of the dispute." This effectively deprived the workers of the legal opportunity to use strikes to advance their wage demands.

And finally, an addition to Penal Code § 222 on coercion, which criminalized almost any measure intended to stop strikebreakers from working. Thus, even the workers who were legally on strike could not prevent the employer from taking in other workers willing to work in their place. In this way, the strike weapon lost its power at the same time as it was criminalized.

The new rule in Section 222, second paragraph of the Criminal Code read as follows:

> With fines from NOK 25 to NOK 25,000 or imprisonment of up to 1 year, whoever intentionally causes or seeks to cause someone to opt out or give up their work or to not apply for work . . .,
>
> a. by harassing him or his household with threats or violent, insulting or intrusive behavior,
> b. by following him from place to place,
> c. by providing public information about who is working or has worked or has applied for work during a work stoppage,
> d. by hindering him in his work or acquisition through inappropriate behavior.

The provision was given to "protect the individual's right to work".[4] The Penal Code aimed to criminalize several conditions when used as means in the workers' struggle for their interests, that otherwise fell outside the general prohibition against illegal coercion in Section 222. Among other things, publishing the names of strikebreakers, picketing, and going to the homes of strikebreakers to encourage them to stop working was forbidden. Of course, striking workers also occasionally used harsher measures such as threats of beatings and direct physical confrontation. However, this was already prohibited through the Criminal Code's general provision on unlawful coercion, threats, and physical insults. Now the criminal law extended to "intrusive" and "inappropriate" behavior.

With this, one of the most effective means that workers had in a labor dispute, namely measures to prevent others from performing the work of the workers on strike, was criminalized. It pulled the teeth of the trade union movement; it knocked the tools out of the workers' hands. The provision was aimed at the workers' most important tool in the fight for wages and better working conditions, namely the solidarity among working people. The law was therefore a great moral provocation. Strikebreakers were considered traitors, and legal provisions that protected them against measures that were otherwise legal in society were bound to create ill blood and aggravate the class struggle.

2.4 The Case of Zacheus Selj

Publishing the names of strikebreakers had been standard practice for many decades and had not been considered illegal. This was confirmed by the Supreme Court as late as in the case in Rt. 1931 p. 129. The case concerned a compensation claim that Zacheus Selj had submitted on the occasion that he had been named and shamed as a strike breaker. On 9 May 1924, Zacheus Selj's name was included on a list in "*Arbeiderbladet*" which had the heading "The striped dockworkers". On 6 June of the same year there was a notice in the same newspaper: "Strikebreaker Sakeus Selj, Vestbygaten 7, does not live there but in Nydalen" signed by the Brewery Workers'

[4] Ot. prp. No. 54 1924 Om utferdigelse av en lov om forandring i straffeloven p. 1.

Strike Committee. On 11 June, the newspaper had a notice with the heading: "Information" signed by the Brewery Workers' Strike Committee. This stated: "Strikebreaker Zacheus Selj, Vestbygt. 7, does not live there, but apparently lives in a hotel. The family must not be molested – it is their son who is wicked." For this last notice, the leaders of the strike committee and the editor of the newspaper were sued at Oslo City Court, which sentenced them to pay compensation to Zacheus.

Seil had originally turned to the ministry and the Storting in vain to receive compensation, see Inst. S. no. 162 1925. When he did not get it, he asked both the government and the Storting for legal aid to bring forward compensation claims, see Inst. S. no. 141 1926. Also, this was denied. The case ended up in the Supreme Court, which ruled four to three judges that it was not illegal to name and shame Zakeus Selj. On behalf of the majority, Supreme Court judge Schjelderup stated that the notice was a regular part of the labor dispute to increase the effectiveness of the strike. "In a case of this nature, where one does not have a positive law to adhere to, but where in society there were and still are strongly divergent opinions about the justification for using the disputed and other means during a labor dispute, I think the courts should be extremely careful in declaring unlawfulness," stated Schjelderup. Using the term "strikebreaker" was not illegal. This was an adequate expression of the fact that the person concerned carried out blocked work during a strike.

In his report on the provision for the Criminal Code Council from 1931, professor of criminal law Jon Skeie argued that the provision did not otherwise entail anything particularly new, as all the actions mentioned in Section 222 II would, in Skeie's view, already be punishable under the current provisions of the Criminal Code (Skeie 1931, pp. 496–499). This was contrary to the view of most of the legislators who certainly intended for the new law to criminalize otherwise legal behavior. The adoption of the provision quite clearly led to the use of the police and courts against workers in labor disputes to a far greater extent than previously.

The Supreme Court thus did not follow the legal opinion that professor Jon Skeie had expressed in his report on illegal means in the fight for working conditions from 1931, where he had stated that the publication of the names of strikebreakers would be contrary to the penal provision in § 250 on violation of privacy (Skeie 1931, p. 350). The judgment is therefore a clear example that the Supreme Court did not always interpret the law against the working class. From a legal point of view, it would have been clearly arguable for the court to reach the opposite result. In this case most of the court did not side with the employers, even if this would have been possible within the law.

With the adoption of the new paragraph to § 222, the law was changed. The new law gave those persons who took up employment with an employer during an industrial action protection from having their names published. The law was crystal clear here, which was confirmed by the Supreme Court in 1934 (Rt. 1934 p. 442). Here there was no possibility of misunderstanding or misinterpreting the law.

Neither were the trade unions in doubt that the new laws broke with previous legislation and case law. LO's chief legal officer, Trygve Lie, later Minister of Justice, Minister of Trade, and Minister of Foreign Affairs, and the UN's first Secretary-General, said at the annual trade-union congress in 1927: "It has never before been a criminal offense to inform the public of strikebreakers. Nor has it been a criminal offense to influence strikebreakers to give up their 'occupation'. That workers have the right to establish a boycott against unorganized workers has been beyond argument. Section 222 of the Criminal Code is therefore contrary to the entire current legal opinion and contrary to a number of Labor Court judgments and Supreme Court judgments.[5] He continued: "Following the passing of the new laws, the trade unions have had to put themselves above the law and the best way to fight today is to show that these laws are not being respected."[6] In other words, the lawyer, and the later Minister of Justice and General Secretary of the United Nations, Trygve Lie, advocated for breaking the law to combat it.

The labor movement, and thus large sections of the population, regarded the provisions as illegitimate and at odds with general legal consciousness. They did not regard the laws as binding law, but as an expression of the legislative power being used by the ruling class to break the organized labor movement. The laws contravened the basic principles of justice, of equal treatment and equal opportunities. While the employers' weapons in the conflict over wages and working conditions remained untouched, the workers were deprived of theirs.

2.5 Laws of Exception and Civil Disobedience

The Labor Party described them as laws of exception. By this they meant that they departed from the general principle of equality before the law. The penal provision did not protect the right to work in general, only the right to take up work during conflict when organized workers refused to work. Everybody's right to work was not protected. It did not prohibit employers' blacklisting of workers who had participated in strikes, and they were often denied work after a conflict. According to the philosopher John Rawls, a law that fundamentally violates the two basic principles of justice; equal basic liberties and social and economic differences that satisfy the requirements of equality of opportunity and the difference principle, can be violated with full moral right, even if it has been democratically adopted (Rawls 1972, pp. 363–391).[7] Such a law lacks legitimacy. This was the case with Section 222 II of the Criminal Code, thought great parts of Norwegian society.

The laws not only challenged the legal consciousness in broad sections of the population, who perceived them as instances of class justice. They also challenged the professional lawyers' perception of the law as neutral. "Among those who have had the opportunity to closely follow our latest jurisprudence regarding coercion in labor disputes, it is probably a general opinion that the judges - and not just the lay judges - have been influenced in their assessment of evidence by the hateful

[5]LO Kongressen 1927 Agenda and minutes p. 233.

[6]Op. cit p, 234.

[7]pp. 363–391.

atmosphere, which is built up against the 'penitentiary law'," wrote Skeie in his report (Skeie 1931, p. 520). Thus, he could claim that the legislation had not strengthened, but on the contrary weakened the legal protection of strike breakers. The perception of the law as biased, targeting one social class to protect another, was widespread far beyond the ranks of workers and socialists. It clearly caused discomfort for lawyers and others who were trained to believe that equality before the law is fundamental to the rule of law.

The instance of the Penitentiary laws is a perfect example of civil disobedience in the theory of the well-known political philosopher John Rawls. He defines civil disobedience as "a public, non-violent, conscientious, yet political act contrary to law usually done with the aim of bringing about a change in the law or politics of the government" (Rawls 1972, p. 364). According to Rawls, civil disobedience is a political action where the purpose is to influence the state to change its policy or laws. Rawls treats civil disobedience in the context of his general theory of justice. His starting point is that even if society has built institutions that satisfy the principles of justice as far as possible, they will in some cases produce results that are contrary to these. Basically, people still owe loyalty to the institutions, but there are certain exceptions. If a policy or a law fundamentally contradicts the principle of equal liberties or equal opportunities, breaking a law to draw the majority's attention to this may be justified.

Civil disobedience in liberal political theory presupposes a society based on the principles of justice with just institutions, i.e. a society based on democratic legitimacy, in the words of Rawls, a "nearly just society" (Rawls 1972, p. 363). In such a society, says Rawls, civil disobedience strengthens institutions and contributes to stability, by counteracting injustice and helping to correct it when it occurs (Rawls 1972, p. 383). As we shall see, Norway emerged strengthened from the conflicts surrounding the penitentiary laws. Ultimately, the authorities treated the labor movement's offenses with tolerance, which should be shown towards civil disobedience that satisfies the justice principles of Rawls (Dworkin 1977, p. 260). This is an important reason why this conflict between labor and capital did not escalate.

References

Andersen K (1965) Arbeidskamp og arbeidsrett et 50 årsjubileum (Labor conflicts and Labor Law A 50 years Anniversary). Johan Grundt Tanum forlag Oslo

Andersen K (1932) Streik og arbeidsboikott efter norsk rett (Strike and labor boycott according to Norwegian law). JW Cappelens forlag, Oslo

Berg P (1930) Arbeidsrett (labor law). Olaf Norlis forlag, Oslo

Castberg F (1974) Rett og revolusjon i Norge (Law and revolution in Norway). Universitetsforlaget, Oslo

Dworkin R (1977) Taking rights seriously. Duckworth, London

Falkum E (2008) Makt og opposisjon i norsk arbeidsliv (Power and opposition in Norwegian working life), Doctoral theses defended at the Faculty of Social Sciences, University of Oslo No. 128, Oslo

Hansteen C, Kambestad S-Ø, Monsen HC, Stueland E (2015) Interessetvist og arbeidskamp (Dispute of interest and labor conflict). Gyldendal, Oslo
Hansteen V (1927) Tukthuslovene Fagorganisasjonen under offentlig administrasjon (The penitentiary law, the trade unions under public administration). Andelsforlaget Ny Tid, Oslo
Hem P (2012) *Megleren: Paal Berg* 1873-1968, (The Mediator: Paal Berg 1973–1968) Aschehoug, Oslo
Johansen PO (1977) Menstadslaget, (The Menstad Battle) Tiden norsk forlag, Oslo
Ousland G (1975) Fagorganisasjonen i Norge 2 De store kamp-åra 1921-1931 (The trade union in Norway 2 The great fighting years 1921-1931). Tiden, Oslo
Rawls J (1972) A theory and justice. Oxford University Press, Oxford
Sandmo E (2005) Siste ord Høyesterett i norsk historie 1905-1965 (Last word Supreme Court in Norwegian history 1905-1965). Cappelen, Oslo
Seim J (1972) Hvordan hovedavtalen av 1935 ble til (How the main agreement of 1935 came about), Tiden Oslo
Skeie J (1931) Ulovlige midler i kampen om arbeidsvilkår (Illegal means in the fight for working conditions). Det Mallingske bokgtrykkeri, Oslo

Chapter 3
The Creation of the Penitentiary Law

3.1 The Praeludium

Attorney General Bernhard Getz was the first to consider and propose criminal sanction for preventing others from doing the work of striking workers.[1] He did so in 1896 in a report for the Ministry of Justice, commissioned by Prime Minister, and his close friend, Francis Hagerup from the Conservative Party. Getz was a brilliant jurist, a great law reformer, and conservative. Among other things, Getz was for a time mayor of Oslo. He was, according to his biographer Adler Vogt, "strongly interested in politics and closely followed the politics of the day." (Vogt 1959, p. 173) His attitude to political issues was "decidedly conservative".

On 15 April 1896, members of the justice committee and the committee for social issues at the Norwegian Parliament (Stortinget) submitted a proposal for a provision on punishment for employers who sought to interfere with the workers' freedom of opinion and association.[2] The trade union movement was still week, and many employers opposed workers' attempts to organize. Workers who took the initiative to form or lead unions were often fired (Skeie 1931, p. 351). Therefore, the workers appealed to the state for protection of their right to organize.[3]

Proposal for such a provision had already been made in 1881 by the fifth Norwegian workers meeting in the city of Drammen. In 1893, the proposal was sent to the Storting from the executive board to the Norwegian Workers Party. On 7 July 1896, the parliamentary committee gave its recommendation on the proposal.

---

[1] Kristen Andersen gives a detailed overview of the legal and political discussions that led to the enactment of the protection of "freedom of work" from 1894 to 1927 in Andersen (1967), pp. 307–349.

[2] See document no. 85 for 1896.

[3] Hansteen et al. (2015), pp. 290–292 give a brief overview of the attempts to have the right of association enshrined in law.

H. P. Graver, *Democracy and Lawlessness*,
https://doi.org/10.1007/978-3-031-69055-6_3

A majority was in favor of the proposal and presented a bill on "protection of workers' political rights and associational life". When the matter came up for consideration in Stortinget, the chairman of the committee was on leave, and the Speaker therefore proposed that the matter be postponed to a later session. The motion was unanimously approved.

In connection with the proposal, prime minister Francis Hagerup requested a report from the Criminal Code Council. Attorney General Bernhard Getz answered this inquiry on behalf of the council on 16 May 1896. The report was sent to Stortinget and printed as an appendix to the committee's proposal.

Getz believed that the proposal to protect workers' political rights and union life in effect prohibited the employer from engaging in political discussions with its workers. Such a ban would not only protect the freedom of opinion and organization but could also prevent the employer from safeguarding its own legitimate interests. Getz feared that the law could be abused by anyone who was fired or not promoted to claim that this happened for political reasons, and the employer would be defenseless against such accusations. Getz believed it would enable workers to "put the dynamite bomb under the factory at the first strike that breaks out".[4]

The behavior the bill aimed to ban was largely "innocent, yes, even praiseworthy", Getz stated.[5] There was therefore no reason to support a proposal for a ban. Getz also pointed out that unions were often unscrupulous towards workers who allowed themselves to be summoned by the employer to work in place of striking workers. Innocent workers would be subject "to the despotism of the trade unions and declared pariahs", with whom the other workers would have nothing to do.[6]

Getz's attitude was clear. It was neither necessary nor desirable to limit activity by employers to prevent workers from organizing. What should be limited, on the contrary, was actions taken by workers to prevent others to work in their place during conflict. The law should protect the employers' ability to keep the company going during a strike. Employers would be defenseless against the unions if the proposal were to be adopted. The employer would be "forced to tolerate the trade unions and their members, without the union members being subjected to any limitation in their right to refuse to tolerate others."[7] Getz had no understanding of the inequality in power relations that existed between employers and employees in the nineteenth-century labor market, or that the law can be used to protect the weaker party without it being biased.

Getz also pointed out that instead of protecting unions, many countries had provisions that criminalized organized behavior to influence wage formation and to prevent others from working, i.e. rules which protected the freedom of work and industry. He skipped over the fact that the international trend had been that many countries with bans on trade union organization had lifted these bans.

---

[4]Tillegg til dokument no. 85 for 1896 p. 5.

[5]Tillegg til dokument no. 85 for 1896 p. 3.

[6]Ibid.

[7]Tillegg til dokument no. 85 for 1896 p. 6.

Getz's opinion was primarily that the state should not interfere with its punitive authority in the parties' solution of the "social issues". The use of punishment would easily lead to "increasing the bitterness of the social contradictions". But if one were to prohibit employers from opposing workers' organizing, then this had to be accompanied by rules prohibiting unions from taking measures to prevent employers from replacing striking workers with others.

The ministry did not follow up with any legislative proposal. But there were others who seized on Getz's proposal to protect the employers from the effects of the strike. The Association of Mechanical Engineering Workshops (MVL) in Kristiania (now Oslo) took the initiative for a demand for a legal provision to protect "freedom of work" to be formally presented to the Storting for the first time in 1899.

MVL was concerned with protecting the employers' interests when workers who were on strike forced unorganized workers who were not on strike not to work while the strike was going on. MVL pointed out that there could be many valid reasons why a worker wanted to stay out of a strike, and that this choice had to be protected.

The proposal was met with strong protests from a number of trade unions, and the parliament unanimously decided not to approve it, but to send the matter to the government for further deliberation. The matter was thus in the hands of the ministry of social affairs.

In its follow-up to the proposal, the ministry decided that such a provision would have no beneficial effects and be out of place.[8] The need for such a provision would in any case mostly disappear with the arbitration scheme the ministry proposed. When the matter came up for consideration in Stortinget, Professor Hagerup put forward a proposal to include the provision in the law. Hagerup, who had commissioned the investigation from his friend and colleague Getz while he was prime minister, was now the representative of the Conservative Party.

Hagerup argued that only around 15 per cent of the workers were organized, and if the unions were to be protected in the law, the workers who were not members of a union had to be similarly protected *against* the unions.[9] He referred to the report by Attorney General Getz from 1896 and the position that the right to organize could not be protected by the law without at the same protecting strike breakers against the unions.

Johan Castberg, representative of the Liberal Party, reacted sharply. "This is the most brutal and tyrannical bill towards the workers that has ever seen the light of day in this country. That is my opinion about it, and I dare to assure that it will be regarded in that way in working-class circles. It is here, through penal provisions, that attempts have been made to knock out of the hands of the workers the moral weapon which they have to seek to advance their economic interests."[10]

---

[8] Ot. Prop. No. 111902–1903 Ang. utferdigelse av. en lov om registrerte fagforeninger samt megling og voldgift i arbeidstvistigheter.

[9] Stortingstidende, forhandlinger i Odelstinget (no. 132) 1902/1903 p. 1069.

[10] Stortingstidende, forhandlinger i Odelstinget (no. 132) 1902/1903 p. 1240.

The bill was nevertheless passed by the majority of the first chamber of the Storting. But back then, a proposal had to be passed in both chambers of the Storting before it became law. Before the matter came up for consideration in the second chamber, Lagtinget, several trade unions mobilized against the law. So did the employers, who were against protecting the workers' right to organize and who had always believed that the ministry's bill was too poorly researched. They also objected to interference by the state through arbitration. On this basis, the second chamber decided to ask the first chamber to set the bill aside.

3.2 The Arbitration Act Committee and the Labor Disputes Act

The proposal was still not dead. Work on designing a legal framework for resolving labor disputes continued. The level of conflict between labor and capital increased in the early years of the twentieth century. In particular, the Liberals and the Labor Democrats committed themselves to legal regulation of labor disputes, which finally came with the Labor Disputes Act in 1915.

The Labor Disputes Act from 1915 came about after thorough deliberations and discussions that involved the parties of the labor market. The law was not biased against the labor movement and was perceived as relatively neutral by the trade unions (Ousland 1975, p. 328). Both the employers and the trade unions wanted an arrangement where the state could intervene when necessary. At the collective level, the law had much in common with market law under a liberal regime (Aubert 1989, p. 196). The law was based on a proposal from the Arbitration Committee appointed in 1908. The committee, which Johan Castberg as Minister of Justice appointed, was led by lawyer Ole Severin Solnørdal. Solnørdal was called Castberg's right-hand man. The other members were Dr. Jur. Einar Einarsen, chairman of the National Confederation of Trade Unions Ole O. Lian, factory owner K. Myhre and member of parliament Thore Myrvang (Labor Democrats). The committee was to find a solution to three questions: an institutional framework for compulsory mediation and arbitration, whether arbitration should be compulsory and a solution to the issue of freedom of association (Alsos et al. 2016, p. 55). The committee submitted its recommendation in 1909.

The Arbitration Act Committee proposed a provision to protect the freedom of association in a separate recommendation.[11] The proposal would make it a criminal offense for an employer to prevent a worker from establishing or participating in a trade union or to make the employment relationship conditional on the employee not

[11]Indstilling fra Den til behandling av. spørsmålet om tvungen voldgift i arbeidstvister m.m. nedsatte departementale komité II Utredning av spørsmålet om beskyttelse av foreningsfriheten og arbeidets frihet, Kristiania 1912 (Innstilling om beskyttelse av foreningsfriheten og arbeidets frihet).

being member of a union. It should also be prohibited to offer organized workers worse conditions than unorganized workers. The proposal stated that trade unions were necessary to counteract the imbalance between the individual worker and his employer. It pointed out that some employers actively opposed trade unions, and thus forced that the workers who were affected had to "make do with a smaller part of the return in the businesses they participate in than is beneficial from a societal point of view".[12] For this reason, the society should intervene with regulation.

The majority of the committee refused to propose a legal provision on the protection of "freedom of work". They pointed out that this would only benefit the employers and was not a protection of the right to work. They rejected the argument advanced by Getz 15 years earlier that a provision prohibiting action against strikebreakers was a necessary counterpart to rules protecting union activity. On the contrary, the majority pointed out that "the more the trade union movement gains support among the workers, (...) the less often the members fall into violence during the industrial struggle.[13] Organization creates discipline, maintained the majority.

The employers' representative on the committee, factory owner K. Myhre, dissented and drew up a proposal for a provision on the protection of unorganized workers in conflict in line with Getz's proposal.

The arbitration committee's proposal was not followed up until Prime Minister Herman Scheel from the Conservative Party in 1911 commissioned then judge in the district court of Oslo Paal Berg to deliver a proposal for an employment dispute law. Berg also acted as special secretary for the parliamentary committee after the ministry had presented a proposal based on Berg's draft. In the follow-up to the draft law, it was particularly the question of compulsory mediation in disputes of interest that was controversial. Both LO and the Employers' Association were against this. The result was, nevertheless, the Labor Disputes Act on 6 August 1915, with the labor court for resolving disputes about the interpretation of collective agreements and forced mediation in disputes of interest before combat means could be used.

3.3 The Penitentiary Laws

The Labor Disputes Act was not aimed at preventing the implementation of the workers' demands but was based on the practice that the main organizations themselves had incorporated. However, the conservatives changed their approach to the labor movement during the 1920s, as increasingly revolutionary statements were expressed by the labor movement. Consequently, conservative politics became more aggressive towards the trade unions. This was in line with a general development in Europe. "A specter is moving in Europe - the specter of communism," Karl

[12] Innstilling om beskyttelse av foreningsfriheten og arbeidets frihet p. 19.

[13] Innstilling om beskyttelse av foreningsfriheten og arbeidets frihet p. 33.

Marx and Friedrich Engels had written in the introduction to the Communist Party Manifesto, and the bourgeoisie believed this. The communists and the revolution in Russia loomed in the background.

On 4 July 1924, a conservative government put forward a proposal to change the Criminal Code and a proposal to change the Labor Disputes Act.[14] *A right of passage for Judas,* LO leader Ole O Lian called it in a protest demonstration against the penitentiary law on 14 July 1924. The background for the proposal was prolonged and bitter labor disputes in 1923 and 1924. A number of the conflicts were illegal. The conflicts strengthened the demand for "increased protection for those willing to work".[15] In the opinion of the government it was required "that more reassuring legal provisions be made available to protect the individual's right to work".[16]

For the first time, proposals for legal provisions on the criminalization of measures against strikebreakers were presented by the government. At the same time, the government proposed to toughen the penal provisions for illegal work stoppages, and to extend them to include incitement and support for such conflicts. The government proposed a dual-track system. Measures against those willing to work during illegal strikes were to be regulated in the Labor Disputes Act, while corresponding actions during legal strikes were to be criminalized by the Criminal Code.

Both bills were presented by Minister of Social Affairs Odd Sverressøn Klingenberg, who represented the Conservative party. The government brushed the dust off the report from the Arbitration Committee from 1912, which had been shelved for over 10 years. Legislative provisions to protect freedom of association had, as we have seen, been a demand of the Labor Party for several decades. Only now, when the trade union movement had grown so strong that it did not really need the protection of the state, did the government put forward a proposal to protect it. At the same time, following the argument of Getz, it proposed to protect the employers with provisions to protect "the right to work".[17] The ministry asserted that "during the ministry's conferences with the police and the prosecutor's office, these authorities have also strongly emphasized that the current legal regulations are not sufficient to be able to effectively intervene in the many cases of abuse and harassment against those willing to work that have taken place during the conflict."[18]

In proposition no. 54, the government proposed an amendment to § 222 of the Criminal Code. This would make it a criminal offense to harass a person or his household by threats or by insulting or intrusive behavior to cause someone to lose or give up their job, or to refrain from applying work. Serious threats were already

---

[14] Ot. prp. No. 54 (1924) Om utferdigelse av en lov om forandring i straffeloven and Ot. prp. No. 55 (1924) Lov om forandringer i lov om arbeidstvister av. 6 August 1915.

[15] Ot. prp. No. 54 (1924) p. 2.

[16] Ot. prp. No. 54 (1924) p. 1.

[17] Ot. prp. No. 54 (1924) p.2

[18] Ibid.

illegal irrespective of whether this was connected to labor relations or other matters. In labor relations, the ministry stated that there were "a number of intimidations of a more or less serious nature that the Criminal Code does not cover at all." Here the ministry mentioned "the mere demonstrative following of the person willing to work, gathering about him, publication of the name of the person willing to work, as well as many cases of intimidation," and "such intimidation can, however, exert equally strong and undue pressure, as an unlawful threat."[19] The intention of the bill was to target behavior beyond what was otherwise punishable as unlawful threats.

The penalty for threats under Section 222 was fines or imprisonment for up to 3 years. For the special prohibition against intimidation of those willing to work, the ministry suggested imprisonment as the mandatory punishment.

At the same time, the government presented a proposal in proposition no. 55 to tighten the penalty provision in section 40 of the Labor Disputes Act, which applied to illegal conflicts.[20] Following a recommendation from the employers' association, the ministry proposed to extend the penalty provision to apply to "anyone who incites or contributes to an illegal labor dispute".[21] The provision should affect "anyone who encourages the start or continuation of such a work stoppage or who expresses his approval or supports it, or collects or distributes collected contributions for its implementation or continuation or contributes to this." The ministry also proposed a new second paragraph to the provision that it should be considered complicity "when someone during an illegal work stoppage stays at or on the way to the workplace to observe who is working or looking for work there or to influence someone to give up work or do not look for work (striker guards)."[22] The proposed bill extended the penalty framework be so that it would be possible to impose a prison sentence.

The social committee of Stortinget split into two factions, where the majority of five members was formed by the representatives from the Liberal Party and the Labor Party, and the minority by the Farmers' Party and the Conservative Party. Stortinget voted to postpone the matter, since it had been presented so late in the session.

3.4 The Final Push

The ministry presented the proposal again in 1925. In the meantime, the Liberal Party had taken over government and a bill was put forward by Lars Oftedahl as Minister of Social Affairs. At the same time, the government presented a bill for a

[19] Ot. prp. No. 54 (1924) pp. 2–3.

[20] Ot. prp. No. 55 (1924) Lov om forandringer i lov om arbeidstvister av 6 August 1915.

[21] Ot. Prp. No. 55 1924 p. 9.

[22] Ot. Prp. No. 55 1924 p. 10.

law on compulsory arbitration in conflicts of interest.[23] This was an old cause for the liberals. According to this bill government could prohibit a labor dispute if it would "endanger significant social interests. The possibility of compulsory arbitration was, in the ministry's opinion, necessary to "protect the public interests against the destructive effects of an open industrial struggle."[24] The ministry pointed out that there had been rules on compulsory arbitration from 1916 to 1923, and that the instrument had been used in "major labor disputes."[25]

The ministry also proposed to reverse the burden of proof in cases concerning the trade unions' liability for compensation for the employer's loss in the event of an illegal conflict. To escape liability, the trade union would have an active duty to prevent and limit a breach of the collective agreement. The proposal for new Section 4 of the Labor Disputes Act read:

> If members of a trade union or employers' association have breached a collective agreement or have been guilty of an illegal work stoppage, the association is liable, unless it proves that it is not itself to blame for or through the means at its disposal, has sought to prevent the breach or the continuation of the violation contrary to the collective agreement or the illegal work stoppage.

The provision was neutral in form, but in practice it was one-sidedly directed at the workers and their organizations. The trade unions perceived the proposal as an attack on unionizing as a means of promoting the workers' interests, and as an attempt to transform unions into bodies for the enforcement of the state's "gag laws".[26]

The ministry maintained the proposal to toughen the penalty provision for illegal actions but proposed to exempt the individual participant from criminal liability. Punishment was thus to be reserved for the managers as well as anyone who supported, or encouraged, or contributed to illegal work stoppages. The Liberal Party would not follow through on the proposal to toughen the punishment to prevent those willing to work in *legal* conflicts. Therefore, the ministry withdrew the proposal to add § 222 to the Criminal Code.

The Social Committee Stortinget issued a recommendation on 20 January 1926.[27] It split into three factions. The three representatives of the Conservative Party believed that "one should be careful with the introduction of coercive provisions when determining pay and working conditions".[28] Experience showed that it would be difficult to gain respect for such rules, and that they would therefore not create peace at the workplace. Forced arbitration would also be a worrisome interference with freedom of business. They also believed that the condition that the bill would not in practice constitute any restriction on the use of compulsory arbitration.

---

[23] Ot. Prp. No. 54 1925.

[24] Ot. Prp. No. 54 1925 p. 14.

[25] Ot. Prp. No. 54 1925 p. 8.

[26] See on the debate in Stortinget, representative Løhre in Stortingstidene, Stortingstidende, forhandlinger i Odelstinget 10. juni 1929, p. 497.

[27] Innst O. III 1926.

[28] Innst O. III 1926 p. 8.

The Labor Party's representatives argued that the conflict between those who sell labor and those who buy it was so great and profound that it would not be possible to contain it with a repressive law. They also found unacceptable that the state should determine the price of labor without also determining the price of the goods the workers needed for survival. The representatives from the Liberal Party and the Farmers' Party supported the government's proposal. Once again, the Odelstinget decided to postpone the matter, after it came up at a meeting on 24 June.

It was not until 27 April 1927 that the matter came up again in for deliberation. Again, there had been a change of government. Now there was a right-wing government at the helm. The responsible minister was Peter Andreas Morell. This time it was serious, and the representatives debated the proposals over 3 days. Morell argued that a permanent right for the government to adopt compulsory arbitration would in practice mean a permanent state regulation of wages and other working conditions.[29] Because of the special situation in which the country found itself, he nevertheless was able to support the adoption of a temporary law with a duration limited to 1 May 1929. Thus, there was a majority in the Storting for a law on compulsory arbitration, but with a limited duration, and not, as proposed by the previous government, as a permanent arrangement.

The debate resulted in a majority in favor of changes to the Labor Disputes Act and a temporary law on additions to the Labor Disputes Act on compulsory arbitration, and the law was adopted. During the debate, Johan Norem from the conservatives put forward the old proposal for punishment for measures against strikebreakers. This proposal was forwarded to the justice committee for consideration there.

The justice committee issued its recommendation on 23 June.[30] The liberals believed that after the Arbitration Act had been passed there was no need for such a penalty provision, and suggested the case be sent back to the ministry. The Labor Party's two representatives opposed the proposal, and alternatively submitted to send it to the ministry. The other representatives supported the proposal.

In Stortinget, the Conservative Party and the Liberal Left had 54 representatives, the Liberal Party 34, the Labor Party 24, the Farmers' Party 22, the Social Democrats 8, the Communists 6 and the Radical People's Party 2. The Conservative Party, with the Liberal Left Party (which was really a fraction of the conservatives) and the Farmers' Party thus controlled 76 of the Storting's 150 representatives.

The bill was debated on 28 June. The proposal to send the case back to the ministry fell by 54 to 52 votes. The 54 were the Conservative Party and the Farmers' Party. When the result of the voting became known, a commotion broke out in the public gallery, with shouts and singing of the Internationale. The well-known communist Otto Luihn gave an appeal, and the demonstrators threw leaflets into the hall. The leaflets were signed by Norway's Communist Youth Association.[31]

---

[29] Stortingstidende, forhandlinger i Odelstinget 27. april 1927 p. 468.

[30] Innst O. No. 137 1927.

[31] See notice in Hamar Arbeiderblad on Thursday 30 June 1927.

Luihn was arrested and sentenced to 21 days in prison for disturbing public peace and order.[32]

The president had the gallery cleared. The Liberal Party's Johan Ludwig Mowinckel then took the floor. He was furious. "The kind of demonstrations that have now taken place for the second time in this parliamentary session must be regretted to the highest degree," he thundered. "If the labor parties think that they are intimidating the country's legislature in that way, they are wrong! We discuss and consider the questions presented to us. Completely to the point, and the position we take towards them is based on objective considerations. We are not intimidated. Based on the arguments and based on the good relationship that I want there to be between the classes, I have wanted the bill in question not to be considered at this time. I think it would have been correct if one had followed the view that I have claimed. However, the demonstration which has taken place, and which has aimed to intimidate the Odelsting from passing laws which it deems justified, made such an impression on me that I, for my part, will now vote for the law that is proposed. For that reason, I will vote for the law and advise my party colleagues to do the same."[33] As Mowinckel now turned, the outcome of the voting was obvious.

The debate became heated. The president had to call for calm and ask the representatives to stay in their seats. In one case, there was so much commotion in the hall that the president could not hear what the speaker said. The Labor Party put forward a proposal to send the bill back to the justice committee. When this also fell, the Labor Party representatives, together with the Communists and the Social Democrats, left the hall. As the Labor Party's Alfred Madsen stated, they would not "participate in the comedy that will be performed here."[34] Madsen also said before he left that "you must remember that it is you who will appear before the court before too long, and then it is the gallery, it is the public that will have the opportunity to pass judgment on your behavior and your politics over the recent years. A more reactionary policy than this which Storting has pursued in recent years with the tacit and sometimes loud consent of the liberals, a more reactionary policy has not been pursued in this country since we got our independence in 1814."[35]

Since the representatives of the labor movement left the hall with this, the law was unanimously adopted in the Odelstinget and the penitentiary laws were a reality.

[32] See Aftenposten Monday evening 12 December 1927.

[33] Forhandlinger i Odelstinget (no. 134) 1927 p. 1065.

[34] Ibid.

[35] Forhandlinger i Odelstinget (no. 134) 1927 p. 1070.

3.5 The Reception of the Law

"1. May this year will be marked by lockout and arbitration", wrote the Oscar Torp as leader of the Norwegian Labor Party and Halvard Olsen as leader of the Norwegian Federation of Trade Unions (LO) in an appeal to the working class on 29 April. "The workers must firmly state that an arbitration and penitentiary law whose main purpose is to maintain the employers' privileged position and reduce the workers' living conditions, which are already bad enough, cannot be recognized by the workers."[36] "The workers have no confidence in an arbitration tribunal appointed by a bourgeois government. And we recognize no right for judges from the ruling class to decide the workers' wages and working conditions."

The call to action was heard by the masses. The whole country mobilized to oppose the new laws. "The May 1st demonstration was an impressive rally against the lockout and the Penitentiary Act," wrote Arbeiderbladet on May 2. The demonstration in Oslo was the largest in a long time, and 25,000 took to the streets. The sun shone over Youngstorget, after several days of sleet and rain, Oslo showed its best side. In Bergen, the largest 1 May demonstration the city had ever seen passed through the streets.[37] The demonstration "mustered to rise and fight against the attacks on the Norwegian working class." There were about 6000 participants. In other cities too, the turnout was record high. In Stavanger, the biggest demonstration ever took place, according to the newspaper 1 May.[38]

The addition to Section 222 of the Criminal Code raised the level of conflict. The main newspaper of the Labor Party, Arbeiderbladet, wrote: "The Penitentiary Act is a punch right in the face of the workers. They will respond in kind to this gross provocation. Those who sow wind will reap storm."[39]

The fight against strikebreakers was a fight for the very right to go on strike. At the same time, it raised deep ideological and emotional concerns. Therefore, the labor movement perceived society's criminalization of this struggle as a violent provocation. There were two fundamental conceptions of justice that stood against each other (Maurseth 1987, p. 478). "It is an unforgivable crime to kill one's brother. Yours is just as great," wrote Ottar Rønning in the poem *Til streikebryteren*, which was published in the Bookbinders' Association trade journal on 1 May 1931. The attitude towards strikebreakers was no different in 1927.The strike-breaker was a fratricide, and now he was protected by the law.

Elsewhere in Europe, fascism was on the rise and now it was knocking on the door in Norway. "We are (...) dealing here with an offshoot of *the general European reaction*, the same reaction against which the struggle of the working class across Europe today is directed" Hansteen 1927, p. 4) This was written by lawyer and later head of LO's legal office Viggo Hansteen in a brochure on the

[36] Arbeiderbladet Friday 29 April 1927.

[37] Bergens Arbeiderblad Monday 2 May 1927.

[38] 1 May Monday 2 May 1927.

[39] Arbeiderbladet Wednesday 29 June 1927.

"penitentiary law". Hansteen referred to emergency laws in Hungary, Poland, Lithuania and the Balkan countries, the terror in Italy and the "reactionary movement" in France. He also pointed to the close relationship between the new laws and the proposal for a trade union law in England, "whose task it will be to castrate the powerful *English* trade union movement" (Hansteen 1927, p. 4). Special laws aimed at trade unions were a European phenomenon in the years after the First World War (Olsen and Lie 1931, p. 5). Trade union historian Gunnar Ousland wrote that the right-wing government had gone on a mission for "a purely fascist-minded reaction (Ousland 1975, p. 364)."

Introducing a right for the government to order arbitration in interest disputes would abolish the distinction between legal disputes and interest disputes and make strikes illegal. "The ban (. . .) will in practice also become a ban in disputes of interest," wrote Hansteen (Hansteen 1927, p. 10). Seen in the context of the tightened rules on trade union liability, this would transform the trade unions' role from fighting for the workers to becoming the lackeys of the employers. What obligations were not imposed on the unions? Were they obliged to go around to every striking worker and ask him to resume work, lift blockades and advertise the positions of the striking workers vacant? Strike allowances for striking workers, for them to maintain their lives and their families, were out of the question.

According to Hansteen, the penal provisions in the Labor Disputes Act and in the Criminal Code were an "attempt to carry out terror" (Hansteen 1927, p. 18). The provision affected not only the participation in an illegal action, but also advocating action at trade union meetings, expressing support for illegal actions and collecting or giving money to striking workers. Now any pressure on strikebreakers was to be punished.

Hansteen pointed out that the labor movement had been met with a cold shoulder when, in the late 1800s, it had asked for state protection against employers' union busting. Then it was said that the state should not intervene in the private relationship between employees and employers. Only when the trade unions had grown strong and become a factor of power did the state intervene, but now on the employers' side.

Also in the debate in the Storting, representatives of the labor movement had used harsh words about the draft laws. The Labor Party's Olav Sæter pointed to the one-sidedness of the government's proposal: "I know of a number of farmers and forest owners in my district who have prevented those who were on strike up there, those organized in the Julussa conflict, from being allowed to work. Should these forest owners now be subject to punishment under this law with imprisonment of up to 1 year or with fines of up to NOK. 25,000? If it is right for one, it must be right for the other. It would be interesting to know.[40]

Ingvald Berentin Aase from the Communists spoke of "the crime that the assembly is about to commit against the working class by adopting these exceptional laws, which are only aimed at the working class and not at anyone else. There is talk

[40] Stortingstidende. Forhandlinger i Odelstinget 28 June 1927 p. 1059.

of practicing terror. No, it is the class that sits here and rules that practices terror, practices terror against the working class; but they have not been satisfied with the terror they have exercised so far, it must be further intensified, they must be given access by law to intensify the terror against the working class, and that is the purpose of the present bill."[41]

The priest and Labor Party representative Kristian Pedersen Tønder from Troms believed that "a bill like this would have been unthinkable 6–7 years ago."[42]

At the annual congress of LO that same year, "The tactics and the fight against the Penitentiary Act" was an important item on the agenda. In LO's archive there are approximately 600 letters from various trade unions protesting the law.[43] The LO secretariat wrote in its introduction to the annual meeting that "The trade union stands as a link in the overall labor movement facing the capitalist social system. Laws passed to hinder the unionized workers' freedom of action in their struggle for economic liberation must therefore be fought".[44] The wording was penned by Legal Consultant LO, lawyer Trygve Lie.

According to the secretariat, the changes in the Labor Dispute Act caused it to completely change character. Whereas before there might have been doubts as to whether the law was one-sidedly aimed at the workers and their organizations, this doubt was now completely cleared aside. Furthermore, it said: "The worst of all the provisions, however, is Section 222 II of the Criminal Code. This is a clean and pure penitentiary clause, after which previous legal actions now are subject to a prison sentence of up to 1 year. (. . .) The lowest-ranking individuals, the strikebreakers, have become the darlings of the bourgeoisie, and are now more legally protected than any other person in our country."[45]

Trygve Lie introduced the debate at the meeting. "Here we face the whole of bourgeois society, whose only purpose is to stop the advance of the working class and put down the struggle for wages", he opened.[46] After explaining the new laws, he moved on to discuss how to get them repealed. The Labor Party had to work for it in the Storting. The question for the meeting was how the organization could support this work.

The laws made it impossible to wage a conflict legally. "Today charges have been brought, or charges are being prepared, against 36 trade union representatives and editors of party newspapers, and this only because of three small conflicts. The trade unions must put themselves above the law, and the best way to fight today is to show that these laws are not being respected, "said Lie.[47] In order to protect those who were jeopardized because they had to go against the law, the secretariat proposed

[41] Stortingstidende Forhandlinger i Odelstinget 28 June 1927 p. 1068.

[42] Stortingstidende Forhandlinger i Odelstinget 28 June 1927 p. 1070.

[43] Ref. ARK-1579 Da 135, Da136.

[44] The Norwegian confederation of Trade Unions, LO Congress 1927 Agenda and protocol p. 220.

[45] LO congress 1927 pp. 220–221.

[46] LO congress 1927 p. 226.

[47] LO congress 1927 p. 234.

creating a fund that would financially support those who came into conflict with the law.[48]

The left and the communists believed that the secretariat's proposal was too lame, that it was a "thin soup". They wanted more direct confrontation with the laws and criticized the management for showing passivity in the work. The management warned against involving LO more directly. "For reasons of liability for damages, there can be no more in what is adopted here at the congress," said Trygve Lie.[49] Oscar Torp, who became Prime Minister of Norway after the war, emphasized that "The national union of workers must take up an organized illegal activity against strike-breaking, a struggle that is organized from the highest management and with the strongest organizations behind it, but a firm plan cannot be adopted and submitted to this Congress. What is printed can be used against us."[50] The means of the fight had to be covert.

The laws were also criticized from academic circles. Professor Ragnar Knoph, one of the most respected legal professors of Norway of all times, characterized a rule restricting boycotts as "a rigorous and poorly thought-out rule that is not aware of its own content and scope." (Knoph 1934, p. 363). According to Knoph, the law was the result of "a legislative preparation in which the conservative parties ultimately completely outbid each other in power and rigor, under the impression of the elections that were immediately at hand". Arnljot Engh wrote that "In the legislation as a whole, the provision is unparalleled. Because of these 'penitentiary laws', Norway can boast of being one of the countries with the strictest laws regarding industrial action." (Engh 1933, p. 63).

Several prominent lawyers on the left went public with criticism. Lawyer and later Supreme Court President Emil Stang wrote in an election brochure for the Communist Party in 1927:

> The Arbitration Act stipulates that workers' wages - but not directors' royalties and capital owners' interest - must be determined by arbitration, not by industrial action. This means that the capitalist class, through its government, can autonomously determine the workers' living and working conditions. (. . .) The trade unions are threatened with prison sentences and fines and an incalculable liability for damages, if they directly or indirectly promote or support or rather, if they do not directly oppose and prevent any illegal strike. And any strike is illegal. In that way, the bourgeois state will take the trade union into its service or else crush and destroy it. At the same time, the state supports and protects the strikebreakers - those 'willing to work' through strict penal provisions, aimed at honest, organized workers. That the state does not shrink back from using even the power of bayonets, the Jullussa affair is proof of that. (Stang 1927, pp. 4–5).

Supreme Court judge Karl Frimann Dahl wrote two critical articles in the newspapers about the Arbitration Act after the construction workers' dispute.

---

[48] Cases from the Workers' Justice Fund have unfortunately been preserved to a small extent - nothing about the Penitentiary Act there (ARK-1736).

[49] LO congress 1927 pp. 240–241.

[50] ibid.

"Stripped off all phrases, the introduction of forced arbitration is tantamount to the restoration of slavery in a form adapted to the capitalist mode of production," he wrote in a scathing criticism of the law, printed in the newspaper Fremtiden, Saturday 16 June 1928. He believed that the law contradicted against the spirit and principles of the constitution, even if it did not contradict the letter of the constitution. To introduce forced labor at a wage fixed by the state was a pure expropriation. Even if it happened against compensation determined by the arbitration court, the constitution could not be considered to authorize the expropriation of labor. The law deprived the workers of free control over their labor power by forcing them to work under conditions they had not themselves approved. The final word on the law's constitutionality would rest with the courts. "The near future will show whether our courts in this vital issue for the entire working class will follow a formalistic literal interpretation or interpret the constitution in accordance with the spirit of freedom that inspired the founding fathers." In the later court case about the Arbitration Act, one of the arguments was that the Act conflicted with the Constitution.

Frimann-Dahl's agitation against the arbitration law drew the ire of right-wing radical forces, and the newspaper Norges Fremtid later wrote about him "It is a dangerous sign that lawlessness has crept in among our civil servants. Either society must now do something to gain respect for the laws and remove the useless civil servants, or else one must be prepared that the part of the people who have hitherto been law-abiding will no longer find themselves mocked and abused by the mob, while a gang of corrupt thugs of Kullmann's and Dahl's type prey on it. The day may come when the poor enforcement of our laws also forces us to resort to the law of fists to protect our existence. And we will not be wearing silk gloves."[51]

"This legislation does not agree with Norwegian legal awareness", wrote district court judge Carl Bonnevie in a comment a few weeks after Dahl.[52] Bonnevie argued that the law violated both justice and people's legal awareness. "The force of the law is unilaterally aimed at the wage workers", he continued. Bonnevie also attacked the rule of evidence which imposed liability on the unions if they failed to prove that they had done everything possible to prevent an illegal action and to bring the workers back to work. "I especially ask jurists to note how this statutory provision conflicts with the general rules on the burden of proof," he wrote. "'Equality before the law' is an unwritten legal fundament. But it is contrary to this when the general rules of evidence are shifted here to the detriment of the trade unions." He pointed out the broad penal provisions and said, "truly our criminal courts will have enough to do, if all offenders here are to be taken, and taken equally. Yes, because the penal provisions are surely not intended as a blanket mandate for the prosecution and the police to select a few from among the thousands of criminals who, at the discretion of the official in question, are considered particularly fit to be the subject of criminal prosecution."

[51] Norges Fremtid Saturday 9 December 1933.

[52] Namdal's Arbeiderblad, Saturday 25 June 1928. Both articles both printed in a number of newspapers from the labor press.

The 1927 parliamentary election was an electoral landslide for the Labor Party. After joining forces with the Social Democrats, they became the largest party in the Storting with 59 representatives, an increase of 27. "The people pass a crushing judgment on the right-wing government," wrote Arbeiderbladet.[53] The election result led to the formation of the first Labor Party government, the minority government of Christopher Hornsrud. However, the government was defeated in the Storting on the declaration of accession, and only sat for 18 days.

Repeal of the Penitentiary Act was at the top of the Labor Party government's agenda. Before the Hornsrud government resigned, it managed to present Ot. prp. No. 21 on repeal of section 222 section II of the Criminal Code. The ministry wrote that "The actions for which it imposes penalties are partly those that are already affected by the penal code's general provisions on illegal coercion. And actions which are otherwise unpunished should also not be punished the moment they are used as means in the workers' struggle for their interests. The law has also created an extremely strong bitterness among the workers, and it has already been shown that it creates far more unrest than peace. In the long run, it will therefore not be able to be maintained under any circumstances."[54] The government fell before the odelsting had time to consider the proposition, and the odelsting decided to ask the government to send the matter to the Criminal Code Council for investigation.

References

Alsos K, Seip ÅA, Nygaard P (2016) I arbeidsfredens tjeneste, Arbeidsretten gjennom 100 år (In the service of industrial peace, the labor court through 100 years). Pax forlag, Oslo

Andersen K (1967) Fra arbeidslivets rett, (on the law of labor relations). Johan Grundt Tanum forlag, Oslo

Aubert V (1989) Continuity and development in law and society. Norwegian University Press, Oslo

Engh A (1933) Fagorganisasjonen og loven (Norwegian law's position towards trade unions and the trade union struggle). Tiden, Oslo

Hansteen C, Kambestad S-Ø, Monsen HC, Stueland E (2015) Interessetvist og arbeidskamp (Dispute of interest and labor conflict). Gyldendal, Oslo

Hansteen V (1927) Tukthuslovene Fagorganisasjonen under offentlig administrasjon (The penitentiary law, the trade unions under public administration). Andelsforlaget Ny Tid, Oslo

Knoph R (1934) Oversikt over Norges rett, (Overview of Norwegian law). Nationaltrykkeriet, Oslo

Maurseth P (1987) Gjennom kriser til makt (1920–1935) Arbeiderbevegelsens historie bd. 3 (Through crises to power (1920–1935) the history of the labor movement 3). Tiden norsk forlag, Oslo

Olsen H, Lie T (1931) De arbeiderfiendtlige lover og Kampen mot dem, (The anti-worker laws and the fight against them), Arbeidernes faglige Landsorganisasjon, Oslo 1931. Oslo

[53] Arbeiderbladet Tuesday 18 October 1927.

[54] Ot. prp. No. 21 1928 Om ophevelse av straffelovens § 222 avsnitt II p. 2.

Ousland G (1975) Fagorganisasjonen i Norge 2 De store kamp-åra 1921–1931 (The trade union in Norway 2 the great fighting years 1921–1931). Tiden, Oslo
Skeie J (1931) Ulovlige midler i kampen om arbeidsvilkår (Illegal means in the fight for working conditions). Det Mallingske bokgtrykkeri, Oslo
Stang, Emil, (1927) Hvad valget gjelder (What the election is about), Andelsforlaget Ny Tid Oslo
Vogt A (1959) Bernhard Getz. H. Aschehoug & Co, Oslo

Chapter 4
Challenging the Arbitration Act: The Construction Workers' Dispute

4.1 Support to Workers in Conflict

Immediately after the Arbitration Act came into force, the government decreed arbitration in all major conflicts. Only in enterprises with a small number of workers did the government allow the workers to go on strike.[1] Those who had claimed that the law, for all practical purposes, would entail a ban on strikes were proven right. The trend continued into 1928, which was marked by one major conflict, the strike against the arbitration award in the construction workers' dispute. Although this conflict was only 1 of 63 in total in 1928, the strike involved 4100 workers out of a total of 8042 striking workers that year.[2] Overall, 1928 was not a particularly conflict-filled year.

The conflict started with collective bargaining in the spring of 1928 in the construction industry and the graphic arts. The employers terminated the collective agreements, a normal step. They demanded a 17 percent cut in wages and a reduction in holidays in the construction industry. The unions could not accept this. The employers' association notified a dismissal of the workers when the parties did not reach an agreement. According to the normal rules of the game, a strike would be the next step in the conflict. On 30 March, however, the government adopted a decree on arbitration and a ban on "any implementation of work closures or closures in connection with these disputes".[3]

According to the unions, the government was abusing the power it had been given in the law. There were no significant societal interests at stake here, it was a relatively limited conflict in the construction industry and the graphic industry, and even here

[1] Norway's official statistics VIII 73, Collective agreements and labor disputes 1927, Statistics Norway, Oslo 1928 p. 16.

[2] Norway's official statistics VIII 99, Mediation institutions' activities 1927 and 1928 Collective agreements and labor disputes 1928, Statistics Norway, Oslo 1929 p. 39.

[3] Norsk Lovtidend (Norwegian Law Gazette), Avd. I 1928 p. 102.

H. P. Graver, *Democracy and Lawlessness*,
https://doi.org/10.1007/978-3-031-69055-6_4

the conflict only affected. a quarter of the employers. That the conflict was too small to justify arbitration was an opinion that had support in the Storting (the Norwegian Parliament) also from representatives from the Liberal Party and the Farmers' Party, at least in retrospect.[4] Even the government admitted it afterwards. By imposing compulsory arbitration, the government effectively abolished the right to strike in the wage struggle. The law became a ban on strikes, as the Labor Party had claimed in the debate the previous year.

The arbitration court reached a salary reduction of 12 percent and a reduction of the piecework wages by up to 21 percent. This was not just a reduction to respond to the decline in prices, but a cut in real wages. The workers responded on 26 May by going on strike against the arbitration award. This was a clear violation of the new law.

The state responded with repression. Now the workers really felt the consequences of the new hard line of the government. Those who did not respect the prohibition were to be struck with hunger. Due to the new rules, the trade unions could not publicly support the strike, and they could not pay out strike contributions. In order not to be liable for damages, the trade unions had to be able to show that they had done what they could to prevent the strike, so of course they could not publicly support the workers.

The government was not content to cut union contributions to starve the striking workers and their families. The Ministry of Social Affairs sent out a circular to the local governments with the following wording: "After the arbitration verdict was handed down, a strike broke out in the building trades. This strike is illegal. As questions have been raised about access to providing poor support to the strikers, the ministry must announce that there is no legal access to this. The conditions in Section 1 of the Poor People's Act are not met, as the strikers are not considered to be unable to acquire what they need. As a result, the municipality of residence will not be entitled to reimbursement for poverty benefits provided during the strike, either from the home municipality or the state."[5] In other words, the door to public support was closed to the strikers.

In another circular, the ministry stated that the health insurance of the strikers was also suspended, as workers on illegal strike could not benefit from the rule that unemployed could retain their membership without a premium.

The circular led some municipalities also to refuse to provide support to the strikers' family members. The Communist Party MP IB Aase raised this in an interpellation in the Storting, but the government refused to answer or to take any action towards the municipalities.

The government also refused to comment on a proposal from Aase to order the government to withdraw the circular. Prime Minister Mowinckel contented himself with saying that the government "will now, as hitherto, use all legal means at its

[4]See the debate in Stortingstidende 1929, forhandlinger i Odelstinget 6 June 1929 pp. 456–457.

[5]Quoted from Stortingstidende 1928, forhandlinger i Stortinget 19 June 1928 p. 2117.

disposal to combat the ongoing illegal strike."[6] The workers were to be forced back to work.

The situation prompted several prominent members of the Labor Party publicly to call for fundraising in support of the striking workers. This was in direct defiance of the prohibition against anyone who "incites or contributes to an illegal labor dispute". On 4 June, the magazine *Den røde ungdom* (The red youth) had an article under the heading "Undeterred by the law" with a list of the initiators. The magazine was sent out as an attachment to the main labor newspaper *Arbeiderbladet*. Among the signatories were several members of the parliamentary group of the Labor Party, the party chairman Oscar Torp, history professor Edvard Bull and several other trustees in the party. Later pillars of the Norwegian society such as Einar Gerhardsen (prime minister 1945–1965), Halvard Lange (foreign minister 1946–1963), Rakel Grepp (journalist and close friend of Alexandra Kollontai), Nils Hønsvald (newspaper editor and chairman of the Nordic Council in 1958 and 1963), and the poets Rudolf Nilsen and Arne Paasche-Aasen were included. The list included around 1000 names of party members who subscribed to weekly contributions.[7]

Since all support for illegal strikers was a crime, this was a massive show of civil disobedience and a call for others to join in. The demand to disregard the law was already pronounced within the party and the unions, but organized civil disobedience as a form of political action was still relatively unknown. Internationally, civil disobedience implemented on a mass basis in a national scale gained currency only in the 1920s and 1930s (Schock 2021, p. 411).

The conservative newspaper Tidens Tegn described the call as a sensational provocation and asked the Minister of Justice what this provocation would lead to. He replied that theoretically charges could be brought against all contributors but left it up to the public prosecutor to decide on that.[8]

The intention of the call was both to raise funds and to protest the Arbitration Act. The appeal spread and gathered many thousands of contributors from all over the country. Money was also raised in other ways. The organizers of the year's first athletics competition in Oslo on 1 June decided that half of the profits from the competition should go to the striking workers.[9] In Oslo alone, over NOK 5,000 had been collected by the end of June.[10] This corresponds to 20,000 Euro in today's value. Socialist newspapers around the country printed appeals and signatures in support of the strike. The direct confrontation with the new provision in the Labor Disputes Act § 40 continued and spread. Both the appeals and the signatures with support and promises of contributions were punishable breaches of the new law. Over 1000 people broke the law with the first appeal, thousands joined in the weeks that followed.

[6] Stortingstidende 1928, forhandlinger i Stortinget 20 June 1928 p. 2198.

[7] The list is reproduced in Norges Kommunistblad on Tuesday 5 June 1928.

[8] Tidens Tegn Tuesday 5 June 1928.

[9] Arbeiderbladet Thursday 31 May 1928.

[10] Arbeiderbladet Thursday 28 June 1928 p. 8.

The appeals received an unprecedented support. "Under our more than 100-year-old constitution, the Arbitration Act is the first law that otherwise lawful citizens, en masse and led by a number of members of the National Assembly, knowingly and willingly have violated. And why? Because the Arbitration Act profoundly violates and upsets the legal awareness of the country's most numerous social class, something which the legislators were surely aware of." These are the words of Supreme Court judge Karl Frimann Dahl in a large article published in several of the country's newspapers after the construction workers' strike was over (Dahl 1928).

Those who were on strike were also denied the holiday allowance to which they were entitled. Together with the fact that the municipalities refused to pay poverty support to strikers and their families, this meant that their children did not have the opportunity to leave the city during the upcoming school holidays. This prompted a few prominent people to rally behind a call for people to offer holiday accommodation to the children of the striking workers and to contribute money so that the children could go on holiday. Among the signatories were notable public figures such as the architect Arnstein Arneberg, the writers Hulda Garborg, Olav Duun and Arnulf Øverland, the women's rights activist and politician Betzy Kjelsberg, the painter Henrik Sørensen, and the psychiatrist and public intellectual Johan Scharffenberg, together with several other famous and unknown people. The call was published in Dagbladet on 4 July 1928 and in a number of workers' newspapers around the country. The call prompted the ministry to send a circular to the municipalities and clarify that it was permissible to support the striking workers' families, provided that the municipality took care that the striking workers themselves did not benefit from this support (Volan 1928, p. 39).

4.2 The Arbitration Act in Court

4.2.1 The Prosecutors and Police

It did not take long before the courts had the opportunity to determine guidelines for penalties for breaches of the Arbitration Act. In total, over the next six months, more than 150 judgments were handed down for violating the penal provisions in the Labor Disputes Act during the summer of 1928.[11] The Arbitration Act reached the Supreme Court in three cases as early as October 1928. All the cases arose out of support for the construction workers' conflict in the same year. The speed with which the cases moved through the legal system shows how important the conflict was perceived by both the prosecution and the legal apparatus.

The government also perceived the conflict as important. Although it did not intervene in the prosecution, it used "all legal means at its disposal to combat the

[11] See Ot. prp. No. 19 Om amnesti for lovovertredelser i anledning av den i 1928 iverksatte streik i bygningsfagene og de grafiske fag 1929 p. 2.

ongoing illegal and anti-union strike."[12] Among these was, as mentioned above, ensuring that the striking workers and their families did not receive any support from the public allowances to the poor.

The prosecution was initially at a loss as to what to do. Should they fine all or a selection of those who broke the law? How would they get the resources to deal with the situation? Attorney General Peder Kjerschow was on the scene already the day after the call for support had appeared in the newspaper and stated on 5 June in an interview with Tidens Tegn: "We have to consider today whether we are going to prosecute everyone or some of those who have participated in this action. It is conceivable that the case now assumes a scope that necessitates extraordinary help. There is no doubt that all those in 'The Red Youth' who have had their names published as contributors to the illegal strike are liable to punishment by the law. The procedure could be that each individual gets a penalty order, if they do not accept this, the case goes to the court and then extraordinary measures are needed. But as I said, the matter will be considered today." In other words, there was little hesitation on the part of the supreme prosecuting authority. Kjerschow was an unpopular man in the labor movement. He was regarded as biased and unwilling to react against fraud and corruption, while at the same time he was harsh against offenses committed by members of the working class and their representatives.[13]

Nor did those further down the ladder hesitate. Police and prosecutors gave the highest priority to pursuing those who broke the Arbitration Act. The police immediately launched an investigation to find those responsible for organizing the call. Among other things, they visited the representatives of the Storting who had signed the petition, but all of them refused to give statements.[14] The following day the public prosecutor presented each of them with a fine of NOK. 500, which they refused to accept. The police sent the cases the same day to the district court for summary proceedings.[15] A recently adopted change in the law had made it possible to deal with cases of misdemeanors without summoning lay judges.

4.2.2 *The Courts*

While the government starved the workers, the judiciary reacted particularly harshly towards the press. On 6 June, Norges Kommunistblad published an article about the construction workers' conflict written by Kasper Dahl. The next day, he was summoned for questioning by the police. On 8 June, the police showed up at the newsroom with an arrest warrant for the editor Henry W. Kristiansen. Charges had been brought against him for breach of the Labor Disputes Act and the Criminal

[12] Stortingstidende 1928, forhandlinger i Stortinget 20 June 1928 p. 2198.

[13] See, for example, Arbeiderbladet on Tuesday 11 May 1926.

[14] See Agderposten on Thursday 7 June 1928.

[15] Aftenposten Friday 8 June 1928.

Code for 14 articles against the Arbitration Act and the arbitration decisions. The court of inquiry imprisoned him. Also, editor Reiersen of Telemark Kommunistblad was summoned to the police and the court of inquiry for having reproduced articles from Norges Kommunistblad. On 12 June, the communist newspaper's acting editor Arvid Hansen was arrested for new articles.

On Saturday 23 June, the case against the four Labor Party MPs was held in the district court of Oslo. The court was administered by district court judge Eystein Hesselberg, the prosecutor was detective chief Sveen and the defense attorney was Emil Stang. The defender argued that the law was an unconstitutional expropriation of labor, and that in any case it did not authorize the government to decree arbitration in the case in question as serious societal interests were not at risk. The district court passed judgment on Monday 25 June and sentenced the four in accordance with the indictment to a fine of NOK. 500. This was a considerable amount, equivalent to 2000 Euro today. The district court stated that it was up to the government's discretion to decide whether to intervene in a conflict with arbitration, and that the courts could not review this discretion. The court also said that the constitution contained no prohibition against state authorities passing legislation regulating working conditions.

The case against editor Kristiansen came up before Oslo City Court on 26 June. The court was also now administered by assessor Hesselberg with Mrs. Ingrid Bakke Gabrielsen and trader Vinsent G. Hansen as lay judges. The prosecutor was Broch Utne, defender Jørgen Dahl. Professor Edvard Bull was subpoenaed as the only witness. The verdict was handed down the next day with 4 months in prison. The defense lawyer requested that Kristiansen be released from custody pending appeal of the verdict. Judge Hesselberg presented Kristiansen with a statement in which he undertook to stop any illegal writing for the duration of the conflict. When he refused to sign this, the petition for release was refused.

Hesselberg administered the court again on 28 June, this time without judges. Now several people from the leadership of the Labor Party were charged with having contributed to the strike. Three people, including Einar Gerhardsen, were also indicted for, as members of the representative council, having taken part in deciding that the party should support the strike. The prosecutor did not find the trouble worth attending.

Defense attorney Emil Stang examined Minister of social affairs Torjus Værland as the first witness. He asked which significant societal interests were at risk that made it necessary to apply the law and prohibit strike. The minister explained that the chief mediator had recommended arbitration. This was a condition in the law for the government to be able to intervene. The government believed it was important that the construction work was not put on hold. "However, the decisive factor was that economic life was very nervous at the time. The minister feared that it could not withstand a labor conflict."[16] Chief Mediator Voss emphasized in his testimony that the question of the use of arbitration fell within the discretion of the government. All

[16] Arbeiderbladet Thursday 28 June p. 7.

the defendants were sentenced to fines between NOK. 400 and 200, somewhat lower than what was stipulated in the indictments.

Most convictions were appealed to the Supreme Court. On 16 October, the Supreme Court rejected the appeal from the four members of the Storting.[17] The Supreme Court rejected the claim that the Arbitration Act conflicted with the Constitution. Supreme Court judge Karl Frimann Dahl, who of course did not take part in the hearing of the case, had explained the argument to the campaigners in an article with the headline "Shall slavery be reintroduced in Norway? And is the Arbitration Act constitutional?"[18] Since the constitutionality of the act was argued before the courts, it is of interest to examine more closely the argument put forward by justice Dahl, as it most probably inspired the defence.

Dahl opened his argument by stating that the law was hardly in direct conflict with the constitution's written sections. But he believed that this was also not decisive for whether the constitution permitted the expropriation of human labor. According to Dahl, such an expropriation was strongly against the spirit and principles of the constitution.

To reach this conclusion, Dahl argued that the constitution was not exhaustive regarding rights. The rights which the constitution expressly protected, such as the freedom of enterprise and the freedom of the press, were rights which, with the power of the absolutist Danish King fresh in mind, the founding fathers found necessary to protect in the constitution. When the constitution did not protect other human rights, such as freedom of expression, freedom of assembly, freedom of association and freedom of religion, it was because the constitution regarded them as self-evident and without the need to be explicitly mentioned. It was, for example, completely unthinkable for the founding fathers that the legislature would introduce slavery. Freedom against slavery therefore had to be protected by the constitution, even if it was not protected by an express provision.

This was not an argument that can be dismissed out of hand. He was undoubtedly right that human rights were an important part of the ideology of the men gathered to write the constitution in the spring of 1814. As Eirik Holmøyvik has pointed out, there was a lack of both time and political incentive to include a catalog of rights in the constitution (Holmøyvik 2015, p. 201). This is completely in line with Dahl's argument that the rights that were included were those that were perceived as urgent at the time. Holmøyvik argues that the founding fathers also regarded the rights as binding according to natural law, so that they lacked a legal incentive to include them. This is also in line with Dahl's argument.

There are many countries where the courts have interpreted rights which are not found in the written text into the constitution. Such a development could well have taken place in Norway too. Nevertheless, it did not turn out that way, in our tradition the courts have been reluctant to take such a dynamic approach to supplementing the constitution's catalog of rights (Opsahl 1968, pp. 49–66.

[17] Rt. 1928 p. 859.

[18] See Fremtiden Saturday 19 June 1928.

Dahl went further in his argument to place the Arbitration Act in a fundamental rights perspective. And it was at this point that the argument failed. According to Dahl, the Arbitration Act constituted legal wage slavery in that, under threat of punishment, it forced the workers to work for a wage they would not accept voluntarily. "If the law imposed compulsory labor for the wages and on the conditions determined by the purchasers of labor, no one could doubt that it had introduced pure slavery. But in reality, it will of course come to the same result if the legislature takes a detour and leaves the determination of working conditions to an arbitral tribunal appointed by a capitalist government," he wrote (Dahl 1928).

The Supreme Court briefly rejected the allegation that the law contradicted the constitution. "The applicable law on arbitration limits the right to use a strike or lockout as a means of struggle, but it does not oblige the individual to work, nor to work for a specific payment. According to his legal position, he is free, whether he wants to work or whether he does not want to work," wrote judge Breien with the agreement of the other judges.[19]

The defenders argued that forcing someone to work for a wage set by the state was a form of expropriation. Judge Schjelderup retorted that the law did not require anyone to work, nor to work for a specific payment. The individual was free to choose whether he wanted to work or not. The Supreme Court also agreed with the state that the courts could not review the government's assessment of whether it was necessary to order arbitration.

When it came to sentencing, judge Schjelderup wrote that "special consideration must be given to the fact that the law in question was given to protect important social interests" and that the accused had acted "in direct defiance or open war against the law, by those who hold the position of legislators."[20] Two days later, the Supreme Court rejected appeals from a number of other defendants, hereunder my grandfather, with the same reasoning. In the opinion of the Supreme Court, the law was in other words well-founded and the protests indefensible.

The case against the newspaper editors came up a few days later.[21] Editor Eivind Reiersen in Telemark Kommunistblad had written articles in support of the construction workers on 23 May, 31 May, 6 June and 11 June.[22] On 25 June, he was put under indictment following a decision by the state attorney in Telemark and Aust-Agder. On 15 August, he was sentenced in Skien's district court. The public prosecutor appealed the verdict on 25 August and the Supreme Court handed down its verdict on 18 October.

The case in the Supreme Court involved three editors, including editor Reiersen from Skien. The Supreme Court significantly increased the penalties in relation to the judgments in the district court, where the defendants were given fines. Judge Paulsen stated that "A call in the newspapers to put themselves above the laws and

[19] Rt. 1928 p. 859.

[20] Rt. 1928 p. 859.

[21] Rt. 1928 p. 862.

[22] Extract from Supreme Court case p. no. 38/II 1928, RA/S-1002/L/La/L0123.

seek to deprive the laws of their meaning has quite different consequences than where individuals act against the laws and seek to put them out of effect. I therefore believe that if the threats of punishment set by the Labor Disputes Act and the Arbitration Act are to be effective against newspaper editors, one cannot avoid using prison sentences, when the newspaper articles have had such a challenging content as in the present case."[23] The sentence was set to prison for 30 days.

In some cases, however, the sympathies of the lay judges may have been with the campaigners. A case from Skien against the district board of the Communist Party may indicate that. Four people were prosecuted for writing a petition in support of the construction workers. Three were sentenced by the district court to a fine of NOK. 50 each, one was acquitted. In the Court of Appeal, the judge found it necessary to admonish the jury in the legal instruction. He said that the Arbitration Act was not a coercive measure and that the Supreme Court in the case against editor Reiersen, precisely from Skien, had decided that it was not unconstitutional. The jury was bound by this. It was impossible for the jury to reach a different result. He maintained that when it came to the law's command "the juries should not go its own way in violation of the law without there being consequences for the juries concerned." It must be said to be extraordinary for the presiding judge to find necessary to so strongly emphasize the jury's duty to follow the law. This says something about the atmosphere that prevailed. The jury returned with an affirmative answer to the question of guilt, but at the same time with a recommendation to pardon the defendants.[24]

4.2.3 Harshness of Sentencing

In other words, the courts reacted quite sharply against the campaigners, without much understanding of their political and ideal motives. The law was well-founded and the protests indefensible. Challenging the law publicly was a particularly seditious act, which should be met harshly by the courts.

Not all jurists, however, agreed that the disobedience should be cracked down on. City court judge Carl Bonnevie pointed out in an article in Arbeiderbladet that the courts should take into account that many of the defendants felt it necessary to defy the law out of respect for the general principles they believed that the Arbitration Act contradicted.[25] "Great weight must be attached to whether these motives (the defendant's motives for the offence) have appeared to the accused to be respectable and morally justifiable. (. . .) If the new provisions in the Labor Disputes Act and the Temporary Act on Compulsory Arbitration, together really form an extraordinary legislation contrary to our general legal and social order, then this must

[23] Rt. 1928 p. 862.

[24] See report from the case in Telemark Arbeiderblad 10 December 1928.

[25] Arbeiderbladet Tuesday 3 July 1928.

be a mitigating factor for those who violate this exceptional law," he wrote in a classic appeal to treat those who commit civil disobedience against unjust laws more leniently than ordinary offenders. This view was clearly not the prevailing view among the judges who ruled in the cases.

According to the instructions of the Supreme Court, the punishment for editors who published petitions and appeals was a minimum of 30 days in prison. Many received more severe punishments if they had also written articles that came under stricter penal provisions. The level of punishment was hardly high enough to have a particularly deterrent effect. Nor was it so high that it could be said that the government used disproportionate means against the campaigners. On the other hand, the Supreme Court's rulings bore no sign of showing leniency or tolerance towards civil disobedience.

The kind of resources that were deployed by the police and the speed with which they reacted against the campaigners was also remarkable. On the other hand, reading other criminal cases may indicate that a short time from apprehension to trial and sentence at that time was quite normal. There are unfortunately no statistics on the processing time in criminal cases. It is therefore difficult in retrospect to judge whether the processing time of these cases was extraordinarily short. What is reasonably certain is that the treatment they were given does not suggest a particular tolerance of their nature as political acts carried out by otherwise law-abiding citizens.

The measures against the striking workers and their families were even more draconian. Admittedly, they were not tried or sentenced. But the law assured that they were without support from the trade unions. It was a criminal offense for others to give them support. In addition, the government ensured that neither they nor their families could receive contributions from the welfare system or benefits from the sickness funds.

4.2.4 Paal Berg and the Labor Court

The conflict ended when the employers brought the strike to the labor court to get a court ruling that the conflict was illegal, so that they could escalate the conflict with a lockout in other sectors. After the negotiations in the court had ended, the chairman of the court, Paal Berg, took the initiative for a settlement between the parties. Under Berg's leadership, the parties approved an agreement which ended with them accepting a proposal that Berg put forward. Here the salary reduction of 12 per cent was split in two, so that 8 per cent was to be taken immediately and the remaining 4 the following year. The last part was linked to the development in the index and was therefore in reality omitted. With this, the settlement ended with the arbitration award being set aside.

For all purposes Berg annulled the arbitration court's judgment as he rejected to establish that a strike against the arbitration court was illegal. This would have been both the ordinary and expected course of action for the Labor Court. Berg chose here to follow his own judgment instead of the law. Negotiating a settlement was not against the law, but it was a creative solution that the law did not expressively provide for. It meant that the outcome of the conflict for the workers was as if it had been an ordinary legal conflict; a forced settlement with the employers with better conditions for the workers compared to the offer that had triggered the strike. In effect, Berg with this undermined the legitimacy of the arbitration court and the use of compulsory arbitration.

Signe Wullf writes that it would have been desirable to further investigate Paal Berg's role here, but that it has not been possible due to a lack of sources (Wulf 1980, p. 17). Berg's biographer Per Hem refers to notes from the CEO of the employers' association Finn Dahl, which became known later, and which indicate that Dahl on behalf of the employers and Trygve Lie on behalf of the trade unions had talked about the possibility of a settlement (Hem 2012). It is therefore not certain that settlement was Berg's initiative or idea. In any case, it is important that he allowed such an unusual solution, and that he put his stamp on this solution and cut through the fact that the workers had defied the arbitration court's ruling and entered into an illegal and punishable conflict. With this, Paal Berg used the authority of the Labor Court to signal that the court did not immediately take the authorities' hard line in this conflict, and that finding a solution was more important than giving the employers a verdict that the conflict was illegal and had to end.

4.3 "Very Law-Abiding Citizens"

District court judge Carl Bonnevie wrote in Arbeiderbladet:

> Now the situation is not that the contributors to the fundraising are people who want to defy our legal order and the laws as such. Most of them are probably very law-abiding citizens. It is because the 'penitentiary laws' are considered in large social circles to conflict with our general legal order, that the fundraising has received so much support.[26]

Bonnevie links here to the classic notion of civil disobedience, a conscience-based, public, non-violent, politically motivated offence, which aims to bring about a change in public authority policies or laws (Rawls 1972, p. 364).

Apparently, there is a paradox in this, both being law-abiding and breaking the law. The key word is conscience, an inner voice that speaks to us with greater authority than the law in the individual case. It is something internal and psychological at the same time as it is social. It is already in the word: *con*, the social, and *science*, the inner knowledge and conviction (Brownlee 2012, p. 52). A well-developed conscience does not allow us to follow our inner voice regardless of what this leads to for others. Thus, the experience of being bound by the law and respect for the law is a core point in the conscience-based political offence, and something that makes it morally respectable.

[26] Arbeiderbladet Tuesday 3 June 1928.

How did a municipal auditor from a small village in Telemark get involved in this? Although many people participated by breaking the law, they were after all only a tiny minority of the population. There is little doubt about my grandfather Torjus' respect for the laws and general law-abidingness. His career choice was a job as a guardian of the law. Haugesund's Dagblad had a presentation of him in 1934 where he was described as "an unsentimental gentleman who has received the auditor's stamp as a cradle gift. (...) The man is surrounded with the necessary respect, and a nimbus that no one can take away from him has already grown around his name."[27] The characterization came after his disclosure of embezzlement in union coffers. He rapidly created an accounting and auditing system for the trade union movement that commanded respect. In 1938 he had a staff of five men after having started alone as an auditor in LO in 1933.

Torjus created for himself a reputation as strict and reliable through his time at Rjukan. In February 1933 he was appointed as the first permanent auditor of the federation of trade union. The board of representatives chose to hire him rather than the person the secretariat had nominated as number one. The choice was political. "As auditor who has to mess around and dig into the accounts, they don't want a man who stands in opposition," he wrote in a letter to his brother Olav.[28] He assumed the position of union auditor on 20 February 1933.

He quickly gained respect. First, he discovered an embezzlement in the construction workers' union. This led him to initiate a larger investigation. He set about reviewing the associations' accounts 10 years back. In December 1933, he discovered an embezzlement of NOK. 52,000 in the Norwegian Wood-Workers' Association. It also turned out that the embezzlement in the construction workers' union was much larger than first revealed. In an interview, he stressed that there was no need to panic because of the embezzlement that was discovered. For the most part, the staff of treasurers in the associations were honorable and capable.

"If you compare with the numerous embezzlements in the private business world, the comparison falls entirely in favor of our organizations," he said in an interview with Arbeiderbladet.[29] The liberal newspaper Dagbladet described him as "a relatively young, energetic man, with great accounting knowledge and a healthy and skeptical view of life."[30]

Most of the embezzlements in the unions were done in need and desperation in times of real hardship. Torjus found the work difficult, he pitied those who were exposed. But dishonesty had to be uncovered and sorted out for the sake of trade union work.

That he was law-abiding and demanded this of others was clear, but where did his conscience come from? And what led him to willingly break with the authority of the law, which was, after all, so embedded in the image he had created of himself as an

[27] Haugesund's Dagblad Tuesday 9 January 1934.

[28] Private letter 25 June 1932.

[29] Arbeiderbladet Thursday 7 December 1933.

[30] Dagbladet Saturday 6 January 1934.

auditor? His upbringing was marked by simple means, hard work, and respect for knowledge and book learning, His background was what we can describe as sobriety, piety, and reflection.

Torjus was born on 9 October 1893 and grew up on the small farm Nedre Gravir in Fyresdal, a somewhat remote municipality of Southern Norway. The farm was modest but provided income for the family who lived there. His parents Petter and Margit were both of families of farmers. They had 5 children, Torjus was the eldest son. He had an older sister and two younger sisters and a brother. Their grandmother Torbjørg also lived on the farm, in addition to a servant girl. In addition to forestry, the farm had had a horse, cows, sheep, and pigs.

The farmers in Telemark were a well-read people, so also at Nedre Gravir. They had, like many other farms, the Bible, a book of devotion, a hymn book, and Snorri's sagas of the old Norse Kings. They also kept a weekly newspaper. In addition, the village library had an unusually large and good collection of books with many classics. It was rumored that Torjus had read through the entire collection twice.

Torjus wanted out of the village to seek knowledge. In this he received support from his father. Petter was eager for the children to have an education, the girls too. Alas, the money was not sufficient, so Torjus was the only one of the children sent out to learn. He was considered particularly intelligent, not least because he read so much. Besides, he was smaller than his little brother, who made himself more useful in the farm work. His little brother Olav was big and strong and capable at chopping timber, and in this way raised money for Torjus to get an education. Torjus brought the togetherness and solidarity with him into the world, together with a solid ballast of piety and culture.

The social element in a conscience-based offense often comes from a religiously based fervor, and Christianity has inspired many to identify and show solidarity with the poor and oppressed. But with Torjus there was also something more. One of his inspirations was Professor Edvard Bull. Bull was one of the central ideologues in the Labor Party in the 1920s and was deputy chairman of the party from 1923. Bull was a historian, particularly concerned with medieval history and the history of Norwegian smallholders. This appealed to Torjus with his background.

The outbreak of the world war in 1914 was decisive for Torjus. He had just finished his conscription military service and could easily imagine the fear and misery of the young boys in the trenches. Once on a hike in the forest, he told me, as he lit his pipe, how lighting a match was the last thing many young lads did because it gave the enemy enough to aim for to put in a well-aimed shot. This thought stuck in him over 50 years after the war.

In 1915, he helped found the Students' Liberal Party at the Norwegian Institute of Technology (Norges tekniske høgskole, NTH), Trondheim where he studied. The aim was primarily to arouse and nurture interest in the Liberal Party. The foundation was welcomed "not least for the reason that it was formed by and will always for the most part consist of young technical academics, future leaders of the country's practical business life," wrote a contemporary local newspaper.[31] On the same day that the newspaper Nidaros reported this, the front page was filled with reports about the war on the continent.

Engineering studies were not for Torjus. He interrupted his studies and traveled to Oslo to attend business school. He did not dare to tell this to his father, and he exchanged letters with home through the girlfriend he had met in Trondheim. He thus feared the authority of his father, but not enough to avoid deception and disobedience. Here his inclination to defy authority showed itself.

His wife Marie became pregnant with my father in the autumn of 1919. It was urgent for them to get a stable living. Luckily Torjus was offered a job as a municipal auditor in Tinn municipality in Rjukan. They moved there at the beginning of 1920. On 20 February they married, and on 30 May their eldest son Petter, my father, was born. Later they had the children Odd and Astrid.

At Rjukan Torjus met what was one of the most vibrant radical intellectual settings of the time. Rjukan was a center for both trade union activities and radical politics. Rjukan was the country's largest industrial town with over 8000 inhabitants at most. This was twice as many as in the second largest industrial town of Norway at the time.[32] Industry had started in Rjukan in 1911 when Norsk Hydro established its plant to produce fertilizer from air and electricity. This process had heavy water as a by-product, something that made Rjukan famous during World War II, since this was a product needed by the Germans in their attempts to make the atomic bomb before the allies.

From the beginning of the 1920s, Rjukan was a hotbed for the organization Mot Dag, an outgrowth of the social democratic student council in Oslo, led by Erling Falk. Several later well-known intellectual communists and socialists were active in Mot Dag. Most of Mot Dag's members were disillusioned sons of the bourgeoisie and ruling elites (Morgan 2020).

The newspaper Rjukan Arbeiderblad was founded in 1922 as the only party organ for the Labor Party in the whole of the county of Telemark. The first editors and editorial secretaries were members of Mot Dag, and the newspaper was called Mot Dag's educational institution. Erling Falk sent people from all over the country to work on the newspaper, so that Rjukan became a living center for the intellectual labor movement. Historian Harald Berntsen has characterized the labor movement in Rjukan at this time as "originally rabble-roused and semi-syndicalist, but at the same time a litterate and theoretically interested labor movement" (Berntsen 1995, p. 87).

The circle around Rjukan Arbeiderblad brought many of the era's socialist intellectuals to Rjukan. The historian Jakob Friis was editor of the newspaper from 1925–1928, sent by the influential Labor Party politician, editor and agitator Martin Tranmæl. The editorial staff of Rjukan Arbeiderblad was from the start a subdivision of the radical student milieu. Torjus also received his intellectual stimulation and inspiration here.

[31] Nidaros Thursday 15 April 1915.

[32] The Census in Norway 1920, first booklet, Statistics Norway Oslo 1922 p. 18.

Friis was the son of the executive director of the Røros copper works, and a study mate and close friend of later history professor Edvard Bull. The labor movement included many who had a background or work in the privileged classes. Many of them had higher education. "In no other western country did the ideas of the labor movement have such an influence in the academic world as in Norway," Trygve Bull writes in his book about Mot Dag and Erling Falk (Bull 1955, p. 58). The attachment to communism and dialectical materialism was particularly significant to the most revolutionary wing of the labor movement. Many of them were the sons of radicals from the heyday of the liberal movement of the nineteenth century (Figueiredo 2002, p. 94).

Torjus got involved in workers' unions in Rjukan. He joined the Labor Party and was secretary of Norway's Communist Association in Rjukan, an association that at the time was collectively affiliated with the Labor Party. After the break between the Communists and the Labor Party in 1923, Torjus remained with the Labor Party. He was for periods a member of the municipal council and on the board of the Rjukan Labor Party.

Torjus early participated in solidarity work to support workers on strike. He regarded solidarity and respect for other people as a constructive force, both for society and for himself. In January 1924 he was appointed to a committee which worked to collect money for the benefit of striking ironworkers. The strike funds were almost sufficient to feed those who were without work and income, nevertheless children and young people fainted in food queues throughout the long winter (Bals 2022, p. 213). The committee was also encouraged to search for families willing to host children of the strikers at Rjukan.[33] In total, the committee at Rjukan collected NOK. 1952.50 and provided space for 3 children.

His background from modest circumstances, a Christian upbringing, and at the same time a great emphasis on seeking knowledge and education, shaped both his respect for the law and his inner voice, which commanded him to break it when injustice was obvious, as with the arbitration law. At the same time, he was in a social environment where it was generally accepted that the law was illegitimate. When he signed the list of contributors he was in good company. Over 1000 key politicians and trustees had taken part in the original appeal. In Rjukan alone, over 1100 people joined the call. Considering that Rjukan at that time had a population of 7800, this was a formidable number.

We know from historical events how strongly social pressure, and a desire not to stand out, can influence people's actions. This would probably not in itself have been enough to push a law-abiding man into breaking the law. But so many generally respected and law-abiding people were at the forefront of the offenders, alongside with known revolutionaries and regular demonstrators. It was precisely the conscience-based support that gave the campaign its power, a power that would lead to the authorities admitting their mistake a little later and to withdrawing the law and the sanctions.

[33] Rjukan Arbeiderblad Tuesday 29 January 1924.

4.3.1 *The Demise of the Arbitration Act*

"The law against illegal strikes has stood the test," wrote Minister Evjenth in a widely published article in Dagbladet on 25 July 1928 after the settlement of the construction workers' dispute in the labor court. "Necessary to maintain the current system of legal remedies in full."[34] He portrayed the settlement in the labor court as a victory for the Arbitration Act and the government's line. There were probably not many who agreed with this. The act had not prevented the strike, and the strike had led to a better deal for the workers.

The Arbitration Act which was adopted in 1927 was, by its content, temporary. On 25 April 1929, the liberal government presented a bill to extend the Act. The Liberal Party's proposal had originally been that it should be a permanent law, and this was still the party line. The Ministry pointed out that compulsory arbitration had been practiced several times throughout the 1920s, and that it was a means of protecting society's interests against the destructive effects of open industrial conflict. Although both employers' and employees' organizations were in principle against arbitration, they had largely aligned themselves with the judgments.

According to the proposal, the events of 1928 were an exception to this. Nevertheless, the ministry would not see this as an expression of a breakdown of the arbitration system as such. "When it proved difficult to get this judgment carried out, this was primarily due to the special conditions within the construction workers organizations," wrote the ministry. The ministry admitted that opinions on whether arbitration should have been used at all during this conflict could be divided.

The Social Committee at the Storting split into three factions.[35] The Labor Party representatives referred to their comments during the debate in 1927. They did not agree that arbitration was suitable for protecting society from the destructive effects of labor strife, but argued that, on the contrary, it intensified the strife rather than softened it. The right-wing representatives were also against extending the law. They referred to their principled objections to arbitration. Moreover, they added that "the further experiences with the temporary law, especially the events that took place during the construction dispute last year, are apt to increase the misgivings one must have about the application of compulsory arbitration." The representatives of the Farmers' Party and the Liberal Party supported the proposal.

During the debate in Parliament, even representatives who supported the proposal to extend the law distanced themselves from the way it had been enforced the previous year. The Farmers' Party's Jens Hundseid said: "Finally, I believe that the penalty provisions for violations of this law are incorrect. Nothing has contributed more to undermining the authority of the Arbitration Act and the belief in forced arbitration in labor disputes than all these sanctions last year and the proposal for an amnesty law this year. For one Krone one could obtain fines and imprisonment and the glory of martyrdom. No wonder the Storting's only woman was among the first.

[34] Dagbladet Wednesday 25 July 1928.

[35] Innst O. X 1929.

Women are accused of being a little bit vain. And a martyr's halo is nice to wear, although this was now a bit of a bargain compared to the good old real halos. But the fact that there is access to this kind of antics weakens the authority of the law."[36] Those who opposed the law committed political crimes, not ordinary crimes. And as political crimes they should be treated as such, not with fines and imprisonment, but with political punishment and loss of privileges, Hunseid argued.

John Norem from the Conservative Pary believed that there were two alternatives based on the lessons that could be drawn from the past year: "*Either* we have to ensure that legal provisions are passed that effectively deter those who put themselves above the law; that is to say, the law's liability rules and penal provisions must be revised and expanded in such a way that the authorities are not once again powerless when it comes to preventing an illegal work stoppage. - I think this road is quite difficult to walk down. *Or,* if you don't want to go that way, you have to admit that the forced arbitration, a state regulation of wages puts our entire legal society to such a severe test, it breeds such bitterness and also entails such great disadvantages that little, or nothing will be won by going that way."

Prime Minister Mowinckel blamed the Labor Party for the lawlessness the law had led to. "I would say that it is regrettable that there is a such a demonstration against a law, and I think that the Labor Party was extremely unwise in its sympathy to support demonstrations against the laws of society," he said. He added that they should use the ordinary parliamentary means like everyone else. He also took the trade unions as support for his view, pointing out that they never supported the strike or demonstrations against the law, but on the contrary warned against them and distanced themselves. He bypassed the fact that he and the others who had adopted the law had ensured the passivity of the unions by making them liable for compensation if the acted in favor of illegal action.

The vote resulted in a majority of 59 votes to reject the proposal to extend the law, 37 voted against. The Arbitration Act was thus history. There is little doubt that the extensive civil disobedience was the cause of this. The obedience was a strong appeal to the majority and showed the injustice of depriving the workers of the strike weapon and the possibility of effective support from their own organizations. The actions had not forced the system to its knees, society had been through harsh and long-lasting labor disputes before, and more were to come. The state had the means to crush resistance if it wanted. One can therefore hardly ignore the moral appeal that lay in the fact that thousands of otherwise law-abiding citizens exposed themselves to society's punishment, and that this situation became intolerable for the political majority. This was also evident in the amnesty that was adopted for those who had taken part in the action, onto which we will immediately turn.

[36] Stortingstidende 1929, forhandlinger i Odelstinget 6 June 1929 p. 458.

4.4 The Amnesty Law

Although the law itself was history, it was still felt by the hundreds who had been fined for breaking it. About half of these had not yet paid the fine or served the prison sentence due if the fine was not paid. For those who believed that the fight against the law was a just fight against an illegitimate law, which was even crowned with victory, it was untenable that those convicted were to pay the fines now that the fight was won. In January 1929, both the Communist Party and the Labor Party proposed an amnesty law. The Odelsting decided to put aside the Communist proposal and to send the Labor Party proposal to the government.

The fact that Mowinckel's damaged prestige had prompted the adoption of Section 222 II of the Penal Code was itself a provocation. Mowinckel would not make that mistake again. In the opening of Parliament on 23 January, he said, "I would very much like to extend a conciliatory hand. I would very much like what happened to be forgotten."[37] He was nevertheless surprised by accusations that the government had been provocative. The government had had no desire to provoke, but had responded to "the ever-threatening move that the Labor Party is taking towards the government," he said. Forgotten was the instruction to the municipalities to cut the poor allowances for the workers and their families. He did not forget what he perceived as threats from the Labor Party. But he was willing to forget. He announced that the government wanted to carry out an amnesty as a special pardon for last year's offence, although he thought it might be difficult.

Mowinckel followed up a few weeks later. The proposal for amnesty for offenses on the occasion of the 1928 strike in the construction and graphic arts was put forward on 15 March.[38] Both the Labor Party and the Communist Party put forward their own proposals for amnesty laws. The Labor Party had previously put forward a proposal for an amnesty law in connection with party leaders being imprisoned in 1925, convicted of inciting a military strike and sedition. The Labor Party primarily wanted a law that gave the government a general mandate to issue amnesty, but alternatively advocated a law that granted amnesty to those who had been convicted of the actions against the Arbitration Act.

Both the government and the Labor Party proposal came up for debate on 10 June. The Conservative Party opposed any form of amnesty. The Justice Committee's chairman, Olav Fjalstad, said that "if one goes to the adoption of an amnesty law today, it could be the first step on a rather slanted level, namely the weakening of the legislative power and thus also the authority of the power of the state."[39] In other words, he was afraid of the consequences of tolerating civil disobedience. The possible effects on general obedience of the law is a classic argument against being tolerant of civil disobedience. He also doubted the labor movement's willingness to reconcile: "Should amnesty be a question in this case: extending a

[37] Stortingstidende 1929, forhandlinger i Stortinget 23 January 1929 p. 86.

[38] Ot. Prp. No. 19 (1929).

[39] Stortingstidende, forhandlinger i Odelstinget 10 June 1929 p. 494.

conciliatory hand - then the prerequisite must be that society's hand is received with the same attitude with which it is extended, one should not reasonably fear that there will be a dagger hidden in the toga of the other party." He thus maintained that punishment is necessary to ensure obedience and respect for the laws.

Those in favor of amnesty argued differently. The Labor Party's Knut Nordanger, later county governor in Hedmark, said that "a state cannot in the long run do without a certain sense of unity among the people, and if the effect of a law is destructive to this sense of unity, then it is primarily in the state's interest to have that situation changed."[40] This is a line of thought that reconciliation is necessary to prevent the conflict from developing, allowing society to move forward.

The amnesty law was passed against the votes of the Conservative Party and the Farmers Party. For the Labor Party it was the final victory over the arbitration act and the use of criminal law against strikers and those supporting them. Trygve Lie and Halvard Olsen called it "one of the more significant facts in the history of the trade union and the political labor movement (Olsen and Lie 1931, pp. 79–80)." The striking construction workers had "shown that there were clear limits to how far the government could go in its attempts to discipline and rein in the trade union movement," writes Jonas Bals in his comprehensive book about the use of strike in Norwegian history Bals (2022, p. 239.) Now remained the fight against the second part of the penitentiary laws, the criminalization of measures against the strikebreakers.

References

Bals J (2022) Streik! En historie om strid, samhold og solidaritet. Res Publica, Oslo

Berntsen H (1995) To liv - en sjebne (Two lives – one destiny). Aschehoug, Oslo

Brownlee K (2012) Conscience and conviction: the case for civil disobedience. Oxford Legal Philosophy, Oxford

Bull T (1955) Mot Dag og Erling Falk (Mot Dag and Erling Falk). Cappelen, Oslo

Dahl KF (1928) Voldgiftslovens sammenbrudd (Collapse of the Arbitration Act), Kongsvinger Arbeiderblad Saturday 4 August 1928

Figueiredo I (2002) Fri mann – Johan Bernhard Hjort, en dannelseshistorie (Free man Johan Bernhard Hjort – a journey of education). Aschehoug, Oslo

Hem P (2012) *Megleren: Paal Berg* 1873-1968, (The Mediator: Paal Berg 1973–1968) Aschehoug, Oslo

Holmøyvik E (2015) Folkesuverenitet, likskap og menneskerettar i 1814 (Popular sovereignty, equality and human rights in 1814), in Eirik Holmøyvik og Dag Michalsen. Lærebok i forfatningshistorie, Pax Forlag, Oslo

Morgan H (2020.) How a Small Student Magazine Helped Build Norway's Social-Democratic Common Sense, Jacobin https://jacobin.com/2020/07/norway-labor-party-social-democracy-mot-dag-magazine

Olsen H, Lie T (1931) De arbeiderfiendtlige lover og kampen mot dem, (The anti-worker laws and the fight against them). Arbeidernes faglige Landsorganisasjon, Oslo

[40] Stortingstidende, forhandlinger i Odelstinget 10 June 1929 p. 497.

Opsahl T (1968) Skal vi modernisre individenes grunnlovsvern? (Should we modernize the protection of individual rights in the constitution? Originally in Lov og rett 1968 pp. 49–66, reprinted in Torkel Opsahl, State power and human rights, vol. 1, Ad Notam Oslo 1995

Rawls J (1972) A theory and justice. Oxford University Press, Oxford

Schock K (2021) Consequences of civil disobedience. In: Scheuerman WE (ed) The Cambridge companion to civil disobedience. Cambridge University Press, Cambridge

Volan E (1928) Kampen mot tukthus- og voldgiftslovene, (The battle against the penitentiary and arbitration laws). Andelsforlaget, Oslo

Wulf S (1980) Tvers igjennom lov til arbeidsfred: bygningsarbeiderstreiken 1928 (Through the law to labor peace: the construction workers' strike of 1928), master's thesis in history at the University of Oslo

Chapter 5
Criminal Law Against Industrial Action

5.1 The Case of Rådhushospitset

It was not long before Section 222 II of the Penal Code was employed against workers and others who participated in labor disputes. Some of the first cases related to the conflict over working conditions at Rådhushospitset, a hotel in central Oslo. The conflict was a test case for the right to a collective agreement for hotel and restaurant workers. Five young campaigners were imprisoned for four weeks for demonstrating outside the hotel and handing out leaflets.

The owner of Rådhushospitset refused to enter into a collective agreement with the Food and Beverage Association. The conflict over Rådhushospitset unfolded as part of one of the most bitter battles in Norwegian history over the neutrality and autonomy of the law. It extended not only to labor law, but also to the law on licensing of premises to serve alcohol. When the strike was rendered ineffective because of the law's protection of the employer's right to employ strike breakers during the conflict, the municipality, where the Labor Party together with the teetotalist movement had the majority, refused to renew the hotel's serving license. The link between the fight over working conditions at the hotels and the right to serve alcohol was not limited to Rådhushospitset in Oslo.

The same happened in Bergen, where the municipal council decided on 27 October 1930 to take away the right to serve drinks from the Terminus, Norge and Bristol hotels, as well as the Børscafeen in connection with the fact that these were affected by a strike in order to establish a collective agreement. The Norwegian Hotel and Restaurant Association appealed this decision to the Ministry of Social Affairs, which declared the decision invalid. Bergen municipality refused to comply with the ministry's decision, but nevertheless gave the four restaurants their licenses back after the labor dispute had been resolved.[1]

[1] See Ot. prp. No. 11 1931 p. 3.

H. P. Graver, *Democracy and Lawlessness*,
https://doi.org/10.1007/978-3-031-69055-6_5

Rådhushospitset, Rosenkrantz gate 21, was located on what is today the corner between Rosenkrantz gate and Otto Sverdrups gaten near the harbor of Oslo. At the time, Tordenskiolds plass was located here, a square that opened onto the city pier and the old suburb of Piperviken, which, with the city council's decision in 1923 to build a new town hall, was doomed to disappear together with the old square. In the summer, Piperviken buzzed with life, with sea bathing and local boats and ferries that carried the traffic between the town and the departure points further out in the Oslo fjord. In winter it was quite quiet. The sea hero Tordenskiold stood on a plinth in the middle of the square, "surrounded by an armada of big smelly regular buses (Overn 1929, p. 75)." The space was described as "a large and congested traffic square." Central to this square was Rådhushospitset. The hotel had 54 rooms, and the price for a single room was NOK. 5 per day, and for a double room NOK. 9 (Christensen 1925, p. 7).

The conflict started when most of the employees at the hotel joined the Food and Beverage Association on 1 December 1927 and demanded a collective agreement. The hotel opposed the demand, and the workers went on strike. The hotel nevertheless continued operations by hiring unorganized workers. Wages in the industry were low and working hours long. None of the companies in the hotel industry in Oslo had a collective agreement. At Rådhushospitset, conditions were particularly bad.

Statistics Norway's survey of wages and working conditions in hotel and cafe operations for 1925 shows that the average wage in 1925 for room maids, who were the lowest paid group, was an average of NOK 69 a month for those under 20, while those over 26 years earned an average of NOK 77 a month.[2] 95 percent of the maids in Oslo had a working day of more than 12 hours. Wages in general in the country had been through sharp reductions and were on average reduced between 10 and 15% from 1925 to 1927.[3] The female workers made up about 90 per cent of the employees in the industry.

The pay and working conditions at Rådhushospitset in 1927 were "unbelievably poor". Salaries for some were reduced by a third at the hotel as a result of the drop in prices.[4] The female part of the staff had a working week of 84 h, the men 90–96 h. The salary for the women was NOK 60 a month plus board and lodging, for the men from NOK 50 to 180 plus board (Medby 1951, p. 51). The staff were treated like slaves.[5]

The battle between employers and employees over organization and pay and working conditions within the hotel and restaurant industry turned Rådhushospitset into a battleground. The conflict was "the first real battle that the Hotel and Restaurant Workers Union waged to bring an end to the shameful looting of the

---

[2] Statistics Norway, Arbeidsfoholdene ved hotell- og kafevirksomhet 1925 p. 15.

[3] Statistics Norway, Lønninger 1927, Norges offisielle statistikk VIII.

[4] See Norges Kommunistblad on Friday 18 May 1928.

[5] According to an article in Arbeiderbladet on Monday 9 December 1929.

workers at the city's hotels, and the battle was waged for months with the greatest determination on the part of the strikers," Norges Kommunistblad wrote.[6]

The fight started after representatives of the Oslo Hotel and Restaurant Workers Union approached the staff at the hotel. They organized the staff and got them to demand a collective agreement. The workers' claim was rejected after the manager had conferred with the board and with the Norwegian Hotel and Restaurant Association.[7] The conflict lasted for four years, until 1931. The manager of the hotel, Miss Berge, was characterized in the newspaper Arbeiderbladet as a "very stubborn woman".[8]

On Tuesday 3 January 1928, the Oslo Hotel and Restaurant Workers' Union had an advertisement in the newspapers with a "warning" in which they announced that "No honorable worker must take emplyment at the Hotel Rådhushospitset, Rosenkrantzgate 19 & 21, as there is a conflict there for the recognition of the right to organize. Transport to and from the hotel is also blocked."[9] The hotel kept going with theology students as strikebreakers. These could be recruited as the hotel belonged to a christian foundation. The strikers organized pickets, handed out leaflets in the streets with the names of the strike-breakers and urged visitors not to enter the hotel. The police, for their part, kept watch day and night at the hotel while the conflict was going on.

On Sunday 22 January, the police decided to act. They arrested five strikers who were handing out leaflets listing the names of strikers who worked at the hotel. The five were released with a warning. On the same day, the police arrested them again and charged them with breaching section 222 II of the Norwegian Civil Code for trying to prevent people from carrying out their work during a work stoppage. This time the police did not release them, but produced them in the court of inquiry, which remanded them in custody for up to a month. They were kept in jail for the whole of this period.

The trial two months later against the five young activists took place before Oslo City Court in Møllergata 19, the city's court and police chamber building. The court session lasted six hours. Three of the defendants were 19 years old, the other two were respectively 20 and 22. The three nineteen-year-olds met with guardians. The professional judge was assessor Nikolai Johan Hoff, later a judge and responsible for the trails against collaborators and traitors after the war at Oslo City Court. He was known for his "restrained, matter-of-fact administration, with a distinct ability to moderate hot tempers and create respect for the court."[10] The defender was Emil Stang. For his work on the case, he was awarded a fee that exceeded the monthly salary of the maids at the hotel.

---

[6] Norges Kommunistblad on Monday 15 October 1928.

[7] See Rt. 1933 p. 548 p. 550.

[8] Arbeiderbladet Thursday 26 January 1928.

[9] Arbeiderbladet Tuesday 3 January 1928.

[10] Aftenposten 6 September 1969.

The five campaigners were accused of breaching Section § 222 II and Section 350 second paragraph on disturbances. The indictment for violation of Section 222 II had been ordered by the Attorney General himself. According to the indictment, they had "provided public information about who is working or has worked during a work stoppage" and disrupted public traffic "by charging and harassing people who came to or left the establishment Rådhushospitset." They had been kept in custody for their performance for over four weeks, from the day they were imprisoned until March 2 and 5.

"We appear here in court, not because we feel responsible to this class court, not because we feel responsible to the prison laws of the bourgeoisie, we despise them as much as we hate capitalist society," said the first defendant when he took the stand after the prosecutor's introduction.[11] He continued that he and his co-defendants hoped to have "contributed so that the fight the striking workers at Rådhushospitset are waging will be a fight not only against the owners of the hotel, not only against the hotel and restaurant association, but also against the state and the judiciary, which so benevolently have helped the employers in their struggle against the just demands of the workers." The reason they had distributed the lists of those who worked during the strike was "so that all workers would become aware of them and shun them like the plague, like the wretched pack they are."

During the trial, Miss Berge denied that the conditions at the hotel were bad. To an "involuntary loud laughter" from the defendants and the audience, she said that the working conditions were better than elsewhere.[12] As an example she pointed out a girl who had been with hotel for 12 years. She had NOK 80 a month. When Mrs. Solberg, who worked in the laundry, said that she had a working day of 12 hours and often more, Miss Berge protested and said that the working hours were from 7 to 4. "If she was kept in meetings in the basement," this was her own responsibility. "But if the work wasn't finished?" asked lawyer Stang. "Then she takes it the next day," was the reply. "But if it doesn't finish then either and it piles up?" "One day it must be finished," replied Miss Berge to great cheers in the courtroom.[13]

The court found four of the five guilty of breaching the Section 222 II. The fifth was acquitted when the court did not find it proved that he participated in the distribution of the leaflets. All five were acquitted of the charge of disorderly conduct. The court did not find it proven that the general peace and order or lawful traffic was disturbed by the defendants speaking to those coming and going from the hotel and making them aware that the hotel was blocked during a labor dispute.

The penalty was set at a fine of NOK 100, which was deemed to have been served by enduring detention. Account was taken that the defendants were previously

---

[11] Norges Kommunistblad Wednesday 28 March 1928.

[12] Norges Kommunistblad Wednesday 28 March 1928.

[13] Dagbladet, Wednesday 28 March 1928.

unpunished and that "the manner in which Section 222 II of the Criminal Code has been violated here must be considered of a less serious nature."[14]

The four appealed to the Court of Appeal, where the case was tried on 18 May. Lawyer Stang pointed out that the hotel and restaurant association's blacklisting of the striking workers after a conflict, and circulation of the lists with a warning to other hotels against employing them, was legal. Publication of names of workers who had been on strike effectively pushed them out of the labor market in a situation with mass employment. This showed the hollowness of the Penitentiary Act's ban against publication *during* a conflict, and thus in practice against the workers alone. The law was biased and contradicted the principle of equality before the law. His arguments were not regarded by the court. The public prosecutor submitted a request for unconditional imprisonment for the four. The jury found the defendants guilty, and the court sentenced them to a fine of NOK 100, like the district court.

This was not the only case originating from the conflict. A few months later, editor Just Lippe of the communist newspaper Klassekampen stood trial, accused of having published a list of strikebreakers at Rådhushospitset. The administrator was again assessor Hoff.[15] The newspaper had published the names of strikebreakers in two articles.

The defender, attorney Jørgen Dahl, said that "the penitentiary clause is an abuse of power, as it must be clear to everyone that the relationship between workers and employers is so complicated and delicate that it cannot be regulated or solved by legal clauses of this nature." He also said that it could not be proved that the publication had been made with the intention of preventing the strike-breakers from working.

Lippe himself showed how the history of the labor movement had been characterized by the struggle for the right to organize as the greatest good and the most sacred right, and that the struggle becomes hard and bitter when you try to rob them of this right with the help of the state authorities and the judiciary. "When the law was passed which will now be used against me, a fight was announced on the part of the workers. When those in power nevertheless thought they could push the law through, it was because their policy to stabilize the economy required a consolidation of all forces and thus forcing the workers' organizations to become their tools. This plan was of course doomed in advance, and we can also see that the law has completely broken down and that it is not possible to enforce it."[16]

The city court sentenced Lippe to a fine of NOK 100, 20 days in prison if the fine was not paid. The verdict was unanimous.

[14] Oslo City Court judgment 28 March 1928, State Archives in Oslo, SAO/A-10456/G/Gc/Gcb/Gcbd/L0117.

[15] See report from the case in Norges Kommunistblad on Wednesday 13 June 1928.

[16] Ibid.

5.2 Penal Code § 222 II in the Supreme Court

The new law was not popular among judges and lawyers. According to Gunnar Ousland, who has written the history of the trade union movement, "neither the prosecuting authority, the prosecutors, nor judges (. . .) liked to enforce this exception law (Criminal Code Section 222 II). They were always told that they sat there and judged as if on command, against their own convictions. Everyone had a feeling that it was an instrument of the capitalist class, whether it was necessary or not (Ousland 1975, p. 368)."

Per Ole Johansen, who has written a book about the battle over the Menstad plant, one of the most famous of the confrontations between striking workers and the police, writes that "judge Nygård, who led the appeal court proceedings against the Menstad protesters, and State Attorney Hartmann, who was the prosecutor on the same occasion, had little sympathy for the second part of section 222 of the Criminal Code (Johansen 1977, p. 329)."

"As a lawyer, I have noticed that the prosecutors often use other provisions, because they do not like to use Section 222, II. It must therefore be possible to say that in practice and action it has almost ceased to exist," said Trygve Lie during the LO congress in 1934.[17]

Professor of Criminal Law at the University of Oslo Jon Skeie also believed that the judges in their assessment of evidence were influenced by the "hateful atmosphere, which has been built up against the 'penitentiary law' (Skeie 1931, p. 520)." A judge in Stavanger characterized the legal provision in a legal statement as a "panic measure that had significant technical deficiencies."[18] How representative were such statements? That even the Supreme Court was not entirely enthusiastic about the new provision can be seen from the judgments where the court had to decide on it.

Section 222 II of the Criminal Code was initially an expansive penal provision. The legislature wanted to expand the framework for the criminal offense of campaigning against strikebreakers. The ministry assumed that there several "acts of a more or less serious nature" that were not affected by the Criminal Code, including stalking the person willing to work, mingling around him and other intrusive behavior. Threats were not covered by the existing laws, unless what was threatened was illegal by its own right.[19] A threat that a person would be excluded from the company of the working community was not a crime under the existing law. The ministry considered it necessary to criminalize such behavior. Any pressure on those willing to work should be punishable.[20]

The Supreme Court's approach to Section 222 II of the Penal Code was characterized by the strong contradictions that underpinned the provision. To some extent,

[17] LO congress proceedings 1934 p. 254.

[18] 1 May, Friday 11 December 1930.

[19] See Ot.prp. No. 54 1924 p. 2.

[20] Ot. prp. No. 54 (1924) pp. 2–3.

such opposite views were also found among the judges. We have already seen how one of the judges, Karl Frimann Dahl, went public against the Arbitration Act. When it came to Section 222 II of the Penal Code, most of the judges urged caution, not to expand the scope of the law's application and to limit the scope as far as possible applying the law. The result was that Section 222 II of the Penal Code did not significantly change the legal situation compared to the situation before it was adopted. As a result, the practical application og the provision went a long way away from the rule adopted by the Storting (the Norwegian Parliament) in June 1927.

As early as January 1929, the Supreme Court received a case from the indictment against four people in connection with a demonstration and action against unemployed people who took log driving work during a conflict in Grytåa in Nord-Odal in May 1928 (Rt. 1929 p. 12). The ruling in this case was not exactly clear, but it provided the basis for the many acquittals handed down by the subordinate courts, which were the subject of strong criticism from the conservative press.

The background for the action and the case was a long-standing struggle for trade union organization of loggers and log-drivers in the Grytåa river.[21] The reason for the case was that the forest owners refused to give work to loggers who joined the union. Instead, they brought in people from the outside to do the job. Unionization was the answer to "medieval" working conditions. Wages were so low that those who had families to support had to get additional support for their families from social welfare, even if they worked full time in the forest. The employers' response to unionization was to dismiss the workers who organized and replace them with unorganized workers. When work in the Grytåa area was to resume after New Year 1928, the forest workers were told that they did not have to show up. They had tools and bedding left in the shacks out in the forest, so this came as a total surprise. Many of those dismissed had worked in the forest for 30–40 years.

When the timber floating started after the spring thaw, requiring more laborers, the unemployed hoped that they would now get work, but again they were not employed. The forest owner wanted to use unorganized people also for this work, although it required many extra men. On May 1, the dismissed forest workers had a rally, and they agreed "to take a walk up into the forest and talk to the blockade-breakers". On 3 May, 200 men gathered and marched to the river Grytåa where the timber floating took place. Many of the participants had struggled since Christmas. There was distress and hardship in many homes, and anger was arising among many of the workers.

The campaigners sought out the floats in three different places: the upper, middle and lower dams. The forest master was present at the middle dam. He explained in court afterwards that timber floaters came down there after having been chased from the upper dam. The campaigners lined up and gave them 15 min to think about whether they really wanted to continue working. The "walking boss", who was in charge of the floating, ordered that the log drivers had to bow to superior force and lay down the work.

[21] See Kongsvinger Arbeiderblad, Tuesday 31 July 1928 (nb.no).

Not all the log drivers would leave their shack. One was dragged out by force, and the rest "followed like a mitten". The drivers put down their tools and went head-to-head between the campaigners who cheered both shouts of victory and words of abuse.

Four campaigners were charged after the action. The one in charge of the whole thing, the other three for the two violent episodes that had taken place. The indictment was brought under Section 222 I and Section 228 of the Criminal Code (bodily violation). According to the indictment, the campaigners threatened the floaters with force if they did not stop the work voluntarily. For the most part, the action took place without the use of violence, except for him who was pulled out of the bunk by the legs and thrown out of the shack. In that connection, the chest of his shirt ripped. Another driver was approached by an activist and pushed out of the berth.

In a unanimous verdict, the district court acquitted the defendants under Section 222 I and held that Section 222 II could not be applied. In the judgment, the court stated that "The approx. 200 men seem to have acted, for the most part, restrained, when considering the conditions, i.e. their desperate financial situation. The fact that there was an occasional unruly act cannot be given any weight here."[22] The court assumed that most of the log drivers had stopped working voluntarily, although there had also been statements from some witnesses that they believed that force would be used if they did not stop working. The court further stated that "the mere fact that so many people, as stated in the evidence, approach those willing to work to stop them working, is not in and of itself a use of force or a threat of violence", and the defendants had not acted brutally, violent or inappropriate. Two of the defendants were nevertheless sentenced for bodily harm. The prosecution appealed the verdict to the Supreme Court, which upheld the acquittals.

In the Supreme Court, where seven judges participated, five reasoned arguments were given that pulled in different directions. Taken as a whole, the judgment implied a clear limitation of the scope of Section 222 II of the Criminal Code. It is, however, quite unclear with its different and partly contradicting opinions. What is clear is that the majority of the judges believed that the fact that many people campaign and march together towards a place where work is taking place, and encourage the workers to stop their work, did not in itself involve coercion or threats. This we can infer from the fact that the court sustained acquittal of the district court.

In his opinion Judge Broch agreed with the district Court that the fact that a large crowd of people approaches unorganized workers and asks them to stop working is not in itself a use of force or a threat of violence. He did not address, however, whether this could be said to be "improper conduct" under Section 222 II.

When the majority in the Supreme Court accepted that the lower court acquitted the leaders of the action, it opened up for a legal view that in order to convict, it had

---

[22] Quoted from Kongsvinger Arbeiderblad on Friday 17 August 1928, where the entire judgment is reproduced.

to be proven that the individual defendant had exercised coercion or committed criminal acts such as physical assault. The sting was in many ways taken out of the Penal Code § 222 II when the Supreme Court accepted such actions as the demonstration of the Grytåa workers against strikebreakers. This case can explain many of the acquittals which by the conservative press and by politicians were perceived as aberrant or as the result of party politics on the part of the lay judges. If a demonstration against strike breakers appeared restrained, the leaders of the demonstration could not be punished, unless they had been personally involved in direct coercion or illegal use of physical force.

Two of the judges, Motzfeldt and Næss, wanted to overturn the district court's acquittal. They believed that the district court had wrongly assumed that such an action could not involve coercion, and that it had mixed up the criteria for criminality in the two alternatives of the law, the old section 222, and the new second paragraph to this provision. Motzfeldt and Næss believed that it was obvious that such a situation could amount to a threat of the use of force. The demonstration was undoubtedly dramatic. As we saw above, over 200 men were involved, and the authorities moved in with police and soldiers on standby to protect against violence. There were also some instances of physical abuse, as we have seen from the facts above.

The conditions under which the penitentiary clause could be applied were not clarified by this judgment. It is quite clear that the district court had set the threshold quite high, and that it sentenced those found guilty rather leniently. There is little doubt that the purpose of the demonstrators was to get the unorganized timber floaters to stop working. The court assessed the evidence systematically in favor of the defendants. There is also little doubt that an entourage of 200 workers could be perceived as threatening, no matter how disciplined they acted. However, the court declined to do so. It seems likely that the judges in the district court were influenced by the desperate situation of the workers in their assessment of whether the action was inappropriate. The court stated in the premises that the demonstration was "fully justified" because of the dire conditions in the district with local people facing hunger because they were denied work by the owners of the forests.

However, the new penalty provision would be ineffective if living conditions were to be included in the assessment of an action against strike breakers as improper behavior or not. By this ruling it could therefore seem that the courts had drawn the teeth of the new weapon which Stortinget had deployed against the trade union movement. Although the Supreme Court did not expressly say, as the district court, that it was legal to demonstrate even if a large demonstration could appear frightening, it was important that the majority did not say the opposite. The judgment of the Supreme Court opened the way to a practice in the lower courts that organizing and leading a demonstration against strikebreakers should not be punished under the new Section 222 II.

In the next case before the Supreme Court, the court was invited to decide whether Section 222 II of the Criminal Code could be applied to a blockade of a company that had provided services to a company where the workers were in conflict (Rt. 1930 p. 1127). When the company promised to stop providing services, the organized workers refused to resume work along with the unorganized, who had been working while the company broke the blockade. They said that the unorganized had to either organize or quit. This fulfilled the criterion in Section 222 II of the Criminal Code to “cause someone to give up their work”.

The starting point was a sympathy action in connection with a conflict between the taxi owners and the drivers regarding the drivers’ pay and working conditions. To support the drivers, the Norwegian Iron and Metalworkers’ Union launched an action where members refused to carry out repairs on taxis during the conflict. The Supreme Court concluded that this action was a legal sympathy action in support of a legal strike. At a workshop where unorganized workers worked, repairs had been carried out and the enterprise was blocked. In that connection, it was stated that the blockade could be averted if the unorganized joined the union. The Supreme Court concluded that this was not affected by Section 222 II, as the purpose was not to force the unorganized into the union, but to make the support for the taxi drivers effective. When the action was not unfair to the company, it could not be “unfair to the workers unless the intention was to punish them in a disproportionate way”.[23]

In 1933, the question arose as to whether the expression “improper conduct” only covered behavior that was improper towards the person sought to be influenced not to work, or whether it also covered actions that could be considered improper in other contexts (Rt. 1933 p. 212). The campaigning workers had persuaded some municipal inspectors to break their contractual relations to an employer in conflict, with the result that the workers targeted by the action could not carry out their work. This could be considered inappropriate towards the municipality and the employer, but the inappropriateness was not directed at the workers who were thereby prevented from their work. The Supreme Court held that this was not affected by the ban.

Casting the first vote, Judge Schjelderup believed that it followed from the wording that the provision only aimed at obstacles for the worker in his work through harassment and the like. According to Schjelderup, that the intention of the legislation was to ban actions of an “intimidating nature” directed against those willing to work. Two of the judges, Judges Bang and (Thomas) Bonnevie, disagreed and argued that the condition of inappropriateness was not limited to actions directed at the person willing to work. Bang pointed out that it was up to the courts to determine the content of “improper”, and that such limits as Schjelderup could not inferred from the wording of the provision.

According to Schjelderup, it was a distinctly legislative effort to decide on all possible meanings of inappropriate besides acts directed at those who worked during a conflict. Schjelderup received support from Chief Justice Paal Berg, who stated that “a different interpretation (than Schjelderup’s) would, in my opinion, give rise to an arbitrary and influenced by the individual judge’s personal preference assessment of what should be inappropriate and punishable.”

[23] Rt. 1930 p. 1127, p. 1131.

The two judgments from 1930 and 1933 showed that the Supreme Court was unwilling extend the application of Section 222 II of the Criminal Code beyond the absolutely necessary. All cases that the court received in the first five years regarding this provision led to acquittals. The Supreme Court's approach indicates a rather hostile attitude towards the provision, rather than the opposite or a more neutral approach. The legislature and the Supreme Court were not in line in the question of use of sanctions against demonstrating workers.

In a case decided by the Supreme Court in 1934, the first judgment came in which the Supreme Court found that the conditions for using the provision were met. The editor of the magazine Ny Dag in Tønsberg was acquitted by the Court of Appeal for having named several men in two articles under the headings "A tenacious strike breaker" and "Several strike breakers", Rt. 1934 p. 442. In the district court he was sentenced to prison for 30 days in accordance with Section 222 II of the Penal Code. In his legal instruction to the jury, the judge had said that there was no "work stoppage" in the sense of the law when there was no work going on in the enterprise at the time the conflict broke out. For publication to be punishable, the law required that there had been "public information about who is working or has worked or has applied for work during a work stoppage". A unanimous Supreme Court overturned the Court of Appeal's judgment with a brief statement of reasons. An employer was covered by the conflict even though he happened to have no work in progress when the conflict broke out.

It was not possible to circumvent the ban on giving public information about strikebreakers. This was previously not an offense, as was seen in the case of Zacheus Selj but was now expressly prohibited in the law. Publishing people's names and work could previously be punished as a violation of privacy, but this was not an offence that was prosecuted by the public prosecutor without the victim's petition (Skeie 1931, p. 512).

The Supreme Court bowed to the legislature where the law was unequivocally clear. The different forms of "offensive", "intrusive" or "inappropriate" behavior, on the other hand, had a more unclear and uncertain content. In and of itself, it was not unusual to use such discretionary expressions in a penal provision. The majority in the Supreme Court, however, interpreted the statutory these discretionary conditions restrictively so that invasive behavior and various forms of pressure were not enough for the statute to have been violated.

Not to apply the provision to a large group of campaigners marching out and standing up against people who were carrying out work that the campaigners wanted terminated, was clearly a restrictive interpretation of it. It is not difficult to imagine that the floaters in Grytåa and elsewhere could perceive this as both intimidating and threatening, especially when we know that there were minor episodes of violence did take place. At the same time as the action in Grytåa, similar conflicts were taking place in Ulvaaen, and the trial after the Julussa action the year before was underway, see more below. The Grytåa action was clearly the least violent of the three. However, this was the case on which the Supreme Court ruled, and the Supreme Court could be interpreted to rule that such actions were not liable to punishment under the law.

Thus, through the interpretation that the Supreme Court gave of the provision in Section 222 II of the Criminal Code, the amendment did not add much new to the prohibitions that already applied against the use of violence and threats. This must probably have disappointed those who were in favor of the provision at the Storting and delighted those who went against it. After all, those who were in favor of stricter rules did not get the expansive protection of strikebreakers that they aimed for with the provision. And the provision did not interfere with the possibilities of protecting strikes against employers' use of strikebreakers to the extent that the opponents of the penitentiary law feared. The only exception to this was the ban on the publication of the names of strikebreakers, which particularly affected the use of the press in connection with actions. Here, the wording was clear and an interpretation disregarding the new law impossible within normal legal means. But sentencing was left to the discretion of the courts, and as we shall see, the punishment for editors was much lower here than for breaching the Arbitration Act.

5.3 The District Courts and the Courts of Appeal

If the Supreme Court's approach was cautious, the same cannot be said about the attitude of the police and prosecution. From the beginning, they came down hard on striking workers. Before the addition to Section 222 of the Penal Code in 1927, according to the crime statistics, there were approximately 40 violations of this provision a year. After the addition, the number rose to 77 a year, which is almost a doubling of the number of cases.[24] The first paragraph of the provision applies to threats in general, also outside of labor disputes, so one must assume that the increase in the use of the provision in labor disputes was even greater.

Professor Jon Skeie gave an overview of court decisions in criminal cases regarding coercion etc. in labor disputes 1920/21 to 1930. The overview is not complete as he has not included cases that ended in acquittal based on the evidence in the first instance (Skeie 1931, p. 466). Skeie's overview includes a total of 103 cases. Of these, there were 47 cases before the change in the law in 1927, that is for the years 1921–1927, and 56 cases for the years 1928–1930. This means that the number of cases took place from just under 7 per year before the change in the law to almost 19 per year after the change in the law. This supports the impression of a much greater effort from the police and prosecutors to bring such cases before the courts after Section 222 II of the Criminal Code was adopted.

One explanation could of course have been a rise in the number of work-related conflicts. This was not the case. The increase in cases was not due to an increase in the number of conflicts in the years after 1927. The level of conflict was lower in the years 1928–1930 than in the years 1921–1927, both by the number of conflicts, and

[24] Crime statistics 1931 and 1932, Statistics Norway IX. 32, Oslo 1934 p. 2.

not least by the number of workers in conflict and lost working days.[25] The increase in criminal cases must therefore reasonably be due to the change in the law and to a change in attitude in the police and prosecutors to bring cases against demonstrating workers. In other words, the penitentiary laws shifted the conflicts between the parties in working life from the places of work and into the courts. The conflict between labor and capital was brought into the law.

5.4 Log Driving Conflict

One of the first cases after the entry into force of the new criminal provision was the criminal case in the wake of the Julussa conflict (Skeie 1931 no. 40). Julussa is a tributary that flows from Nordskogbygda in eastern Elverum down towards the main river Glomma in Åmot. After the contract for timber floating in the spring of 1927 had been awarded to a team of unorganized workers, the trade union organized a demonstration to stop the work. The conflict took place the year before the conflict in Grytåa, which ended up in the Supreme Court, see above (Skeie 1931 no. 34). The case was brought under the old law, as the new law was not yet enacted under the conflict. It is still interesting to examine the case as it illustrates the difference in attitude to such conflict between the legislature and the courts.

The economic crises in the 1920s and 30s were a disaster for the villages and settlements in Eastern Norway. Timber prices fell and the forest owners had to cut expenses. This of course also affected the wages. Many forest workers were pushed into destitution, poverty, and unemployment. In the counties of Hedmark and the Oppland, only around 25% of the forest workers were employed. From the mid-twenties, work on trade union organization and demands for collective bargaining for forest workers gained momentum, and in 1927 the Forest and Land Workers' Union was founded and registered with LO (Ousland 1975, pp. 479–493). The Julussa and Austmarka conflicts were the first major conflicts about organizational rights and collective agreements. These were conflicts that became known nation-wide.

On 10 May 1927 the timber floating began in Julussa, and on 11 May the campaigners moved out from Elverum "to watch the driving of logs". Many of the demonstrating forest workers were armed with hunting rifles and shotguns. They brought the rifles as the strike breakers were armed and as armed troops had also arrived from Elverum. The demonstrations lasted several days. One of the days, the leader of the demonstration stopped the driving by preventing the floaters from dropping timber through the bilge. A later day there was a scuffle between two demonstrators and two log drivers, where the two drivers were "given a thrashing" according to the police. The two activists were arrested and later charged with assault.

[25] Collective agreements and labor disputes 1930, Statistics Norway, Oslo 1931 p. 25.

Who was the most aggressive was a matter of debate. "On Thursday when it started here, I stood with two officers facing a force of 120 demonstrators on one side, and 50 log drivers on the other," said Sheriff Høye from Elverum to the daily newspaper Dagbladet on 18 May. "It was almost hardest to keep the drivers in line; they are tough guys who are not afraid to fight."[26] There is still no doubt that the two log drivers Nyberget and Bjørnstad were beaten by demonstrators.[27]

As the protests continued the sheriff called for reinforcements. The authorities in Oslo sent the state police with dogs. Eventually there were also 150 soldiers who were accommodated at Terningmoen. The atmosphere was tense, and the demonstrators had the feeling that they could fear the worst because of the position of the authorities by calling in the police and military.

The demonstrators had a negotiation group that negotiated with the local police. The mayor and parliamentary representative for the Labor Party, Olav Sæter, participated in this group. Although it seemed that the conflict might find a local solution, central authorities stepped in with police and soldiers and ensured that the unorganized drivers who had been given the contract could carry out their work (Ousland 1975, pp. 493–498). Not least because of Olav Sæter's role and involvement both in and outside the Storting, the Julussa conflict had a defining role in the debate and development of the penitentiary clause in the Storting.

The conflict received national attention. Member of Storting Eivind Petershagen from the Communist Party took up issue with the government in the Storting on 18 May, where he asked if it was with the government's approval that police with police dogs from the Oslo Police Corps were sent to intervene in the conflict. He also asked what the government would do to prevent such provocations from the police in the future.[28] This led to a long debate where the Labor Party's representatives attacked the government. Petershagen's proposal that the Storting should demand that the police be withdrawn nevertheless fell with 89 to 31 votes.

The public prosecutor brought charges against five organizers in November 1927 for threats, violence and rioting. The case was to go directly at the Court of Appeal. On 2 May 1928, the criminal case against the five began in the Court of Appeal in Gjøvik. State prosecutor Faye Hansen led the prosecution, lawyer for the defense was Emil Stang. The defendants were charged with having prevented the log drivers at Mørstaddammen from opening the bilge, for having threatened the floaters with beatings and for causing a riot.[29] Two of the activists were acquitted. The leader of the action, Peder Vestad, was convicted for having held onto the pike pole that one of the floaters was going to use to open a jam. In this way he prevented the float from dropping timber through the bilge. For this he received a 21-day suspended prison sentence for the use of violence. Two were sentenced for violence and bodily harm against two log drivers. This resulted in 40 days and 21 days of suspended

[26] Dagbladet Wednesday 18 May 1927.

[27] See Vestopland on Thursday 3 May 1928.

[28] Stortingsforhandlinger forhandlinger i Stortinget 18 May 1927 pp. 1441–1469.

[29] Report in Arbeiderbladet on Wednesday 2 May, Thursday 3 May and Friday 4 May 1928.

imprisonment. All were acquitted of the charge of rioting. Immediately after the verdict was handed down, the convicted demonstrators went to Ulvåen to campaign against the timber floating which had started there.

Aftenposten was outraged by the mild reactions to violation of section 222. "Even those who lead the charge against the timer floating go pretty much free. In any case, the punishment is so small that it in no way corresponds to its purpose, namely to prevent repetition. Some get NOK 25 in fines, others get nothing. On Saturday, three men drove from the courtroom in Gjøvik, where they received a suspended sentence, directly to Ulvåen to besiege a team of drivers, which had received a tender for work there in the river. They left with the verdict in their pocket – to a new violation of the law."[30]

Although the judgment was handed down before the judgment in the Supreme Court on the action in Grytåa, we see that the expressed the legal opinion that was later confirmed by the Supreme Court: the fact that a large crowd of people addresses unorganized people and asks them to stop working is not in itself a use of force or a threat of violence. However, the judgment was based on the old provision on coercion in section 222 first paragraph and therefore did not take a position on the applicability of the requirement in the new section 222 II.

There were many similar actions in connection with timber floating in Eastern Norway during this period. The public prosecutor in Elverum brought charges against Peder Vestad for the action in Ulvåen. Here he had again led 300 protesters. The demonstration attracted a lot of attention. The police moved out against the demonstrators with 26 men, and during the night 60 guards from Terningmoen army base with full field equipment came up to the dam. The police asked the protesters to leave the scene, which they did. The police and the guards remained at the scene. The next day the minister of justice came up and had a conference with the chief of police and the sheriff.[31]

The protesters cut the telephone line to the site. Vestad and another went into the bunk of some willing to work and told them to stop. The protesters shouted that if they dared to open the dam they would be thrown into the river. The log drivers opened the dam despite this, but no action was taken against them by the demonstrators.[32] Over the course of the evening the unrest escalated, stones were thrown and dynamite fired. Vestad was brought before the district court in Elverum on 19 July 1929 (Skeie 1931 no. 43). Here he was unanimously acquitted. The court said that he could not be held responsible for the unlawful acts committed during the demonstration even though he a leading position in the demonstration. On the contrary, he had tried to calm the mood and advised the protesters to stop throwing stones at the drivers' berth. "According to current law, this legal assessment is unassailable," commented Skeie (Skeie 1931, p. 513).

---

[30] Aftenposten Tuesday 8 May 1928.

[31] Vestopland Gjøviks Blad og Samhold, Monday 7 May 1928.

[32] Østerdalens Arbeiderblad Monday 22 July 1929.

In one case, the defendants were sentenced to prison for violating Section 222 II of the Criminal Code in connection with a conflict over log driving (Skeie 1931 no. 56). On Saturday 7 February 1931, 5 men stood trial in the Court of Appeal in Hamar for harassment of men willing to work in connection with a conflict in the Torpa watercourse the previous year. In the district court, all recieved fines. In the Court of Appeal, the case went on for three days. The court sentenced one of the defendants to 120 days of unconditional imprisonment and another to 60 days. The others received 30 days in prison, with a suspended sentence.

The campaigners had joined a demonstration against a group who carried out log driving. They had made threats, thrown stones, taken the peavy hooks from several of the log drivers and molested the drivers with punches, spanks, and abuse. The police giving witness in court said they had perceived the situation as life-threatening. One of the defendants was also charged with assault, but the prosecutor dropped this part of the charge after the evidence was presented. The court emphasized that the demonstrations proceeded in a particularly malignant manner. This distinguishes this case from the many other court cases about timber floating conflicts, where accused protesters largely behaved restrained and calm.[33]

The cases that unfolded in the wake of a conflict in the Trysil watershed in May 1929 give an example of the imposition of very severe sentences in the district court and of acquittals in the court of appeal (Skeie 1931 no. 47). The acquittal was highly criticized in the conservative press at the time, and may have contributed to the impression that juries illegitimately acquitted demonstrating strikers for political reasons. A total of 30 people stood accused in the district court. The judge was the former state attorney Jørgen Grøner. The case concerned demonstrations at four different locations over four days, and judgment was delivered on 16 October 1930.

Magistrate Grøner "acted as a prosecutor in the case", "with a cunning cross-examination to make the defendants acknowledge that they had acted against those 'willing to work'," wrote Østerdalens Arbeiderblad in a report from the first day of the trial.[34] The case was widely reported in newspapers across the country.

Grøner and one of the two lay judges convicted 29 of the defendants and acquitted 1. The convicted all received prison terms, 25 of them were suspended. In the judgement, the court majority, Magistrate Grøner and one lay judge, state that "to proceed in such a way under the agitated situation that existed in May 1929 here in Trysil, between demonstrators and work-willing log drivers, had to be perceived and understood as coercion. Likewise, that such conduct was unlawful as a manifestation of the will of the strongest to exert pressure on others in an inappropriate manner and by evoking fear of the most serious physical consequences. These considerations, together with the great importance of the fact that every citizen can carry out his legal work unimpeded by others under the protection of the legal order,

[33]The case is referred to in detail in Østlendingen for Monday 9 February, Tuesday 10 February, Wednesday 11 February and Thursday 12 February 1931.

[34]Østerdalens Arbeiderblad Saturday 11 October 1930.

are determining reasons for the sentencing of the court.[35] The majority then went on to hand down prison sentences for all of them. The minority opinion, the other lay judge, held that there had been no unlawful coercion.

The verdict ranged from 25 to 100 days in prison. As we can see from other similar cases, the punishments were unusually strict, particularly taken into account that none of the accused were charged with assault. "A sentence so hair-raisingly brutal that you have to go to Finland to find anything similar," wrote Østerdalen's Arbeiderblad.[36] In Finland, the fascist Lapua movement has a strong influence on politics, and the Communist Party was outlawed. "It becomes clearer with every sentence Magistrate Grøner pronounces that he has been sent here to the district to organize terror against the timber workers," the newspaper continued. All 29 appealed to the Court of Appeal.

The proceedings before the court were not very different from other conflicts dealt with by the courts at this time. What set them apart was the large number of defendants and the severe punishments imposed by the court. The demonstrations that had taken place had followed a familiar course. On four occasions, groups of demonstrators had gone up to floating points. The groups varied in size from around 100 men to around 30. The march through the forest had in all cases proceeded in good order. Once there, they had given the log drivers 15 min to finish their work. There had been some shouting and commotion and some threats had been made that log drivers would be thrown out and that they would have to take the face the consequences of defying the mob. The campaigners tore the pikes from some of the log drivers and broke them. There were some episodes of violence where drivers were punched and butted.

The appeal court case began on 5 May and was covered with great interest by the press. The audience bench was full. Also many of the defendants had to sit as there was not room for everyone in the defendant box. The case was administered by judge Rolfsen with the magistrates Andersen and Wiesener as co-judges. The prosecutor was state prosecutor Faye Hansen, defender Trygve Lie.[37] The case went on for 5 days with examination of the defendants and dozens of witnesses. The last day, Saturday 9 May, was set aside for the legal argument of the prosecution and the defense.

The public prosecutor reviewed the law's requirements for criminal liability in his argument. He admitted that the demonstrators initially contented themselves with attempts at persuasion, but when that didn't work, they had "started to shout and scream. Some swung their sticks amid deafening screams and shouts as they came up the road. Inarguably, this could be the prelude to a violent attack."[38] In his argument for the defense, attorney Lie said that it was a social drama that had unfolded. The demonstrators had behaved calmly and with dignity. The relationship between the

[35] Sør-Østerdal District Court's judgment in criminal case no. 71/1930 16 October 1930.

[36] Østerdalens Arbeiderblad Saturday 18 October 1930.

[37] Hamar Arbeiderblad Wednesday 6 May 1931.

[38] The voter on Saturday 9 May 1931.

protesters and the log drivers was friendly, and they ate and drank together. When the police arrived, the log drivers refused to go down to the river to resume work. Three months had passed from the action until reports were filed, which showed that it was the company, and not the offended log drivers, who had pushed for a formal report to the police.

The arguments took three and a half hours. More than 100 questions were put to the jury, which spent 4 hours in its deliberations, before it returned and issued a verdict of acquittal for all the defendants. "An appalling ruling", said State Attorney Faye Hansen to Dagbladet. "And it is just as appalling that, according to the new criminal procedure system, there is no opportunity to do anything about it."[39] The acquittal received a lot of attention and was one of the cases that formed the basis for the attack on the jury system by the Conservative Party and the Farmers Party, see more on that later in this book.

Was the verdict political? Both this case and the case against the demonstrators in the Torpa waterway went before the Court of Appeal in Hamar a few months apart. The result in the two cases shows that in any case there was no automatic acquittal for charges under Section 222 of the Criminal Code in labor disputes in this Court of Appeal.

No indictment for violence had been brought against any of the campaigners. The case was solely about Section 222 of the Criminal Code. When one compares this demonstration with the demonstrations in Grytåa and Ulvåen, the acquittal does not appear striking in any way. That intimidating protests by gangs of demonstrators not in itself constituted illegal threats is in line with the ruling of the Supreme Court in the Grytåa case. Another matter is that those who were involved in bodily harm and damage by destroying the pikes of the log drivers would probably have been sentenced for this in another court. But before the Court of Appeal there was no separate charge for this.

Mention can also be made of a case before Nes District Court on 13 December 1930, where a man was convicted for having grabbed hold of the bridle of a horse and screamed at another who was plowing the field on a farm that was under boycott "You look like you've been lying in whey all your time" and asked him why he was working. The reason for the comment about whey was that the man otherwise worked at a dairy. To another he had said "it is dangerous to work there". (Skeie 1931, p. 31). The case was linked to a conflict over timber floating in Søndre Høland. The prosecutor stated that it was not particularly doubtful that the defendant's statements were covered by the law, and that he made them in order to get the aggrieved to stop working, in which he also succeeded. The man received a fine of NOK 50.[40]

[39] Dagbladet Monday 11 May 1933.

[40] See minutes in Indre Akershus Blad on Tuesday 16 December 1930, parts 1 and 2.

5.5 The Folldal Mines

Not all conflicts at the time were about timber floating. The conflict at Folldal mines was one of the bitterest and longest in the era surrounding the penitentiary laws. The origin of the conflict was that director of the plant, Worm H. Lund, did not want to submit to the collective agreement for the mining industry and broke out of the employers' association. He began, according to trade union historian Gunnar Ousland, "a war against the union that is almost unprecedented in the history of the trade unions (Ousland 1975, p. 569)." Elsewhere, Ousland characterizes the conflict as "a classic example of how a monomaniac employer could keep a war going against the trade union month after month despite all mediators and courts (Ousland 1975, p. 564)."

The conflict was not primarily about pay, but about matters of principle such as organizational rights and the legality of the conflict. Already in connection with a conflict in 1923, director Lund refused to accept the general, nationwide mining agreement and withdrew the company from the employers' association Bergverkenes Landssamslunning. In 1929 it struck again. From 1926 there had been annual wage reductions. In 1928, director Lund wanted to reduce wages by a further 10 per cent, while the workers demanded an 8 per cent increase. The result was a strike. The conflict became particularly bitter because the director recruited workers from outside the area and kept the mines going despite the strike, while at the same time the local workers were locked out of the housing made available by the utility and their children denied access to the utility's school (Bækkelund and Kalvatn 1998, pp. 185–189). Almost all the company's employees stopped working. The local population in the surrounding villages showed solidarity with the strikers, so that it was difficult for the company to recruit strikebreakers locally.

The conflict has been described as "one of the most stubborn and sensational conflicts we ever had in Norway (Bekken 1977, p. 91)." The company initially refused to negotiate with the union and claimed that it had individual employment agreements with each worker. The conflict lasted over 20 months and was one of Norwegian industry's longest-running conflicts. In total, there were 14 court cases in the wake of the conflict, most under section 222 of the Criminal Code, and the number of formal complaints made to the police by the company was far higher.[41] The company also asked the authorities to send state police to the conflict.

What Skeie refers to as case 45 concerned a case that arose out of the conflict in Folldal mines. Nord-Østerdal District Court at Tynset had sentenced the chairman of Foldal's mine workers association and two of its board members to pay fines for their conduct towards strike breakers during a conflict.[42]

The union decided to make efforts to put an end to the strike-breaking. They tried to get the strike-breakers to stop working by talking to them, appealing to them with information about the conflict and the situation of the workers on strike and so

[41] See Folldal AOF-forening (1981), pp. 43–44 for an overview of the 14 cases.

[42] Hamar Arbeiderblad Monday 11 November 1929.

on. The company responded with reporting union members to the police. In addition to reporting union members, the company reported the newspaper Hamar Arbeiderblad for having published the names of strikebreakers.

The case against the management of the miners' union came up in the Court of Appeal on 10 February 1930.[43] The public prosecutor argued that there had been a breach of Section 222 II in that two of the defendants had approached two of the workers and said that it was bad for them to work, and that if they continued they had to face the consequences. A few days later, the leader of the union had approached another strike breaker and told him that the striking workers thought 20 days in prison for assaulting a strike-breaker "was totally worth it" and that he should think about this on the way home. The next day they had entered the drawbridge of the mine and told the workers that they had to face the consequences if they continued to work.

The prosecutor said in his procedure that this behavior was intrusive behavior in the meaning of the law because those willing to work were intimidated. The statement that the strikers would not be deterred by a sentence of 20 days in prison had to be perceived as a threat and was perceived as a threat by the man who had been told so, according to the prosecutor. The judge said in his legal statement to the jury that the evidence in the case indicated that threats had been made. If the jury found that the chairman had made the statement about 20 days in prison, this was, in the judge's opinion, a very serious threat. A statement that those willing to work would have difficulties in the future to find work anywhere else, had also to be perceived as a threat.

When the jury withdrew, the defender Trygve Lie made a bet over a case of whiskey with director Lund that the workers would be acquitted. The jury ruled for the acquittal of all three and Lie got his whisky (Amundsen 1946, p. 66).

Based on the court reports, it may seem that it would have been wrong to sentence the defendants if one takes as a basis the legal opinion of the Supreme Court in the Grytåa case. This ruling was handed down on 10 January 1929 and should thus have been well known to the legal actors in the Folldal case, but it was not necessarily known for the District Court which gave its ruling in November 1929. As the ruling by the Supreme Court could be interpreted, seeking out people willing to work with a large crowd was not considered a use of force or a threat of violence, even though it could seem both threatening and intimidating. The Supreme Court ruling also gave support to the understanding that nor was it intrusive behavior in the meaning of section 222 II. A statement that people would not be intimidated by a prison sentence was not very specific and hardly a concrete threat. It is not clear that the District Court ruling was correct and the Court of Appeal was wrong in this case. Again, therefore, we see an acquittal that is better explained by a legally defensible restrictive interpretation of the law than by an indefensible disregarding of the law by a politically biased jury, although the conservative press at the time saw it in the latter way.

[43] See Hamar Arbeiderblad Tuesday 11 February 1930 and Wednesday 12 February 1930.

The leader of the union stood trial again on 26 February, this time for refusing to comply with an order from the police to stop a demonstration, which he led. For this he was fined NOK 80 by the Nord-Østerdal District Court. The sentence was appealed to the Supreme Court, which upheld the fine. The case is referred to in Rt. 1930 p. 1076. The case is a pure case of refusal to comply with police orders and of obstructing the police in their work. The Penitentiary Act was thus not engaged as a legal basis.

Another case that arose out of the Folldal conflict is referred to as no. 44 by Skeie. On 9 May 1931, Nord-Østerdal District Court sentenced a man for having approached three people who worked at the plant and asked them if they knew that there was a strike at the plant and stated that they should pack away and that they had been given a place in hell. The incident took place at a cafe in Folldal, and the man was heavily intoxicated. After a long speech, he swept down with his hand what was on the table in front of the three workers and broke a glass vase and a beer glass. When one was about to leave, he grabbed him by the coat collar and tried to kick him in the back. The defendant was convicted of breaching both Section 222 II of the Penal Code and Sections 16 and 17 of the Vagrancy Act.

The union fight against the strike breakers was not very effective, and the work at the mines continued. However, the workers received support from the rest of the trade union movement, which launched boycotts at the companies that were purchasers of pyrite from Folldal. In the end, the company could not sell its pyrite in Norway, and the trade unions also increased their boycott of the exports. Finally, the company had to suspend operations because it could not dispose of its product, and the conflict was resolved through negotiation, after it had been going on for over 22 months.

5.6 The Battle of Menstad

The well-known Menstad battle revolved around Norsk Hydro's use of contract workers to ship goods out of the port of Menstad at the Skiensriver near the city of Porsgrunn in Southern Norway. There was a strike going on in the factory, and the union wanted to block products leaving the plant.[44] Between 2000 and 3000 people gathered on 2 June 1931 in front of the gate at Menstad port, pushed past the police and the fences and physically took out the contract workers to abuse and mocking remarks. Hydro demanded better protection of the contract workers and the Minister of Justice sent reinforcements. On 4 June, people gathered for a large demonstration in the cities of Skien and Porsgrunn, despite the fact that the police had banned demonstrations. The demonstrations continued for the next few days and there were clashes between demonstrators and the police.

---

[44] The presentation here is based on Johansen 1931.

On the morning of Monday 8 June, the contract workers had resumed work. The workers' leaders immediately mobilized for a demonstration and marched to Menstad, where the police had posted a guard. The police were informed that the demonstration was en route with workers armed with sticks. Demonstrators and police rammed together, demonstrators throwing stones, police with water cannons and batons. It soon degenerated into hand-to-hand fights. In the evening of the same day, the government decided to send soldiers to Menstad, who arrived early the next morning. The navy sent warships.

The demonstrations had their legal aftermath in the Court of Appeal, where 28 people were prosecuted and 20 sentenced to prison terms ranging from 30 days to 10 months. Vestlandske Tidende had a headline "The Menstad guys got off cheaply".[45] In addition to indictments for violence, indictments were issued for violations of Section 136 of the Penal Code on rioting with the intent to commit violence against persons or property and Section 222 I and II of the Penal Code. For rioting, imprisonment was mandatory. However, the court also imposed prison sentences of 30 to 60 days for some of the defendants who were only convicted of breaching Section 222 II.

The conflict is one of the better known labor conflicts of the time, not least because the acting minister of defence was Vidkun Quisling, who later betrayed the nation by staging a coup during the Nazi Occupation of Norway in 1940 and led a fascist collaborative government throughout the war. After the war he was executed for treason. The conflict of 1931 was a show of strength by the communists, with the Labor Party and the Federation of Trade Unions calling for moderation. In the history of Section 222 II it is in a way a "grand finale" in that the provision at this time was going out of use, and at the same time was used to impose the most severe penalties that were meted out under the provision.

5.7 Naming and Shaming of Strike Breakers

One of the new crimes introduced by Section 222 II of the Penal Code was that it became an offense to provide public information about people working or had worked or had applied for work during a work stoppage. The courts convicted for breaking this prohibition several times. In Skeie's list, there are 16 cases where the defendant was sentenced under Section 222 II for publishing names as a means of combat in a labor dispute.

Skeie's case no. 46 concerned a case about the publication of the names of 115 strikebreakers in Folldal. The publication was made by Hamar Arbeiderblad and Østerdalens Arbeiderblad. In the district court, the defendant was sentenced to 24 days in prison. He appealed the verdict. In the Court of Appeal, the defendant admitted that he had published the names, but said that it had not been done with the

[45] Vestlandske Tidende, Thursday 10 December 1931.

intention of getting the strikers to stop their work. He was fully aware that they would not stop for the reason that he published the names, and that he did so "almost as a neutral reporting of facts."[46] The defense laywer in the Court of Appeal submitted argued for acquittal, which "the majority of workers in the jury naturally accepted," wrote the conservative newspaper Østlandet in a comment.[47]

However, the verdict of the jury was not obviously incorrect. The law required that publication should be committed in order to cause or seek to cause "that someone quits or gives up their work." The defendant's explanation of his motive for the publication had not been countered by the prosecutor, and in the opinion of the defense counsel, it had to be taken as the proven fact. In that case, the conditions for applying Section 222 II of the Criminal Code were not met. It may seem though, that the jury interpreted the facts in a way friendly to the defendant.

The case that Skeie refers to as no. 49 concerned the publication of the names of two people who worked for a number of blocked timber enterprises in Elverum. The defendant, editorial secretary at Østerdal Arbeiderblad, explained in court that he had published the names as he believed that the trade unions had a right to know them. He had no intention of putting pressure on those willing to work or to get them to organize, even though the article contained a recommendation for those willing to work to settle their affairs with the organization as soon as possible. According to the judge, the defendant had "given a fairly unclear description of what the motive for the articles had been."[48] The judge in his instruction to the jury nevertheless believed that the defendant could not be found guilty, as there was no conflict and work stoppage at the company in question, which was a condition for applying Section 222 II to the publication of the names of those willing to work. The reactionary paper Norges Fremtid described the sentence as "a shocking acquittal".[49] Again we see that an acquittal which was based on the professional judges' interpretation of the law was criticized in the press as an incorrect acquittal.

The provision was not only used against publication in the press. In the conflict over Rådhushospitset, we saw that it was used against demonstrators distributing leaflets with the names of strikebreakers. We have another case from the Court of Appeal in Stavanger in a judgment handed down on 11 December 1931.[50] During the great lockout in 1931, butter worker Elias Gabrielsen had stood up in the main square of the city of Stavanger on 30 June and read out the names of the strike breakers from the newspapers Stavanger Aftenblad and Stavanger. For this he had to answer in the Court of Appeal.

In the district court, he had been acquitted by the lay judges against the vote of the professional judge. In his defence, he claimed that he knew it was illegal to publish such names in the newspapers, but he did not know that it was illegal to read out

[46] Hamar Arbeiderblad Saturday 15 November 1930.

[47] Østlendingen Saturday 15 November 1930.

[48] Østlendingen on Friday 13 February 1931.

[49] Norges Fremtid Friday 13 February 1931.

[50] The case was handed down after Skeie completed his overview.

names that were already published. The names were of course widely known in advance. The lay judges had argued for the acquittal Gabrielsen on the grounds that reading out what was in the newspaper was not covered by the provision. The professional judge did not agree with this interpretation of the law.

The jury found Gabrielsen guilty of the charges after discussing the case for only fifteen minutes. This is despite the fact that the judge had said in his instruction that he had not the slightest doubt that it was not as punishable to read out the names of those willing to work on the square as to publish the names in the newspaper. He also said that it was difficult to see the protection of union rights as unjust. "The is often much to blame those willing to work, when they betray class solidarity," said the judge.[51] Gabrielsen was given NOK. 300 in fine. Here, in other words, the majority of the jury decided on a stricter interpretation of the law than that which the judge recommended. It is thus yet an example of how it was often the professional judge who argued for a restrictive interpretation of the law.

The judge was obviously critical to the law adopted by the legislature. In this he was not alone. In some cases, this led to judges and juries failing to judge apply the provision, also in cases where it should have been applied both according to the law and the evidence.

On 26 November 1930, the Drammen city court acquitted an editor even though the newspaper in three notices had published the names of a number of strike-breakers during a timber conflict. The majority of the court, the professional judge and one of the lay judges, found not to be proven that the editor personally had any involvement with the notices that were included in the newspaper, despite the fact that he had explained in the trial court that he assumed the criminal responsibility for them being published.[52] The other lay judge dissented and believed that the explanation in the court of inquiry and other circumstances in the case proved that the editor had knowledge of the content of the notices that were inserted.

5.8 Other Conflicts

Apart from the conflicts in forestry and the Folldal mines, the years 1928–1930 were relatively quiet years as far as labor conflicts are concerned. The number of conflicts was fairly high, but workers involved were limited, and with few lost working days.[53] This is naturally reflected in the cases before the courts. This does not mean, however, that no cases arose out of conflicts in other industries.

---

[51] 1st May, Friday 11 December 1931. Based on the sources, there may be some doubt as to what the judge actually said in the instruction. Stavangeren writes in the report on Friday 11 December that "he maintained that there was not the slightest doubt that this was publication within the meaning of the law." If one looks at the statement in the context of what 1ste Mai writes that he otherwise said, I believe that it is most likely that the reporting in 1ste Mai is correct.

[52] Fremtiden Wednesday 26 November 1930.

[53] Statistics Norway p. 25.

At Jæren, in the South-West, the prosecution brought charges against six workers for having threatened strikebreakers at Fjeldberg Bruk with publishing their names in the newspapers and for having spoken in a threatening tone of voice about "certain consequences." Even if all six had not spoken, they were all guilty of having emphasized the threats by their presence. All six were acquitted by a unanimous court.[54] The indictment stated that the strike breakers had been threatened with "the force from the city" which would beat them to death if they did not stop working. The court did not find this proven and held that the defendants had, on the whole, acted in a controlled manner.[55]

The case derived from a labor dispute at Fjellberg Bruk, a canning factory in Hundavåg, Hetland outside Stavanger in the days 31 December 1930 to 2 January 1931. On Saturday 3 January, the lawyer Hille filed a report on behalf of Fjellberg Bruk to the police that the Stavanger and surrounding professional district union had decided a blockade of the company from 2 January.[56] In the report, the factory claimed that several workers had been threatened to stop working, both on Friday 2 January and on New Year's Eve. Hille requested that the police establish a guard at the company to prevent trespass and to protect the workers.

The police sent the case to the Hetland sheriff's office for investigation. The Police Chamber asked for a separate notification "in the event that guard duty is deemed required". The sheriff returned with a report two weeks later, on January 15. The report is not in the archives, but from the record we can conclude that no police guard was posted.

Fjellberg Bruk was part of Johan Tostensen Østbø's canning empire. From 1920, Østbø controlled two factories in Buøy/Hundavåg in addition to a branch in Verksgata in Stavanger (Johnsen 2000, pp. 185–187). The company withdrew from the canning industry in the mid-1980s.

According to the trade union, Østbø ran a rough practice towards his workers. At Fjellberg, the work was from 80 to 113 h a week. Young workers under the age of 18 also had working hours that were in breach of the law. Østbø did not follow the usual practice in the industry of paying extra for overtime work. He objected to the workers organizing, and the wages were far below what was the practice in other companies where there were unionized workers. When the workers went on strike, he would throw the strikers and their families out of the homes they rented through the company.[57]

In the judgment that Skeie refers to as case no. 63 we have what is probably an example of an acquittal that is at least partially incorrect. Telemark Arbeiderblad gives a good record of the proceedings in the Court of Appeal in the 15 and

---

[54] 1st May, Tuesday 8 September 1931. The case is too late to be included in Skeie's overview.

[55] The State Archives in Stavanger, Jæren magistrate's office, SAST/A-100310/01/3/31/310B/L-0008.

[56] The State Archives in Stavanger, Rogaland Police Chamber, sast/A-1001403/G/Gab/Gaba/L-002.

[57] An acquittal and a verdict, article in the newspaper 1ste Mai 8 September 1931 p. 4.

16 September 1930 issues. Two people stood accused in the case in the Court of Appeal in Skien. They had both been convicted in the District Court. After the indictment, they, together with a number of others, had turned up at Tjønnå's dried peat factory in Lunde in Telemark, where the union had initiated a work stoppage. One defendant had told two workers that they could risk their lives if they continued to work, and that one of them was a "damned Judas". The other had called the aggrieved strikebreakers and also said that they could risk their lives if they continued to work. The first defendant had published the names of several of the strikebreakers in an article in Telemark Arbeiderblad.

During the negotiations, it emerged that it was the factory's management who had reported the case to the police and had workers sign them. Several of the aggrieved said that they would not have reported the incident if the company had not asked for it, and that they did not take the threat to their lives literally. During the proceedings, the defender pointed to the Supreme Court judgment in Grytåa and that showing up in large numbers and telling those who worked that they were strike breakers was not punishable, and that statements about "risking your life" were not concrete threats. As for the publication, the defendant claimed that he did not know that it was a criminal offence. According to the defender, he therefore did not have the necessary criminal intent to be punished.

The jury acquitted both defendants. The acquittal for the publication of names was obviously wrong, as both the law and the facts were clear. The reactionary newspaper Norges Fremtid, referred to the ruling as an example of "a typical outcome of these class judgments that have been witnessed in recent times. The jury consisted of no fewer than five members of the socialist and communist parties, all of whom voted for acquittal."[58] The business paper Handels og Sjøfartstidende described the verdict as "startling". According to the newspaper, the vote of the jury was purely partisan, and the verdict had caused considerable attention.[59] The same notice appeared again in several other newspapers across the country in the following days.

Another case that received a lot of attention, because the jury handed down an acquittal while elections for jury members and lay judges were going on in the municipalities, emerged from a demonstration in Lillehammer during the great lockout in 1931. During the lockout, a joint newspaper was published by the newspapers Gudbransdølen, Laagen and Hamar Stiftstidende, which were all affect by the conflict.[60] The paper was published with the help of unorganized workers. This caused exasperation and resentment in the ranks of the trade unions. In the days 21–24 April there was a constant gathering of people outside the premises of Gudbrandsdølen.

[58] Norway's Future, Wednesday 17 September 1930.

[59] Norges Handels- og Sjøfartstidende Tuesday 16 September 1930.

[60] The presentation here is based on the minutes of the newspaper Gudbrandsdølen 7–11. November 1931.

On Saturday 25 April, a meeting was held among the organizers, and they approached the leader of Gudbransdølen and asked if he was willing to receive a deputation. He agreed to this. On this basis, the police gave permission for a demonstration to be held. The police had cordoned off an area in front of the newspaper's premises, but the protesters broke the cordon and pressed the police against the building. Demonstrators started shuffling and shouting, and the police characterized it as a riot. There were occasional clashes between demonstrators and the police, and a state police officer was pulled into the crowd and dragged down across the square to the Mesna Bridge, where he was about to be thrown into the river. However, some clear-headed people were able to prevent this.

During the trial, the chief of police testified and explained that the demonstrators were not regular workers, but people familiar to the police beforehand. Many of the defendants had previously been fined for violence, drunkenness and illegal home-production of liquor. One had been convicted of theft. The leader, on the other hand, was a former Member of Parliament. The police chief explained that the state police officer had unleashed his club on protesters, causing them to turn on him in rage. He believed that life of the officer had been at risk.

All 10 who were prosecuted had been leaders of the demonstration and active in it. The leader and one of the others had not themselves been involved in the violence against the state police officer, but had, according to the prosecutor, helped to stir up the masses. The others had been directly involved in the assault to a greater or lesser extent. The lawyer for the defense argued believed that the evidence was unclear and that there was no evidence that any of the accused had used violence. After three hours of deliberation, the jury returned with an acquittal for all the defendants.

The ruling and the sentence were sharply criticized in conservative newspapers.

Another acquittal was delivered by the Court of Appeal in Oslo on 15 October 1931. Before Christmas 1930, construction work began at Smestad in Oslo.[61] The work was carried out by unorganized workers, and the work was blocked by the trade union, as the employer would not allow organization. Over the winter and spring there was constant trouble at the site, repeatedly visited by picket guards and others. On 16 May, a demonstration was organized from the Monolith at the Frogner Park. The demonstration comprised 250–300 men. When they arrived at the construction site, they encountered a police roadblock. Three of the protesters were allowed through to speak with the construction workers. They encouraged them to cease work. Among the deputation was the Swede Carl Johan Söderström, a well-known communist agitator. After talking to the workers, he mounted a stump and made an appeal. Here he stated that workers had the right to fight the Penitentiary Act by all means.

During the negotiations with the protesters, the workers asked to continue working until the evening. To that it was answered that the comrades would be "excited" if they did not stop immediately. Despite the presence of police with dogs,

[61] The description of the demonstration and the trial is based on a report in Aftenposten on Monday 24 August 1931.

one of the workers stated that he became "somewhat anxious" as there were so many protesters present. They were also told that the demonstration would return the next day with 1000 men if the work continued. Under these circumstances, they chose to quit to avoid further disturbance.

An indictment was brought against Söderström for violation of § 222 II of the Penal Code, and the was tried in the Oslo District Court on 24 August 1931. The prosecutor asked for fines for Söderström. The defender, lawyer Viggo Hansteen, pointed out that the demonstration had taken place in decent manner, which was also proven by the fact of the police letting a deputation into the construction site. Hansteen also pointed out that it was remarkable that charges had only been brought against Söderström. He had had no leading role in the demonstration, and there had been two men besides him who had spoken to the workers. When Söderström was singled out, it had to be because he was a known agitator and accused in the press as a dangerous man. The court delivered a unanimous verdict and sentenced Söderström to 30 days in prison. Söderström appealed to the Court of Appeal, where he was acquitted by the jury. In light of the understanding of section 222 II in the courts this was obviously a correct decision.

5.9 Reinterpretation and Mild Torture

In Jon Skeie's overview, we find several cases in which the Court of Appeal has acquitted defendants on appeal after they had been convicted in the District Court. Particularly striking are the cases he refers to from the Court of Appeal for Hedmark. He refers to a total of 4 cases from this jurisdiction (cases no. 45,46,47 and 49) where the defendants were convicted in the District Court and acquitted by the jury. In two of these cases, the evidence was completely clear, as defendant had admitted to publishing names of strike breakers in the newspaper. It is difficult to find another explanation for these acquittals than the jury refusing to apply the penitentiary law.

In newspapers reports from trials, we find more information about the other cases. The reports show that these, and other acquittals in the Court of Appeal concerned demonstrations and riots to get unorganized workers to end work that had been blocked by the trade union. Although such demonstrations were clearly within the scope of what those legislators who had advocated the Penitentiary Act intended to criminalize, the Supreme Court in its decision in the Grytåa case opened for acquittal on legal ground in such cases. When the consequently acquitted in subsequent cases, this was therefore that had support in the Supreme Court. The criticism that was directed by the conservative press at juries at the time was therefore often misplaced and should have been directed at the Supreme Court and the professional judges. It was the Supreme Court and the professional judges of the lower courts who were responsible for the many acquittals, although some professional judges also believed that such behavior should be punishable. However, they were in the minority and out of line with the majority of the Supreme Court.

Nevertheless, there were acquittals that cannot be explained in this way. There were acquittals that can only be explained by a politically biased jury. As we have seen, the penitentiary laws were perceived as illegitimate by the labor movement and large parts of the population. It is no surprise that such views also influenced members of the juries. Cases where a jury acquits in violation of a clear law are not unknown when a jury is used to decide the question of guilt, even if it is contrary to both the law and the assurance given by jury members before taking office. This was also the case in Norway in the 1920s and 30s. The experienced appeal court judge Chr. L. Rolfsen pointed out in a lecture at the law association in Oslo that "if the legislation under social pressure goes too far in severe punishments, it is difficult to avoid that a court which does not need to justify its decision on the question of guilt, reacts in the face of such strictness in the complete opposite direction (Rolfsen 1931)." He claimed that there were plenty of examples of this from recent times and highlighted in particular cases regarding crimes of immorality and violation of the prohibition legislation. From the First World War until 1926, the controversial ban on spirits and strong wine applied in Norway. Labor Party members were happy to highlight examples of debatable acquittals in cases of violations of the liquor ban when juries were accused by conservative politicians of disrespecting the law in cases against demonstrating workers.

On the other hand, there are also examples of the courts stretching the provision quite far to get the defendants convicted. Some lower court judgments in the cases on the Folldal conflict are an example of this.

The examples that have been reviewed show that there was a wide range of how section 222 II was interpreted in the lower courts. In some cases, the provision was applied to circumstances where the accused would obviously not have been convicted had the case reached the Supreme Court. In other cases, in line with the guidelines drawn up by the Supreme Court, arguments, abuse and general threats were not considered sufficient for conviction. On the other hand, there were also cases where more abstract threats such as "It could be dangerous for you" or "You must take responsibility for what might happen" led to conviction. The fact that situations arose which those willing to work could perceive as threatening or intimidating, for example large groups om angry and demonstrating workers, were generally not punished, although there were also exceptions here. Publication of the names of strikebreakers was usually punished, but even here the practice was not consistent.

The level of punishment was consistently low. Only a few cases led to a prison sentence. In Skeie's list, there is only one example of a prison sentence for the violation of Section 222 II of the Penal Code (Skeie 1931, p. 516). After the Torpa conflict, the protesters received prison for after an encounter that was "particularly malignant". The Menstad battle occurred after Skeie completed his list, so it is not included. This is the case with the most severe sentences for violating section 222 II. Prison was also imposed in the judgment after the conflict in Julussa, but then according to the penal provisions against violence and bodily harm. Prison sentences occurred more often where the defendant was convicted for violating section 222 first paragraph, the general prohibition against illegal coercion. In Skeie's material, this is the case in 7 out of 23 cases. Where section 222 I or II of the Criminal Code was applied in concurrence with another penal provision, there is a prison sentence in 16 out of 29 cases.

The punishment for violating section 222 II was therefore most often a fine. The fines imposed were consistently low mostly between NOK. 50 and NOK 100. On the other hand, there were a number of cases where the prosecution requested, and the accused was remanded in custody before the hearing in court. In this sense, there were many who went to prison for violating Section 222 II.

Nor did editors and others who published the names of strikebreakers receive a prison sentence. This is a clear contrast to the sentencing in the cases concerning the actions against the Arbitration Act, where the Supreme Court determined that prison should be the regular punishment. Skeie mentions 16 cases where people have been convicted of having published the names of those willing to work. In none of the cases was a prison sentence applied. The editor von der Lippe in Klassekampen was fined NOK. 100 by the Court of Appeal for having published the names of the strikebreakers during the conflict at Rådhushospitset. This reaction is indicative of how the provision was applied in such cases, both in the district courts and in the courts of appeal.

The Supreme Court never ruled on the level of punishment for editors who published the names of strikebreakers in violation of Section 222 II. But in Rt. 1928 p. 862, the court stated that the punishment for editors who supported an illegal action in violation of the Labor Disputes Act § 40 had to be punished with imprisonment on the grounds that "an invitation in the newspapers to put themselves above the laws and seek to deprive them of their meaning, has quite different consequences than where individuals act against the laws and seek to deprive them of their effect. I therefore believe that if the threats of punishment set by the Labor Disputes Act and the Arbitration Act are to be effective against newspaper editors, one cannot avoid using prison sentences, when the newspaper articles have such a challenging content as in the present case." Although different penal provisions were involved, the law's level of punishment was quite similar in the Labor Disputes Act in the Penal Code. It would therefore not have been striking if the punishment for newspaper editors had been more severe than for individuals also according to Section 222 II. However, it did not turn out that way.

On the other hand, there are examples of Section 140 of the Penal Code being used against articles in connection with labor disputes, and then the punishment was imprisonment. Section 140 of the Criminal Code covered incitement to a criminal offence. The provision was used several times against calls for refusal of conscription and military strikes. In connection with timber floating riots in Dokka-Etna, the Oslo Court of Appeal sentenced a newspaper secretary in the newspaper Arbeideren to prison for 60 days. He had written an article that said, among other things: "The Torpa workers have not yet taken the rifle down from the wall. But they will and must use this means when the bourgeoisie intervenes with its military strength," and "The workers must everywhere strike hard, and the striking log drivers must intensify the fight against the strike breakers and the police and the social fascists.

Every strikebreaker must be chased out of the rivers, and every police constable must be chased out of the villages. Whatever it takes!"[62]

Although the picture is not clear, the general picture is that courts did not particularly follow up the intentions behind Section 222 II of the Penal Code. The provision quietly became "the object of mild torture on the part of the judges", its content was "rewritten" by the courts and, in some rare cases, was openly sabotaged, to use the prediction made by professor Ragnar Knoph for the destiny of legislation in grave contradiction with a general conception of justice.[63] The reason for this was not primarily, as was often claimed at the time, that politicized jurors acquitted in violation of the law. The main reason was that professional judges, from the Supreme Court downwards, adopted a skeptical attitude towards the law and interpreted it restrictively. This is also reflected in the mild sentencing. Although there were judges who stood out, eventually it became obvious to the prosecution that they would not have the defendant convicted in such cases. As Trygve Lie said at the LO congress in 1934, the use of the provision therefore ceased almost by itself.[64]

5.10 Did the Legislators Achieve What They Wanted?

Jon Skeie characterizes Section 222 II of the Criminal Code as an "in several respects mitigating exception from the main rule (Skeie 1931, p. 494). What he meant was that compared to the main provision on threats, the new second paragraph provided a milder punishment for threats uttered during a labor conflict. He points out the second paragraph set a lower penalty than the first paragraph, that the procedure was more favorable to the defendant and that many circumstances which were punishable under the general rule on threats were not punishable under the amendment. It is, however, clear from the bill and the debates in Stortinget that the legislators did not intend for it to be a modifying provision.

In his legal analysis of the provision, Skeie concludes that the provision brought little new. According to his assessment it was both narrower in scope and milder than what applied under the existing, more general rule. Since the second paragraph specifically applied to labor conflicts, the general rule of interpretation that a special rule supplants the more general rule would lead to the first paragraph was unapplicable in labor conflicts even in situations covered by both rules (Skeie 1931, p. 496).

Although Section 222 II authorized higher fines, it reduced the maximum penalty from three to one year of imprisonment. For crimes specifically addressed to

[62] See minutes of the case in Vestopland on Friday 5 September 1930.

[63] The formulations are from an article by Ragnar Knoph in 1923, see Knoph (1923), pp. 24–25.

[64] LO congress 1934 p. 254.

employment relations, there had never been a stricter penalty than 120 days in prison before the amendment was adopted.

Compared to the general provision on threats, the new provision had a narrower scope of application. It only affected coercion aimed at influencing someone to stop working or to prevent someone from getting work, and only the publication of names in connection with a labor dispute. On the other hand, it was not necessary that the threat communicated an intent to inflict something illegal. Also threats of perfectly legal acts were covered, provided that they in the situation could be regarded as insulting or intrusive.

In Skeie's opinion, the adoption of the new section II had to mean that one could not apply the general part of the provision in section I in employment relations. It became what the lawyers call "lex specialis", a special provision that displaced the more general provision within its area. Skeie argued that this applied because Section 222 II was a special provision for labor conflicts, an exception from the general rule, which also criminalized conditions that were not covered by the general rule. This interpretation clearly contradicted with the purpose that the majority in the Storting wanted to achieve with the change in the law. But the fact that those legislators had intended to toughen the penal rules against workers in battle could not prevail against ordinary legal principles of interpretation. "Legislative intent is not law," wrote Skeie (Skeie 1931, p. 496). Skeie's argument illustrates an important element of the autonomy of law: Although the legislature is free to make laws, it is up to the judiciary and the legal community autonomously to determine the law's further content through interpretation.

Skeie also argued that the inclusion of the penitentiary clause in the provision against threats in the Criminal Code limited its application to where there was intimidation or coercion. If a person spread a rumor about another who was fired as a result of this, the provision would not apply since there was no coercion. Although there was no condition in the law that the offended party should be "molested" by being followed from place to place, having his name published or as a result of inappropriate behaviour, this had to be interpreted in the provision. Otherwise, one could not talk about any form of coercion. The Supreme Court also based this understanding in the judgment in Rt. 1933 p. 212, where the court set conditions that it was not enough that a behavior was improper, it had to be improper towards *the offended party*. Encouraging others to stop work, so that the victim could not carry out *his* work, was not caught by the provision.

Otherwise, Skeie argued that most conditions covered by the penitentiary clause could be affected by other provisions such as the prohibitions against threats, bodily harm, defamation and violation of privacy. Instead of toughening the criminal provisions against measures to prevent those willing to work during a conflict, in other words, it narrowed the area of what was punishable without adding anything particularly new, was Skeie's position. According to Skeie, the requirement to prevent someone from working due to "improper behavior" brought nothing new. He believed that it would always be unlawful to prevent someone from carrying out a useful, or at any rate legal activity, through behavior that was inappropriate (Skeie 1931, p. 499). Here, however, the Supreme Court did not follow Skeie.

In most ways Skeie went further than the courts in restricting the application of section 222 II than the courts. On the other hand, he interpreted other provisions more extensively than accepted by the courts. He does not comment on the Supreme Court's ruling in the Grytåa case, but it is obvious that he would disagree that intimidating masses of people gathering around a few workers did not in itself constitute a threat under the general provision, and he also regarded this as covered by the new provision. Skeie stated that the "gathering of large masses of people on a public road at the entrance to a factory premises" is considered a disturbance of public peace and order and therefore inappropriate and intrusive behavior within the meaning of the provision (Skeie 1931, p. 497). The same would have to be the case if someone trespassed on a private area and remained there despite an order to leave. Skeie also stated that providing public information about a person's employment would be punishable, even without the special provision in Section 222 II (Skeie 1931, p. 498). Unlike the Supreme Court, he regarded this as an illegal breach of privacy to publish the names of strike breakers.

The fact still remains that both the courts and the academic lawyers (there were not many in Norway at the time) severely restricted the scope of the new provision. Why did they do this? We shall return to this question in the next chapter. What we can say here is that there are many indications that Section 222 II of the Penal Code was not suitable for achieving the goals the ministry and those who advocated the change wanted. It was too poorly worked out. The questions Skeie raised had not been thought through in the preparation of the law, it was simply the result of poor legal technical work.

Furthermore, the review of court cases show that the courts were largely in line with Skeie's opinion. Overall, it can be said that both the Supreme Court and the other courts adopted a cautious approach to the new provision and that it therefore did not lead to any major legal changes. Many of the situations that those who advocated the provision had intended to be affected were not considered punishable. This was clearest when the Supreme Court determined that lining up a large crowd and confronting strike breakers was not covered by the provision.

The biggest change after it was passed was in the number of cases, which rose dramatically. This suggests that the provision primarily affected the practice of the police and the public prosecutors, and to a lesser extent the courts. Since the accused were often remanded in custody, there was a widespread use of prison. The other clear change was that publication of the names of strikebreakers was punishable. But overall, the change in the law did not have much significance compared to the already applicable rules. Both those who meant to expand the area of criminal liability and those who feared this, were wrong. This did not, however, prevent the adoption of the provision leading to an expansion of the use of the penal system through the intensified follow-up by the authorities. We must not forget that many were detained, and thus in prison, in connection with the police investigation. Thus, the adoption of section 222 II initially lead to an increase in the legal repression of the fight against strike breakers, albeit not as extensive as intended by the proponents of the law. This increase in intensity was, however, reversed by the resistance that the prosecutor faced in the courts, which led them to eventually giving up indicting workers for offences against provision 222 II.

References

Amundsen H (1946) Trygve Lie Gutten fra Grorud som ble generalsekretær (Tryygve Lie The boy from Grorud who became general secretary). Tiden, Oslo

Bækkelund B, Kalvatn SJ (eds) (1998) Bygdebok for Folldal, vol. IV Folldal verks historie ca. 1745-1993 (Folldal works history ca 1745-1993). Folldal kommune, Folldal

Bekken T,(1977) Folldalkonflikten 1929-31 (The Folldal conflict 1929-31), Tidsskrift for arbeidebevegelsens historie, No 1

Christensen H (1925) Reisehåndbok over Oslo (Travelguide for Oslo), H. Aschehough & Co, Oslo

Folldal AOF-forening (1981) Arbeiderforeningen i Folldal (The workers union in Folldal), Folldal

Johansen PO (1977) Menstadslaget, (The Menstad Battle) Tiden norsk forlag, Oslo

Knoph R (1923) Rett og rettsbevissthet (Law and legal conciousness). Olaf Norlis forlag, Kristiania

Medby J (1951) Norsk hotell- og restaurant-arbeider-forbund 1931-1951. utgitt av Norsk hotell- og restaurant-arbeider-forbund, Oslo

Ousland G (1975) Fagorganisasjonen i Norge 2 De store kamp-åra 1921-1931 (The trade union in Norway 2 The great fighting years 1921–1931). Tiden, Oslo

Overn AM (1929) Boken om Vika og nærmeste omegn. Stranberg & Co, Oslo

Rolfsen CL (1931) Lagmannsretten i dens virke, dens fortrinn og mangler, foredrag holdt i Juristforeningen i Oslo 20. april 1931 (The Court of Appeal in its work, its advantages and shortcomings: Lecture held at the Oslo Bar Association 20 April), Oslo

Skeie J (1931) Ulovlige midler i kampen om arbeidsvilkår (Illegal means in the fight for working conditions). Det Mallingske bokgtrykkeri, Oslo

Chapter 6
The Battle for the Lay Judges

6.1 Abuse and Fraud

The many acquittals led to accusations that the courts, the juries in particular, acted politically and acquitted in violation of the law. It was believed that lay judges and jury members sabotaged the law by acquitting people who were obviously guilty of breaking it. The reason why there were so many disloyal lay judges, it was said, was that the Labor Party had abused its power in local councils to get cadres elected as lay judges. An illustration of this was the document published by the Conservative Party, "The trade union terror rule and the unions' monopoly policy, a document" (Gotaas undated). This document was published by the central governing body of the Party. Under the heading "the denial of the right" the document states that the Labor Party had used its power in a number of municipal councils to fill the lists of lay judges and jury members with reliable people, and that this had borne fruit "where the professional terrorist heroes have been brought before the courts" (Gotaas undated, p. 40). The belief that the Labor Party acted in this way and that this explains the number of acquittals has prevailed through the ages, se for instance Castberg (1974).

Even members of the Labor Party publicly boasted that they controlled the juries. In the Storting (the Norwegian Parliament) in May 1930, Olav Sæter from the Labor Party stated that "I, for my part, have been prosecuted twice under the penitentiary clause, and I am among the most law-abiding people I know in the world! The only wrong I had done was that I had included in the newspaper a list from the union in Hedmark county, a list of those willing to work in the Folldal conflict and those willing to work in Moelven. Fortunately, I and other accused have so far been acquitted, because in our county we have quite a lot of influence over the composition of the courts."[1] Olav Jørgen Sæter was a parliamentary representative for the Labor Party from Hedmark in the period 1921–1945. He was also mayor of Elverum

[1] Stortingstidende, forhandlinger i Stortinget 22 May 1930 p. 1689.

H. P. Graver, *Democracy and Lawlessness*,
https://doi.org/10.1007/978-3-031-69055-6_6

municipality 1932–1940. He was trained as a teacher in 1906 and worked as a teacher in Dovre 1906–1911 and later in Elverum. He was the editor of Østerdalens Arbeiderblad until the newspaper was merged with Hamar Arbeiderblad in 1932.

The records suggest that his claim that he had been prosecuted twice was a brag. As we shall see, however, he was not boasting when he said that the Labor Party in Elverum had great influence over the composition of the courts. He apparently confirmed the view that the Labor Party had abused its power where it could, to secure influence over the composition of the courts.

The opinion that the Labor Party had influenced the courts through political appointments of lay judges and jurors formed quite quickly. "As you know, the municipal councils elect the men, from among whom the lay judges and jurors are selected," said president of Stortinget CJ Hambro when he opened the election campaign for Conservative Party in the World Theater in Trondheim on Sunday 2 November 1931. "These elections have never before been political. But now the people of the Labor Party have been ordered to clean out all the lay judges who could not be considered reliable party members."[2]

As we saw from the review cases in the previous chapter, it is difficult to find clear examples of wrongful acquittals, though there were some. Today it is not possible to verify the evidence of the lower courts. Still, the impression one is left after looking at court records and detailed reports in the local newspapers is that the jurors mostly followed the law as it was determined by the Supreme Court and the professional judges. The acquittals in the courts of appeal often seem to be due to a different interpretation of the law, and it is often not obvious that the jury was wrong.

The accusations of political manipulation of the election of lay judges were serious accusations, which, to the extent they were valid, meant that the courts had become a venue of class struggle. Selecting lay judges according to their party loyalty was obviously a misuse of power in municipal councils. According to the law, the councils should elect persons with integrity, skill and independence. An understanding that they should act as jurors according to party preferences was incompatible with this. On the other hand, it was clear that at the time the selection of lay judges did not reflect the general population, as workers and people from the lower classes were grossly unrepresented. To keep a social class out or leave it obviously underrepresented was also not in accordance with the law. The Jury Commission, which prepared the bill for the current Criminal Procedure Act in which the jury system was a main element, stipulated that the jurors "should be drawn from all backgrounds and circles and thus presumably would come to represent all views and nuances of opinion within society."[3] The idea was thus that the lay judges and jurors should reflect society in all its nuances and not just be made up of representatives of the bourgeoisie or the rural landlords.

[2] Adresseavisen Monday 23 November 1931.

[3] Document No 1 (1885) Recommendation from the jury commission containing a draft law on the procedure in criminal cases p. 493.

Were the accusations of abuse of political power to ensure politically loyal judges correct? To answer this, we must look more closely at the election of co-judges and lay judges in the years 1928 and 1931.

Threats that the socialists would go hand-picking loyal people were clearly there. After the use of Section 222 II of the Penal Code against workers in several major conflicts, such as the conflict over Rådhushospitset, there were demands that the labor party should use its power to influence the composition of the courts through the selection of lay judges and jurors. Worker representatives had to be included in the list of lay judges. "The workers in Elverum have seen how their trustees have been chased like wild animals and thrown into prison out of the clear blue sky. Therefore, the workers in Elverum cannot contribute to the election of members of the bourgeoisie to the courts," wrote Østerdalen's Arbeiderblad, Friday 16 November 1928.

Some would even go so far as to exercise party discipline over lay judges. The Norwegian Union of General Workers put forward the following proposal at the LO annual meeting in 1931:

> In connection with the conflicts that unionized workers have waged against the labor buyers in order to improve their wages and working conditions, the justice system of the capitalist state has been used to a large extent against the workers and their representatives.
>
> In the various district courts and courts of appeal, which have unanimously sentenced the accused workers in accordance with the Penitentiary Act to fines or imprisonment, there have also been workers affiliated to both the workers' professional and political organizations as judges.
>
> In the District Court of Bærum, which unanimously sentenced the forestry and agricultural workers' trustees to fines or imprisonment, one of the judges was a member of Bærum's municipal civil service group affiliated with the Norwegian Association of Municipalities and the Labor Party's branch in Bærum.
>
> In Ålesund city court, which unanimously sentenced the editor of a workers' newspaper to fines, alternative prison terms, because he had published the names of strikebreakers, one of the judges was also a member of the trade union and a prominent member of the Labor Party.
>
> The trade union cannot under any circumstances tolerate such a situation, but must consider the voting of these workers in city and county courts as a breach of solidarity and class-hostile behavior, which can only work to the advantage of strikebreakers and strengthen the bourgeoisie and labor buyers in their reactionary push against the working class and their trade unions.
>
> Accordingly, the Congress makes such decision:
>
> Congress states:
>
> That the Penitentiary Act is a reactionary push against the workers' trade unions and cannot be tolerated.
>
> That the workers who, together with the bourgeoisie, convict unionized workers and their trustees according to the Penitentiary Act, are committing a non-solidarity and class-hostile

act, which is incompatible with membership in the workers' professional and political organizations.[4]

Trygve Lie commented that such a decision would disqualify all members of the trade union and workers' parties as lay judges and advised the congress to vote against it. The proposal was defeated by 10 votes. There was nevertheless a great will in parts of the labor movement to handpick loyal people as lay judges and jurors. This was particularly prominent among the Communists. This will was strongly and publicly expressed and made an impression in bourgeois circles. But how far was this will followed up in practice? There is much to suggest that Trygve Lie's moderate line was the one that succeeded in the local elections of lay judges and jurors.

Regardless of what actually took place, such statements from the labor movement about hand-picking judges and securing their loyalty may nevertheless have helped to create an impression in conservative circles that this happened to a large extent. This was a simple way for conservatives of explaining acquittals that one disagreed with or found incomprehensible. The acquittals thus became a confirmation of the perception that the elections were politically manipulated. The juries acquitted because they were biased, and the fact that they acquitted proved their bias. To find out whether such a politicization of the election of lay judges actually occurred, we must go into more detail about what actually happened in the municipalities.

The elections of lay judges and jury members was the task of the municipal councils and took place every three years after the municipal elections. No reasons were given by the councils for their decisions, and there are no official records of the debates that took place in the councils. To find out of how the elections took place, we can, however, look at the press coverage at the time. Before the time of TV and the internet, there were a myriad of local newspapers that reported from the debates in the municipal councils. These papers are now digitalized and available through the website of the Norwegian National Library. A search for "lagrettemen" (Norwegian for jury members) in the national library's newspaper database yields 202 hits in October 1928, 468 hits in November and 380 hits in December. Most of these hits concern the election of lay judges and jury members in the municipalities. In many cases, there are several hits for a municipality. In 1928, there were over 700 municipalities in Norway. With over 1000 postings, we see that this does not provide a complete overview, since the election process was two step, first an announcement of a proposal by the executive council and then a debate and vote in the full council. In many cases there was no debate as there was inter-party agreement on the proposal, and thus no report in the newspapers. Some of these hits mention the term "jury member" in connection with court reporting, and are therefore not relevant for our purposes. There are also some cases where the elections in a municipality are covered by several newspapers. Nevertheless, we can assume that the newspaper reports cover over half of the municipalities and thus provide a representative picture. If anything, we must assume that the municipalities where

[4] LO Congress 1931 Agenda and protocol, Oslo 1931 p. 369.

there was a political dispute about the elections are overrepresented in the newspapers' coverage, and that we therefore get a good picture of the extent to which the elections for lay judges and jurors were politicized by going through the newspaper reports.

The elections in 1931 were also widely covered in the newspapers, in fact to a greater extent than in 1928. The search for "lagrettemenn" in the database yields 365 hits in October 1931, 719 hits in November and 515 hits in December. Again, it must be taken into account that the proposal of the executive council should be announced before the election in the municipal council.

Some of the articles report discussion and controversy surrounding the elections. Most of the notices, however, only neutrally report the names of the people elected. Sometimes reports expressly state that the election was unanimous. Where the election was unanimous, one can safely assume that the selection of jury members and lay judges was not a political issue. Presumably this is also the case where the newspapers only refer to who has been elected without comment, and also for the elections in those municipalities that are not referred to in the newspapers at all. There was quite a lot of public attention regarding the politicization of these elections, both from the conservative side and from the Labor Party and the Communists. I therefore assume that most cases where the election of lay people to the courts was politicized have been picked up and referred to by local or even national newspapers.

The cases where the papers report of politicized elections make up only a small number of the total of over 700 municipalities. This is also consistent with what the ministry writes in connection with a proposal to change the rules in 1932 that "the current rules must be assumed to have worked satisfactorily in a large number of municipalities."[5]

Furthermore, it was not only questions of political affiliation and class background that could be subject of discussion in the municipal council. In several municipalities, there was discussion about whether the proposals for lay judges and juror reflected the different areas of the municipality well enough. People wanted their local community to be represented. In Flekkefjord, at the election in 1931, they had a discussion about whether also women should be represented on the list.[6] The same was the case in Ålesund[7] and Bærum.[8] In Bærum, it was the Labor Party's Halfdan Koht (later foreign minister from 1935 to 1940) who raised the issue of the representation of women.

[5] Ot. prp. No. 18 1932 Om forandring i rettergangslovene p. 4.

[6] Agder, Friday 4 December 1931.

[7] Sunnmørsposten Friday 11 December 1931.

[8] Arbeiderbladet Wednesday 16 December 1931.

6.2 Election of Lay Judges and Jury Members

In 1927, a completely new system came into force with the new Courts Act of 1915. It is not only in our time that major legal reforms are being implemented slowly. The Act determined in section 64 that court judges and magistrates were to be elected every three years for the following three calendar years. The first election was nevertheless to be held in the first half of 1927 and only apply until 1928. A new election was then to be held in the autumn of 1928 for the following three calendar years. Sections 74 and 75 of the Act determined that the municipal council was to elect members to the list from which the courts would draw the lay judges and jurors. The number of people on the list from each municipality was calculated from the number of people entitled to vote in the municipality.

The law prescribed that the only people eligible for election were those "who, because of their integrity, skill and independence, are considered particularly suitable for the position," section 76. The ministry highlighted this requirement in a circular about the new procedure and underlined the importance that "those who participate in the elections do not have any other considerations in mind than this."[9] The proposal of the executive council should be available for public inspection for at least two weeks before it was presented to the municipal council.

The elections in 1927 apparently proceeded normally. With few exceptions, there seems to have been little political controversy surrounding the elections. Oslo was an exception, where Arbeiderbladet refers that "almost all workers and white-collar workers were excluded" from being selected for the lists of lay judges or jurors.[10] The Labor Party proposed replacements on the list that had been proposed by the executive council but lost the vote. The conservative newspaper Aftenposten reported from the election in Fet municipality and wrote that only communists had been elected.[11] The newspaper also claimed that there were "a couple" of other examples of this, but it is not easy to find traces of this in the reports of the elections in the local newspapers. The notice was in any case inaccurate as it was not the Communists who had a majority in Fet, but the United Norwegian Workers' Party, that is, a merger of the Labor Party and the Social Democrats. That the labor parties forced their people through in the elections may have occurred in 1927 but was hardly particularly widespread.

---

[9] Circulars from the Ministry of Justice on the new trial system, Grøndahl & son's printing house Oslo 1927 p. 46.

[10] Arbeiderbladet Friday 10 June 1927.

[11] Aftenposten Friday 10 June 1927.

6.3 The Elections of 1928

In 1928 there was somewhat more controversy over the elections. On 11 July 1928, the Ministry of Justice sent out a circular to the municipalities stating that, due to the new procedural system, elections for court judges and magistrates had to be held during the autumn. The election this time was to take place for the period 1929–1931. The ministry drew attention to the fact that the preparatory election meeting was to be held no later than 15 November. The municipalities would be notified of the number to be selected by August at the latest.

In most municipalities the elections did not give rise to political controversy. The following report from the newpaper Grømstadposten seems quite representative of the process in most places: "You 'work together', and you can say that only in exceptional cases is there dissent. The decisions are usually unanimous. Municipal committees are set up, jurors and lay judges are chosen without regard to party color."[12]

The discussion in Stange municipal council can give a picture of the attitudes that prevailed in many municipalities. The executive council had put forward a split recommendation, with the majority nominating a list of 5 workers and 3 others, while the minority wanted to nominate 6 workers and 2 others. A short debate arose in the council. Representative Røe (Liberal) said: "My view is not so bourgeois that I will not take my hat off to any of those that the Labor Party has nominated. To that extent, I would have liked to have voted for a pure party list, but I cannot agree to such a principle. I don't think those of the Labor Party opposition will ever pass any class judgment, they are all men of integrity, but the opposition provokes us who represent the liberals and the conservatives!" The representative Lilleng (Labor Party) replied: "There may be something in what Røe says, but when we see who is chosen for the list, we see that few are working people. In Ringsaker (a neighboring municipality), only bourgeois are elected. I think the minority have been quite considerate." Then the mayor concluded: "It is precisely a certain principle that we have followed, as Røe said. The proposal accurately reflects the relative position of the parties in the new council!"[13]

The reference to Ringsaker was correct when it came to the recommendation from the executive council. But in the municipal council this changed and the conservative majority agreed to a compromise along the same line as in Stange. The result in Ringsaker was an election with equal numbers from the two camps.[14]

The view that the list should reflect the overall composition of the municipal council seems to have been quite widespread in the municipalities where politics entered into the picture at all. In Hol municipality, a written election was demanded because "both in Ål and Hol there has been a general dissatisfaction with this election that the liberal party is favored and has received too many

[12] Grømstadposten on Monday 3 December 1928.

[13] Reprinted from Hamar Arbeiderblad on Wednesday 7 November 1928.

[14] Hamar Arbeiderblad Saturday 17 November 1928.

representatives."[15] In the Gjerpen town council, the mayor threatened that it could be "difficult to get together and cooperate in the future" if the farmers' party did not get their man on the list.[16] The Labor Party was thus not the only political party in demanding "its" share in municipalities where there was a political dispute over the election.

In Ålesund, the communists pressured the Labor Party to strike non-workers from the list. The Labor Party's representatives voted against a proposal to this effect. The Communists also proposed striking a strikebreaker off the list of judges in exchange for a unionized worker. The Labor Party also voted against this. "The social democrats prefer capitalists and strikebreakers to unionized workers as judges," was the comment by Norges Kommunistblad.[17] In Lillehammer, the communists put forward a proposal to increase the number of trade union members. The Labor Party voted against this and supported the proposal from the executive council together with the conservative parties.[18] The same thing happened in Røyken. The Communists' representative Smedsrud pointed to "the class judgments that these days are passed on the men of the working class. The worker who votes for bourgeois judges is in reality signing these class judgments." The Labor Party's Olsen said that he "personally" could probably agree but believed that the fairest thing was a proportional election. The mayor agreed with that and pointed out that in other municipalities had followed the principle of proportional representation.[19] In Skoger municipality, the Labor Party put forward a list compiled according to the principle of proportional representation. Previously the lists had consisted only of non-workers, but now the Labor Party had a majority and would not accept this. But the party did not go to the other extreme and exclude non-workers from the selection.[20]

But in some municipalities, there was clash over the elections. First out was Odda, which had a socialist majority. In the proposal from the executive council that was announced on 1 November, only workers were proposed. The proposal was adopted by the municipal council on 20 November. "The labor parties in Odda will introduce class courts," wrote Haugesunds avis on Wednesday 21 November 1928. The election received a lot of attention and was mentioned in several newspapers around the country. The Labor Party newspaper 1. Mai called the attention and outrage on the bourgeois side hypocrisy, and pointed to the result in Time municipality, where the Labor Party had received a third of the votes, but where the council nevertheless only appointed bourgeois persons to the positions of lay judges and jurors.[21]

---

[15] Buskeruds Blad, Thursday 6 December 1928.

[16] Telemark Arbeiderblad, Tuesday 11 December 1928.

[17] Norges Kommunistblad Monday 3 December 1928.

[18] Norges Kommunistblad Tuesday 13 December 1928.

[19] Buskeruds Blad, Tuesday 18 December 1928.

[20] Fremtiden Monday, April 2, 1928.

[21] 1 May, Saturday 24 November 1928.

Soon after came Elverum. The executive council proposed a list draw only from the working classes. "The majority of the executive council confronts the class law," wrote Østerdalen's Arbeiderblad in its report on 14 November.[22] The proposal was debated in the municipal council meeting on 17 December. "Not considerate" and "maybe it will backfire", said a representative from the podium. "Strange that Elverum should take the lead here too by being as extreme as possible," said another. Sheriff Høye stated that the majority took other considerations than the law allowed when choosing lay judges. Major Sæter defended the proposal by saying that "as long as we have forest owners who want to use the military against the forest workers, the bourgeois must accept that we use the means of power we have."[23]

There were also municipalities where the situation was reversed and where a conservative majority ensured that no lay judges or jurors with connections to the labor party or the trade union movement were elected. This was, among other things, the case of Horg in Trøndelag and Hetland in Rogaland.[24] In Nes municipality in Akershus, "the conservative assembly was so strong" that only farmers and no workers were elected.[25] In the conservative newspapers, it was nevertheless the impression from Odda and Elverum that took hold and formed an image that the Labor Party was pushing its people into the courts.

There was also conflict in Oslo, where the Labor Party pointed out that their candidates were grossly underrepresented. The arrangement in Oslo was that the proposal for lay judges and jurors was drawn up by a separate committee on the basis of names put forward by the clerks at the tax office. Only 10 percent of those proposed were workers, even though they constituted the vast majority of the population.

Karl Frimann Dahl, Supreme Court judge and representative of the Labor Party, argued against the proposal. He emphasized that one had to strive for a social representativeness of the list of lay judges, as the courts must give expression to "the legal consciousness alive in the broad layers of the people."[26] He also believed that there was as much skill and fairness among workers as among the middle and upper classes, "an assertion to the contrary will drown in its ridiculousness." The majority's proposal could only be perceived as an abuse of power and an attempt at class dominance, which would destroy confidence in the courts. "The broader the basis, the greater the trust," he said, referring to Johan Sverdrup, the great liberal leader of the nineteenth century who had pioneered the jury system. He believed that the majority's proposal was "a danger to our legal order." The vote ended with the proposal gaining a majority with 43 votes, against the Labor Party's 42 votes. The election was an illustration that if one only followed the traditional way of appointing lay judges, the working class would continue to be grossly

[22] Østerdalens Arbeiderblad Wednesday 14 November 1928.

[23] Østledningen Tuesday 18 December 1928.

[24] See Trøndelagen Monday 3 December 1928, Stavangeren Thursday 29 November 1928.

[25] Romerikes Blad Friday 26 October 1928.

[26] Dagbladet Friday 14 December 1928.

underrepresented. This was portrayed as apolitical by the Conservative Party. Changing it was portrayed as politicizing the elections.

6.4 The Elections of 1931

Before the election in 1931, the Ministry of Justice stressed in a circular to the municipalities that only "insightful, fair-minded and independent people should be elected to the public offices in question here, and that those who participate in the elections should have no other consideration in mind than this."[27] Not everyone was willing to heed this. Again, the Communist Party mobilized to fight against class law and fascism. The party put up as their aim for the municipal elections was that "Only revolutionary workers, small farmers and fishermen are elected as judges and jurors" and "Fight against the reactionary ministry dictatorship and all provisions and measures that stand in the way of the interests and struggle of the working people."[28] The communists complained that in elections where they had a majority together with the Labor Party, the Labor Party voted with the bourgeois securing proportional share for class enemies, whereas pure workers' lists could have been obtained together with the communists.[29]

Again, the election took place without controversy in most municipalities. In Oslo, the unanimous recommendation of the executive council was this time adopted without debate by the city council.[30] The debate of last time had left its impression and the conservative had clearly taken the criticism from the election in 1928 to heart. The Labor Party's representatives received criticism from the Communists for having fully safeguarded the "interests of class justice".[31] In Sigdal municipality, the farmers' party was dissatisfied. The Conservative Party and the Labor Party agreed to elect 3 right-wingers and 1 from the Labor Party. The Farmers' Party got none, and criticized this as a political choice, motivated by an intent to offend the Farmers' Party.[32]

Otherwise, in most cases where there was a political debate, it was where the dissatisfaction of the Labor Party was strongest. There were several examples of a conservative majority nominating no one, or only a few representatives from the working class to the lists.

[27] Quoted from Akers-Posten on Thursday 1 October 1931.

[28] Arbeideren on Monday 12 October 1931.

[29] See, for example, Arbeidet Saturday 28 November 1931.

[30] Aftenposten Wednesday 16 December 1931.

[31] Arbeideren Thursday 17 December 1931.

[32] Buskerud og Vestfold on Thursday 15 October 1931.

At the election in Risør, the Labor Party tried to get workers elected to the list. The newspaper Folketanken reproduces an illustrative exchange in the city council:[33]

Abrahamsen	The Labor Party will now demand to get some of its own in the elections, we have the strongest group in the city council. I suggest Norli, Stiansen, Jonassen and Karlsen.
Kringlebotn	In Norwegian law, there is no indication of anything that justifies demands from political parties in the election of lay judges. The Labor Party can probably point to the fact that they have the strongest group, but if they want to establish a new principle and demand proportional representation, they will risk never getting any of 'their' on the list. The Labor Party's proposal is considered premature as a 'demand'. A totally other matter is that I recognize that Abrahamsen will certainly never make proposals about someone who cannot be personally approved. I will of course vote for Gunnar Karlsen.
Larsen	It is peculiar that all committees we otherwise elect must be filled by the proportional principle. When it comes to elections to the courts, the man from the workplace must be kept out. But the court of appeals should really be a people's court. It is the bourgeois who take political considerations into account here.
Grasaas	For my part, I have never thought about politics when appointing lay judges and jurors.
Kullerud	Abrahamsen's proposal covers the intent of the law. The different interests and legal awareness must be represented in these elections.

In Skjeberg municipality, one of the members of the council opposed the recommendation of the executive council. The speaker could not vote for "the bourgeois-proposed" candidates, as "the election of lay judges is very important for the working class, not least in the times we are now facing."[34]

In Tromsø, the newspaper Nordlys called the executive council's proposal "a shameful challenge to the city's working people."[35] In the proposal for 16 jurors, 13 from the middle and upper classes and 3 from the working class were proposed. The newspaper pointed out that the city council had 24 worker representatives and 28 representatives from the other parties and believed that the proposal should reflect this ratio. "The position of the executive council is not just a shameful challenge to the city's working class. It also shows a disturbing contempt for everything that underpins the jury system," the newspaper wrote. The recommendation of the executive council was passed with the double vote of the mayor. The newspaper

[33] Folketanken (Risør) Wednesday 11 November 1931.

[34] Sarpsborg Arbeiderblad Friday 13 November 1931.

[35] Nordlys 13 November 1931.

Vestfinnmark Arbeiderblad called the result an “abuse of power” by the conservatives.[36]

The Labor Party was kept out of the election of judges also in Nore municipality. During the debate, one of the Labor Party’s representatives pointed out this had not happened before, and wondered if it was punishment for the position the Labor Party had taken in the debate over the municipal budget some time earlier.[37]

In Vestre Toten, the conservatives came to their senses, and let a workers’ representative into the list. Member of Stortinget Erik Andreassen Knutsen Strand from the Farmers’ Party participated in the council meeting as census taker. “I have said it before, and I repeat it now, that I will support an election of Labor Party member M. Johansen,” said Strand. “It is the case that we bourgeois have the power, but we must not be petty. We look beyond political considerations and when the Labor Party has such a skilled and upright man as Johansen, then he should be elected.”[38]

In Grimstad, too, the Labor Party complained about the proposal of the executive council. Representative Honoré Pettersen pointed out that only one of those proposed was from the Labor Party and that workers should be more strongly represented. The mayor replied that party considerations had not influenced the proposal. To which Honoré Pettersen replied that “as long as the workers have an electorate in the country of around 2-3 million, it is strange that the representation here is so tiny.”[39]

On the other side, there were cases where the Labor Party used a majority to force its people onto the lists. In Elverum there were again two proposals, one from the Labor Party and one from the other parties. The Labor Party’s proposal won a majority. The newspaper Østlendingen wrote of a “tyrannical political abuse of power.”[40] Temperature during the debate was high.[41] Representative Berntsen made a lengthy speech and claimed that this was “the grossest abuse of power he had seen.” He believed that conditions were now totally lawless and that the Labor Party was following Russia’s example. Sæter responded by asking why the parallel was drawn to Russia and not Finland, where the fascist Lapua movement and the bourgeois held power. (The Lapua movement was clearly fascist and was later banned in Finland in 1932 after an attempted coup d'état). “We have to act as we do to protect the poorest in our society who are threatened by the bourgeoisie’s penitentiary laws simply because they are fighting for livable conditions,” Sæter continued. A civic representative asked if the Labor Party would protect criminals, to which Sæter replied that he did not consider violators of the Penitentiary Act to be criminals. But he wanted to protect society by being hard on crime and criminals

[36] Vestfinnmark Arbeiderblad Wednesday 16 December 1931.

[37] Kongsberg Tidende Tuesday 17 November 1931.

[38] Oppland Arbeiderblad Tuesday 24 November 1931.

[39] Grimstad Adressetidende Thursday 3 December 1931.

[40] Østledningen on Wednesday 2 December 1931.

[41] See Østerdalen Arbeiderblad Tuesday 1 December 1931.

such as rapists and people who are dangerous to public safety. In any case, he believed that it was no use discussing this matter with the conservative fraction.

Nord-Odal's municipal council also chose a list of lay judges that had been proposed by the labor party.[42] In Vang, only 1 out of 9 elected citizens was not working class,[43] and in Hof there were none.[44]

6.5 Did the Labor Party Politicize the Elections?

In 1927, Supreme Court judge Edvin Alten wrote an opinion about the independence of the courts. The opinion was published in Dagbladet and other newspapers. The article was primarily aimed at the widespread practice of hiring judges on a temporary basis. This threatened independence since many judges did not have the protection that permanent employment provides. In addition, he addressed judges' salaries and how important it is that judges are financially independent. In the introduction to the article, however, he commented on the appointment of judges and lay judges. "Any political consideration, any thought of party reward must be banned by those who are responsible for the selection og judges," he wrote. "Not all municipal councils and not all governments can say they are free of having sinned against this requirement."[45]

Alten did not direct his criticism towards any specific political party. As we have seen from the accounts, he was right in that were sinners against the requirement of political neutrality in all camps. The main picture is, however, that the principle of neutrality and independence was respected.

In the public debate it was different, especially in the conservative press. Already in connection with the elections in 1927, there were conservative newspapers that claimed in more general terms that the labor parties sought to politicize the elections for lay judges. Aftenposten had an article on the front page on 10 June 1927 under the heading "An apple of discord" in which it wrote that "the elections of lay judges and jurors, which are now taking place around the countryside, are more and more marked by pure and cutting party politics."[46] The paper claimed that the communists intended to fill all the positions with communists and were in the process of doing so during the elections. "If the balance is to be fairly maintained, the conservative parties will soon be forced to follow the communists' example. The conservatives must also abandon the proportional election and use the majority where they have it to the fullest," wrote the newspaper. The newspaper also raised questions as to whether the development would force the institution of lay judges and juries out of

[42] Kongsvinger Arbeiderblad Thursday 10 December 1931.

[43] Østlendingen Friday 11 December 1931.

[44] Innlandsposten Post on Tuesday 15 December 1931.

[45] Dagbladet Saturday 11 June 1927.

[46] Aftenposten Friday 10 June 1921.

the court system. Thos had long been the preferred position of the Conservative Party.

The allegation that the elections were politicized was also raised in the Storting in the same year, when the Storting debated with certain changes to the Criminal Procedure Act. A bill was proposed to change the rules on the attorney general's competence, public defenders and simplified processing of misdemeanor cases.[47] The ministry also announced "a change in the rules on the election of lay judges and jury members", but stated that it was not possible to adopt new rules in time for the new procedural system to come into force.

During the debate the conservative representative Mr Eyvind Getz, expressed that he "very much missed in this proposal a closer treatment of the question of the appointment of jurors and lay judges. It is not an unknown phenomenon around the country's municipalities, both in the countryside and in the cities, that strong political considerations influence when appointing jurors and lay judges to the criminal courts. Whether these considerations are taken from one side or the other, they are apt to damage the reputation of the courts around the country, and this has been exploited in many municipalities and in many newspapers to the point that it is said that the judgments that have been handed down are pure class courts."[48]

The government followed the following year in Ot. prp. No. 15 (1928). Here the government emphasized the importance of preventing "that the courts are composed in a way that leaves room for doubt that the judges take into account other factors than law and justice when making their decisions." It continued: "In most cases, one can probably assume that the court and judge meet the requirements that must be met. But it has also been shown that considerations have been taken during elections which are incompatible with an impartial and safe administration of justice."

The bill was withdrawn by the short-lived Labor Party government Hornsrud. In a message to Stortinget on 10 February, the government pointed out that "in the opinion of the current government, in practice there have so far been no such disadvantages with the current arrangement that it would be required for the time being to make changes to the current provisions."[49]

The matter did not end there. Storting representative Odd Bærøe from the Conservative Party tabled the withdrawn proposal as a private bill in a letter to Stortinget on 15 February. The Justice Committee followed up in Addendum 2 to Inst. O. 1928. The committee was split into two factions. The majority proposed changes to the rules. They pointed out that the ministry had in the meantime sent the rules for consultation to all municipalities. Most of the municipalities were in favor of keeping the rules, but a large minority supported a proposed amendment put forward by the government. Against this background, the majority of the committee proposed rules whereby the ministry could decide that the new rules should be applied in municipalities where at least one third of the members of the municipal

---

[47] Ot. prp No. 28 (1927) Om forandringer i straffeprosessloven og løsgjengerloven.

[48] Stortingstidende, forhandlinger i Odelstinget 23 June 1927 p. 970.

[49] Ot. prp. No. 6 (1928).

council requested it. After a debate on the proposal on 15 June, the proposal was rejected by 55 to 31 votes. The Labor Party and the Liberal Party voted to reject the proposal while it was supported by the Conservative Party and the Farmers' Party.

The committee's chairman, Fjalstad from the Conservative Party, claimed that the courts had been politicized in recent times: "What has primarily raised the demand for a more reassuring procedure in the selection of lay judges and jurors is, as is well known, that in several municipalities in our country the communists and the Labor Party have used its greater or lesser power in the municipal councils to appoint only or substantially only their own people and then, as far as can be understood, with the intention that it is the party view and party considerations that should rule, when their judges and jurors operate. I don't think there can be any justified doubt that this premise and this intention have been reflected in practice. Several examples of rather inexplicable acquittals have been highlighted in the newspapers, which seem to speak a fairly clear language."[50]

As we have seen, there was no real basis for the fear that the election of judges was politicized, and it was not the case that the workers' parties were about to take control of the courts. In 1927 elections received little political attention. The attention was somewhat greater in 1928. The election of lay judges was slightly more politicized in 1928. But there are no grounds to claim that the Labor Party consistently used their power over the composition of the courts. In most municipalities where the Labor Party had a majority, they implemented the principle of proportional representation, if anything. The municipalities that deviated from this were mostly municipalities with a conservative majority, often in the continuation of a long tradition. The situation in Oslo is significant in this respect. The selection of lay judges was ostensibly and in form neutral, but in reality it more or less excluded workers. The municipalities where the Labor Party deviated from proportional representation were very few, but they received a lot of attention and created the impression that the Labor Party was willing to politicize the composition of the courts in its fight against the Penitentiary Act.

Before the elections in 1931, the Communist Party had stated in its program that they would take control of the lay judges. However, they had little power and therefore little ability to put their promise into practice. Also, they received little support from the Labor Party, and often directed their criticism of the elections at the Labor Party. The cases where the Labor Party used its majority to elect pure worker lists were few and confined to certain municipalities in Eastern Norway, particularly in Hedmark county. Elverum municipality became a symbol. Pure labor lists were elected here both in 1928 and in 1931. It was the home municipality of member of the Storting Oddmund Sæter, who made a political point out of the fact that he had taken control over the lay judges and juries.

The conditions in Elverum were special. As we have seen from the review of the criminal cases, there were a number of sharp conflicts in the years 1927–1930 around

---

[50] Stortingstidende, forhandlinger i Odelstinget 28 May 1932 p. 782.

the use of strike breakers in timber floating, and many of the cases under Section 222 II of the Criminal Code had their origins in these conflicts.

But there was also another circumstance that contributed to intensifying the conflict over the courts, namely the appointment of state attorney Grøner as magistrate in Sør-Østerdal in 1930. Grøner was a well-known enemy of the labor movement from his time as district attorney in Oslo, and he had prosecuted a number of high-profiled cases against representatives of the working class. Oddmund Sæther described the elections of co-judges in Elverum and surrounding municipalities as a "guerrilla war" against the magistrate.[51] "If the Minister of Justice can get us in Sør-Østerdal a magistrate of the good, old, type, then I promise for my part, and I also oblige the other party members up there, that we will choose according to the proportional principle, and we will let all those fences fall that we have had to put up against the magistrate, we will act as pious sheep of peace," said Sæther in a debate in the Odelstinget. Sæther was not completely accurate in the chronology, as Elverum chose a pure labor party list two years before Grøner took office. The statement is perhaps colored by the fact that Sæter was in the middle of a libel case he and four other workers had brought against Magistrate Grøner. That Grøner was controversial in these matters is nevertheless beyond doubt. He was one of the few judges who applied prison sentences in cases of violation of the Penitentiary Act. Grøner remained in Sør-Østerdal until 1947, when he was appointed magistrate in Kragerø.

To the extent that it can be said that the elections in 1931 were politicized, it was mostly not the Labor Party voting in members of the working class, but the other parties voting them out. They were able to do this with the support of a mistaken belief that the Labor Party had politicized the elections in 1928. Regardless of whether the elections were politicized, there was still a development, however, where the composition of the lists of lay judges and jurors came to be more representative of the population at large. This was a natural consequence of the development in society with the introduction of universal suffrage and the Labor Party's increased representation in municipal councils. There was, as expressed by Gunnar Ousland, "a new legal awareness in development (Ousland 1975, p. 93)." Many municipalities practiced proportional representation, and this led that the Labor Party got to nominate more of the judges. As an experienced judge pointed out in a public lecture in 1931: "the new layers of our democratic society naturally have, within the limits of the law, the same right to participation in public life and public positions of trust as other political factions. It is a natural feature of this that the new layers do their utmost to get 'party members' also elected to what is supposed to be the court of the people (Rolfsen 1931)." What is questionable is when those who are selected to the list are bound to vote in accordance with a given opinion or interest, not that the selection of members of parliament represents the population as a whole.

---

[51] Stortingstidende, forhandlinger i Odelstinget 9 June 1933 pp. 519–520.

The development had as a result that those accused of violating the penitentiary legislation more often faced a court of appeals which had members who sympathized with their case than before 1928. The requirements for conviction meant that it was necessary for only 4 members of the court of appeals to vote for acquittal because the requirement in the law that more than 6 of the members of the 10-man jury had to vote for conviction. Using the right to expel members, it was therefore often the case that at least four members of the jury were from the working class. A greater involvement of worker representatives could therefore lead to acquittals where a jury without worker representation might have voted for conviction. As we saw in the previous chapter, this does not necessarily mean that the acquittal was wrong. In any case, this was not the result of the Labor Party abusing power in municipalities where they had a majority, but of a development where there was cross-party agreement that the co-judges should reflect the entire population and not just the privileged classes. This was a development that some conservatives had difficulty accepting, and which they fought against.

6.6 The Change in the Jury System

The battle over the jurors in 1928 and 1931 had a curious aftermath. On 28 August 2018, a police officer stood trial in the Borgarting Court of Appeal, charged with gross corruption and complicity in the importation of large quantities of hashish. This was the last case in Norway that was tried by a jury. Many years of disagreement over the jury system had finally led to a new law where the jury was abolished and substituted by a large panel of professional judges and lay judges.

The case was first heard in the Oslo District Court in 2017. There, the police officer was convicted. The court found that he had contributed to the smuggling of almost 14 tons of hashish. He had also been paid to do illegal services, in other words corruption. The policeman appealed the conviction to the Court of Appeal. This was a jury trial. After six months of proceedings, the jury withdrew. Six days later it returned and acquitted the policeman of complicity in the drug crime. The three professional judges withdrew for deliberations, and after half an hour they returned to set aside the jury's acquittal. The judges found that the jury's assessment was obviously incorrect, and that the policeman was "undoubtedly" guilty.

When the jury system was introduced in Norway, the professional judges could set aside a conviction by the jury if they believed it to be manifestly incorrect. In this lay an important guarantee, in that a defendant could not be convicted unless both the jury and the professional judges were convinced that the person was guilty. The possibility to set aside an acquittal was of a more recent date. This rule could not be justified in a presumption of innocence. What was the rationale for such a rule, and when did it enter our criminal process?

As we have seen, from 1928 there several proposals in the Storting to change the jury system. The proposals were partly due to the controversies over the election of jurors, but partly they also had their background in the traditional opposition against the jury system in the Conservative Party.

In February 1933, the government led by a prime minister from the Farmers' Party put forward proposals for changes to the Criminal Procedure Act. The proposals consisted, among other things, of repealing the right jury selection and reducing the number of jurors. The ministry indicated that it at a later stage might propose to do away with the jury altogether and switch to a court with lay judges sitting together with the professional judges. However, this would require more investigation.

In the proposal, the ministry stated bluntly that "in the past, wrongful jury verdicts have occurred to a considerable extent. And while there previously have been more scattered and random occurrences, in recent times there have been conscious efforts to put law and justice aside for political and class considerations."[52] The government put forward yet another bill, on the election of lay judges and jury members. Trade union historian Gunnar Ousland called the bill an outright "assassination of the jury system" (Ousland 1975, p. 91). Instead of the municipal council, the election of lay judges was to be made by a special electoral committee of 5 members. Two of the members were to be appointed by the local magistrate, while the other three were to be appointed by the municipal council. The proposal for changes in the election of lay judges and jurors was aimed at remedying what the ministry perceived as "abuse that has resulted from the fact that these elections have largely been politically determined."[53]

The government was shortly afterwards replaced by the third liberal government of Ludwig Mowinckel, who recalled the two proposals. The Liberal Party had always fronted the jury system and it was by its efforts that the jury had been introduced in Norway in the second half of the nineteenth century. Instead, it put forward proposals in a somewhat modified form in a bill on changes in the Criminal Procedure Act and the Courts Act. This government had a somewhat more nuanced view of the problem. It believed that the irregularities had only occurred in certain districts, and that they therefore did not provide a basis for a general restructuring of the jury system.

As documentation for the "failures", the ministry referred to a statement from the Attorney General. He claimed that it could not be overlooked that had have been several jury rulings which could not be explained other than by a failure of the jury to apply the law correctly, and that this was due to extraneous considerations. According to the attorney General, the information available partly through press reports and partly through statements from people who, in the course of the service, had the opportunity to follow cases from beginning to end regarding acquittals despite clear evidence of guilt, were far too numerous and far too clear to be disregarded.[54] He added that complaints about baseless and incomprehensible jury

[52] Ot. prp. No. 26 1933 Om forandringer i straffeprosessloven m.v., etc. 2.

[53] Ot. prp. No. 39 1933 p. 1.

[54] Ot. prp. No. 60 1933 p. 9.

verdicts were not new, but that it must "probably be said that they have become stronger and more frequent in recent years."[55] He also claimed that complaints about wrongful rulings were limited to certain counties and municipalities.

In response to the problems with unfounded acquittals, the ministry proposed an expansion to the rule that the professional judges could set aside a conviction by the jury: "The same applies if the defendant is found not to be guilty of a crime for which he is charged, but the court finds beyond doubt that he is guilty." In an explanatory note to the provision, the ministry emphasized that it should only be applied "where the jury has shown gross misunderstanding or acted contrary to its duties to rule according to the law or the evidence of the case." The government did not follow up on the previous government's proposal for changes in the election of court judges and magistrates.

The majority in Stortinget supported the government in that no changes were necessary in the way lay judges were selected. The minority, representatives of the Conservative Party and the Farmers' Party, argued that it was "urgently necessary to get away from the current system, which has undoubtedly resulted in a number of abuses in the establishment of the lists of lay judges and jurors, with resulting incorrect verdicts that offend the sense of justice."[56] As is well known, the sense of justice is subjective, something that was well illustrated by the debate on the Penitentiary Act. The proposal to give the judges the right to set aside an incorrect acquittal was, however, unanimously approved by the committee.

In the debate, it became clear that the proposal was aimed at the Labor Party and the protests against the penitentiary laws. The representative Olaf Fjalstad from the conservatives said: "It is a fact that in several municipalities a larger or smaller majority of the Labor Party has abused its power to fill the positions with exclusively or predominantly their own people with the specific intention that their lay judges and jurors, when they serve in court, must make their decision based on class and party considerations."[57] He then referred to Sæter's statement that he had never been convicted because the Labor Party had control over the juries. He also referred to statements that had been made during the elections for lay judges and jurors in Elverum and Åmot and to certain court cases where he believed that incorrect acquittals had been handed down. Åmot was not one of the municipalities where the Labor Party had forced through a list of workers, so Fjalstad was mistaken there. Another representative objected that there were also examples of municipalities where the conservatives used their majority to keep out people proposed by the Labor Party. To this Fjalstad replied that he was not familiar with any examples of this. What he was afraid of, he said, was that the abuse, which he believed took place, would spread and undermine the legitimacy of the courts.

Carl Hartmann from the Liberal Party, state prosecutor, lawyer and later extraordinary judge in the Supreme Court, maintained that it was impossible to keep the

[55] Ot. prp. No. 60 1933 p. 10.

[56] Set O. XIII 1933 p. 4.

[57] Stortingsforhandlinger, forhandlinger i Odelstinget 9. juni 1933 p. 502.

political out of the judge's mind, it is something that "sticks to it". The proposal to have an election board appointed by the municipal council, under the direction of a magistrate, would increase the politicization of the elections. Those who were elected to such a panel for a party would inevitably feel themselves to be representatives of that party and therefore take political considerations when appointing lay judges. One had to, said Hartmann, tackle the evil at its root. The solution was to "not enact laws that conflict with a generally widespread concept of justice.[58] If the jury ruled against the law, in other words, according to Hartmann, it was not the jury that was at fault, but the law.

The Conservative Party's and the Farmers' Party's proposal fell by 56 to 53 votes and the system for electing lay judges and magistrates was maintained.

There was a much shorter debate on the proposal to give professional judges the right to set aside an acquittal. Here, only the representatives of the Labor Party were against, so the amendment passed with a large majority. Only one of the Labor Party's representatives took the floor in the debate, Torvald Haavardstad from Aust-Agder. He said, among other things, that "if the case is so doubtful that jury comes to the conclusion that it can find the defendant not guilty, I think it is against the idea of the jury system that he can be dragged before a new court for a retrial, so that the prosecutor gets at second shot at having him convicted."[59]

If the Penitentiary Act did not lead to a politicization of the courts, it in any case led to a common perception that the courts were politicized. The Labor Party perceived the law as a class law, and perceived the courts that applied the law as class courts. Strong voices advocated using the power to secure lay judges who would judge in accordance with the legal view of the labor movement and refuse the law, which they believed was a unilateral attack on workers' freedom of association. There was also an increased awareness in the people of the fact that juries were consistently composed in disfavor of the working class. Conservatives perceived the statements from the labor movement as threatening. They saw debates on the composition of the list of lay judges as undue politicization, and they took the labor movement's rhetoric at face value. The policy of the liberals was primarily a defense of the jury system as such. The jury system should ensure that criminal justice was grounded in the people. Therefore juries should represent the population, and the best was to ensure this was election of lay judges and jury members by the municipal councils. They did not want to change this this, despite some cases where the majority in a municipal council abused the power to influence the composition of the list.

One change nevertheless came out of the fight over the juries; the possibility to set aside an acquittal. Erroneous acquittals had been a part of the jury system since it was instituted. The Labor Party had taken this up in the mid-1920s, prompted by spectacular acquittals of violations of the alcohol ban and charges of corruption. At the time, the question had not aroused political resonance in other parties. In 1933,

[58] Stortingsforhandlinger, forhandlinger i Odelstinget 9. juni 1933 p. 516.

[59] Stortingsforhandlinger, forhandlinger i Odelstinget 9. juni 1933 9 June 1933 p. 542.

the tables were turned and we got the rule that was applied in the very last case that went before a jury in Norwegian criminal law practice. This was a small nod from the dispute over the penitentiary laws in the nineteen-twenties to the legal community in 2018.

References

Castberg F (1974) Rett og revolusjon i Norge (Law and revolution in Norway). Universitetsforlaget, Oslo

Gotaas B (undated) Det faglige terrorvelde og fagforeningenes monopolpolitikk, The trade union reign of terror and the unions' monopoly policy, a documentation by Høires Centralstyre, Oslo

Ousland G (1975) Fagorganisasjonen i Norge 2 De store kamp-åra 1921–1931 (The trade union in Norway 2 The great fighting years 1921–1931). Tiden, Oslo

Rolfsen CL (1931) Lagmannsretten i dens virke, dens fortrinn og mangler, foredrag holdt i Juristforeningen i Oslo 20. april 1931 (The Court of Appeal in its work, its advantages and shortcomings: Lecture held at the Oslo Bar Association 20 April), Oslo

Chapter 7
Civil Disobedience and the Legitimacy of the Actions

7.1 Victory, Regardless of the Law!

The history of the penitentiary laws is often presented as an example of how the labor movement, through its actions, forced the state to its knees. Many have explained the fate of the Arbitration Act by that it was defeated by trade union action (For instance Furre 1992, p. 108 and Maurseth 1999, p. 466). Jonas Bals, who has written the book "Strike" (*Streik*), a central work on the significance of the strike for social development in Norway, writes that "the striking construction workers (had shown) that there were some clear limits to how far the state could go in its attempts to discipline and rein in the trade union movement (Bals 2022, p. 239)."

However, the development cannot be explained as a pure power play. It is obvious that the strike did not coercively limit the policy options available to the authorities and that bourgeois society was not defeated. The state and the employers obviously had resources to continue the conflict. Major conflicts continued to flare up. To understand the development, one must also include the actors' perceptions and normative assessment of the situation. It was the loss of moral values, shame, and damage to the authority of the state, which led to the defeat of the champions of the law (Dahl 1928). As trade union historian Gunnar Ousland writes, the authorities met a "new sense of justice" they had not anticipated. "In a democratic country, where the authorities cannot simply introduce a rule by force, the implementation of the laws depends on the large majority of the people agreeing with them or at least do not actively object. It (the sense of justice) must approve of them, so that at least in its innermost soul it is not upset by them and refuses to obey (Ousland 1975, p. 367)."

The story of the penitentiary laws is one of the clearest examples in Norwegian history that the conditions were right for civil disobedience, that civil disobedience was carried out on a large scale and that it reached its aim. "These laws are the only example of laws which otherwise law-abiding citizens, in thousands, and led by several members of the National Assembly, have knowingly and willingly violated." This claim was made by Supreme Court judge Karl Friman Dahl in 1928, and it is

H. P. Graver, *Democracy and Lawlessness*,
https://doi.org/10.1007/978-3-031-69055-6_7

still holds, except for episodes during the German occupation (Graver 2024, pp. 65–72). At the same time, this is an example of how members of the legal profession can mobilize as a legal complex, "a cluster of legal actors related to each other in dynamic structures and constituted and reconstituted through a variety of processes" for fundamental rights (Karpik and Halliday 2011, p. 220). We shall explain this in more detail below. First, however, we shall take a closer look at the concept of civil disobedience.

7.2 Civil Disobedience

Civil disobedience has a long tradition, but its implementation on a mass basis is held to be a phenomenon of the twentieth century (Sharp 1973, pp. 315–319). Well known examples are the suffragettes in England before the first world war and in the US in the nineteen-twenties, Ghandi's protests in India against the British rule, Rosa Parks' famous bus-ride defiance in 1955 against racial segregation laws in the South of the United States, the marches led by Martin Luther King Jr. in Birmingham, Alabama, the many anti-Vietnam war protesters, anti-Iraq war protesters, animal rights defenders, and anti-abortion activists (Brownlee 2012, pp. 18–19). Recent examples are the protests by climate activists in many European countries.

Both in Norway and internationally, civil disobedience was passionately debated in the 1970s and 1980s, and the topic was analyzed and discussed by liberal philosophers such as John Rawls and Ronald Dworkin (Rawls 1972; Dworkin 1977). At that time, the hot topics were the peace movement and nature conservationists, and in the United States also the civil rights movement. In Norway we had the Alta case, a series of protests in the late 1970s and early 1980s to protect the Alta-Kautokeino River against hydro power development, and which involved the deep conflict between majority rights and the rights of the indigenous Sami population (Nykänen et al. 2022). The protests have recently been celebrated through the film "Let the river live" from 2023, "A drama with deep conflicts, about a young person's courage in the fight for Sami rights in one of the most important events in Sami and Norwegian history," as the cinema poster declares.

The well-known German social philosopher Jürgen Habermas wrote his famous article on civil disobedience in 1985 based on the demonstrations against NATO's so-called "double-track decision", where NATO reacted to the placement of Soviet medium-range missiles armed with nuclear warheads and aimed at Western Europe by both threatening to use its own latest-generation missiles and offering to sign an agreement for both sides to destroy all weapons of this kind. At the same time NATO decided to deploy over 500 nuclear missiles in Europe (Habermas 1985). In Norway, the book "The difficult disobedience" was published in 1981 with contributions from Norway's foremost philosophers and social scientists (Hagtvedt 1981).

One might immediately think it anachronistic to analyze a conflict that took place in 1928 and the years immediately following based on theoretical discussions that took place in the 1970s and 1980s and today. A *legal* assessment of past events based on the legislation and case law of our time makes little sense. But a discussion of the legitimacy of the action based on normative political theory does make sense, at least when it concerns a theory of justice with a claim to more general validity, such as the theories of John Rawls and other more contemporary philosophers. In addition to his normative theses, Rawls has some hypotheses about the impact of civil disobedience actions for the democratic system. These are empirical assumptions, which can be tested, both on past and future cases.

The discussion at the end of the last century was held as part of the liberal tradition in political philosophy, with the theoretical approach of the philosophy of John Rawls setting the tone. Civil disobedience is a form of protest against government decisions that is given a moral justification (Hagtvedt 1981, p. 29). Rawls defines civil disobedience as a conscience-based, public, non-violent, politically motivated offence, which aims to bring about a change in the policies or laws of public authorities (Rawls 1972, p. 364). According to Rawls, civil obedience must also be guided by principles of justice. For this reason, Rawls's theory, and theories based on it, have been criticized for not providing room for actions aimed at environmental and climate policy (Scheuerman 2021; Lysaker 2022). The actions against the penitentiary laws can be justified within the framework of Rawls's theory.

Even though "civil disobedience" is a contested concept with many rivalling definitions, Rawl's concept still captures the essence of its mainstream meaning when the context is action to correct unjust majoritarian decisions within liberal democracy. This is not to say that it is impossible to make a case for the justifiability of civil disobedience that does not conform to Rawl's requirements. The Canadian philosopher Kimberley Brownlee in her book on civil disobedience defines civil disobedience as "a conscientious communicative breach of law motivated by steadfast, sincere, and serious, though possibly mistaken, moral commitment," that is without the requirement of non-violence (Brownlee 2012, pp. 23–24). She goes further than Rawls, in that she not only sees civil disobedience as a right to remedy deficiencies in the democratic processes, but as a primary democratic right for individuals and groups when their well-formed claims are not respected (Weinstock 2016). In any case, civil disobedience involves unarmed nonroutine political action in which obedience and submission are withdrawn from authorities and laws (Schock 2021, p. 407).

Civil disobedience can take the form of defying the law that one is in opposition to, for example by refusing to attend military service or by actively seeking to prevent a measure by standing in the way for construction machinery or preventing ships hunting whales. In other cases, one does not oppose the activity that a protest is directed at, but a law is broken to draw attention to another matter, such as when one blocks traffic to draw attention to the climate issue or blocks the entrance to government offices to protest the state's actions or omissions.

Since civil disobedience presupposes that one breaks the law, a public protest or demonstration will not in itself be civil disobedience, even if it obstructs public transport or other legal activities. A public demonstration will inevitably entail a restriction on normal traffic or traffic management. Freedom of expression gives the right to such demonstrations, and the blocking of traffic that this entails therefore does not represent an offence. It is only when the activists block a business for a longer time than society must tolerate for reasons of freedom of expression, that it makes sense to talk about civil disobedience. The European Court on Human rights has held that:

The freedom to take part in a peaceful assembly is of such importance that a person cannot be subject to a sanction—even one at the lower end of the scale of disciplinary penalties—for participation in a demonstration which has not been prohibited, so long as that person does not himself commit any reprehensible act on such an occasion (see Ezelin, § 53; Galstyan, § 115; and Barraco, § 44, all cited above). This is true also when the demonstration results in damage or other disorder (see Taranenko, cited above, § 88).[1]

Guidance on what can be seens as a "reprehensible act" is given in the following passage (paragraph 172):

In Steel and Others (cited above) the first and second applicants had obstructed a hunt and had impeded engineering work for the construction of a motorway, respectively. In Drieman and Others (cited above), Greenpeace activists had manoeuvred dinghies in such a way as to physically obstruct whaling, forcing the whalers to abandon their lawful exploitation of the living resources in Norway's exclusive economic zone.

We therefor only talk of civil disobedience when the disruption of public or private activities and interests are greater that what must be tolerated in a democratic society according to the freedom of expression and association. It follows that the civil disobedients go beyond their protected right to demonstrate, and that the state may prohibit and sanction their action without infringing on their human rights. Civil disobedience is not a human right, and it is illegal to the extent that laws are broken. But this is not the whole story.

Rawls treats civil disobedience in the context of his general theory of justice. Civil disobedience presupposes a society with just institutions, that is, a society based on democratic legitimacy. In such a society, civil disobedience strengthens institutions and contributes to stability, by counteracting injustice and helping to correct it when it occurs, Rawls believes (Rawls 1972, p. 383).

As mentioned above, this is not only a normative defense for civil disobedience, but also an empirical assumption about its effects. Although inherently difficult to measure, experience seems to indicate support for this assumption. Protests that involve civil disobedience seem to succeed more often than both protests without disobedience and protests involving organized armed resistance. At the same time, regime change brought about by armed resistance is more likely to result in a new autocratic government compared to changes brought about by unarmed resistance, which more often lead to democracy (Schock 2021, pp. 417–418).

Rawls' starting point is that even if society has built institutions that satisfy the principles of justice as far as possible, they will in some cases produce results that

[1] EctHR Case Kudrevicius and others v. Lithuania (Grand Chamber 2015).

conflict with these. Basically, people still owe the institutions loyalty, but with certain exceptions. If a policy or a law fundamentally contradicts the principle of equal freedom rights or equal opportunities, breaking a law to draw the majority's attention to this may be justified.

Is this not just a theory of natural law which presupposes that the law must give way to certain overriding moral principles? If so, it is of little value to those who subscribe to more positivist views about the law. The Norwegian sociologist Vilhelm Aubert has pointed out that Rawls's theory has a clear affinity to natural law and that this shows in his discussion of civil disobedience (Aubert 1989, p. 52). However, an obligation to follow or break the law can also be constructed as a personal, moral obligation, as a conflict between legal and moral requirements, without claiming that society's legal system must respect this (Feinberg 2003). You accept that society can have legal rules that you yourself feel morally obliged to break, knowing that you are committing an act that is illegal. Rawls is not clear on whether he believes that one can derive clear legal consequences from the theory of justice. He says that "courts should take into account the civilly disobedient nature of the protester's act, " (Rawls 1972, p. 387), but this is not saying they should recognize that it is lawful. In other words, it is not necessarily the case that justice trumps law in Rawls's theory. His argument for civil disobedience does not presuppose that one takes a natural law position.

In any case, when analyzing the actions against the penitentiary law, we must take into account the fact that the lawyers in Norway between the world wars of the twentieth century were not as dismissive of ideas inspired by natural law as was legal realism in the post-war period. Ragnar Knoph, a major name in Norwegian jurisprudence between the wars, in 1923 formulated a theory about law and legal awareness and set "man's deep desire for justice" as a limit to the legislative power's authority to determine the law (Knoph 1923a, p. 12). A law that contradicted this would, according to Knoph, "quietly be subject to mild torture by the judges", have its content "rewritten" by the courts and, in some rare cases, be openly sabotaged (Knoph 1923b, pp. 24–25). This, as we saw, was largely the fate of Section 222 II of the Penal Code.

Paal Berg, who we have seen played a major role in undermining the Arbitration Act, believed that "the judge should not be a lifelong slave under the letter of the law. It is the spirit of the law that he must give life to, seen in the light of the legal needs of his own time, and he must never forget that the law was given to serve the constantly changing conditions of life (Berg 1947, pp. 11–13)." The judge should, in Paal Berg's opinion, based his verdicts both on the applicable law and on the general legal awareness.

Interactions between civil disobedience and the legal system to facilitate change is not uncommon. Consider the civil disobedience of Rosa Parks in 1955 where she refused to yield her bus seat to a white person, which lead to public mobilization, legal challenge, a Supreme Court decision striking down bus segregation laws, and later to the passing of the Civil Rights act by the US Congress (Schock 2021, p. 412). But are the connections normative or causal? In order to analyze the connection between law, legal awareness, disobedience and the judges' approach regarding the

Norwegian penitentiary laws, it is hardly decisive whether the perception that the penitentiary laws contradicted basic principles of justice was a normative limit for the legislative authority, or whether it was an expression of "the legislature's relative dependence on social forces that set a bar for his legal-formal perfection of power", in the words of Danish legal philosopher Alf Ross (Ross 1953, p. 444). Historically speaking, it is nonetheless significant that key actors within the legal institutions believed that legal awareness constituted not only a factual limit for the legislative power, but also a normative limit, which justified a correction of the law.

7.3 The Penitentiary Laws and John Rawls' Principles of Justice

In 1927, Norway was a democracy with universal suffrage, political parties, and freedom of expression. Laws were passed by procedures laid down in the Constitution, which then as now gave legislative power to a simple majority in the Storting (the Norwegian Parliament). The political institutions in Norway largely satisfied Rawls' criteria for fair institutions.

The Penitentiary laws; the Arbitration Act with its broad authority to prohibit strikes, the rules in the Labor Disputes Act with criminal liability for those who expressed their support for an illegal action and liability for damages for a trade union that could not prove that it had sought to prevent the conflict, as well as Section 222 II of the Criminal Code on punishment for those which sought to prevent someone from taking up work during a conflict, were provisions aimed unilaterally at the workers' ability to fight for improved wages and working conditions. The workers were deprived of all opportunities to take effective measures, while at the same time the law ensured the employers' ability to replace protesting workers with others willing to work during the period of mass unemployment. Since the power relationship labor and capital was fundamentally unequal, "one party was handed over unarmed to the arbitrariness of the other party (Berg 1930, p. 29)."

The society aimed its coercive measures, penalties, and liability for damages, against the workers in order to protect the interests of the employers. In addition, the government hounded striking workers by depriving them and their families of contributions to the poor and benefits from the health insurance funds. The use of the Arbitration Act in such a small and insignificant conflict as the construction workers' conflict showed the hollowness of the government's argument that the law was necessary to protect society from the harmful effects of major conflicts.

This legislation contradicted what Rawls calls "the two principles of justice", namely equal freedom and equal opportunities (Rawls 1972, p. 372). Although the law was formally neutral, it did not prevent employers from unilaterally dictating the employees' wages and working conditions, without the employees having any effective opportunity to promote their interests. The burden of injustice was not evenly distributed, and the hardship of the unjust law weighed heavily on the workers (Rawls 1972, p. 355). The parties were not equally treated in their conflicts over labor relations. The employers could legally advance their interests by opposing the workers' organization and by keeping business going during conflict with the aid of people willing to work as strike breakers. The "freedom of work" that the penal provision purported to protect was not a general protection of the right to work. The provision only applied during conflict, and it also did not protect workers from employers' blacklisting and reprisals in the form of denial of work. In practice, it was usually not strikebreakers, who were the formally wronged party, who reported the matter to the police, but the employers who used this as a weapon against striking workers. That the laws conflicted with basic requirements of justice was a perception that extended to large sections of the population, and far into the legal profession.

Also, the legislative process itself did not live up to the ideals of a fair procedure. As we saw, Section 222 II of the Penal Code was adopted after an emotional outburst where Mowinckel and the Liberals turned in rage against a demonstration in the Storting gallery. For many years, the Liberal Party had been against this proposal and they had for a long time succeeded in preventing it from being adopted. Then Mowinckel suddenly turned. Against Mowinckel's anger, appeals and rational argument were of no use. The usual democratic path towards this legislative decision was therefore abruptly closed to the labor representatives in the Storting. The result was that the overall legislative package became even more draconian than what the government had planned, and the counter-reactions and anger in the labor movement perhaps more extensive than they would otherwise have been. The government was even accused of "terror" against the working class (Hansteen 1927, p. 18).

According to Rawls, when an otherwise just system produces laws that are instances of substantial and clear injustice, lawbreaking to appeal to society's sense of justice can be justified as civil disobedience (Rawls 1972, p. 372). Breaking the law is the measure of last resort that remains when the democratic and judicial channels have been exhausted. The fact that otherwise law-abiding citizens go to the extent of breaking the law is a strong message to ruling majority's sense of justice. In the case of the arbitration act, the appeal was successful as can be seen by the later amnesty that was granted the demonstrators. That the actions against the other parts of the penitentiary laws were successful is not equally obvious. However, since the new law was rendered more or less ineffective through the way it was interpreted by the courts, also this must be deemed a success as seen from the workers' perspective.

7.4 Violations of the Penitentiary Laws as Justified Resistance

The civil disobedience actions partly took the form of public appeals and fundraising in support of the striking construction workers. Both actions violated the law's prohibition against expressing "approval or support" and "collecting or paying collected contributions" to workers in conflict in violation of the law. The demonstrations and actions towards strikebreakers during the various conflicts from 1928 onwards can also be seen as civil disobedience. They openly and directly defied the prohibition against intentionally causing "someone to quit or give up their work" by insulting or intrusive behavior or by giving public information about who works. The intent to defy the law was also clear. At the annual trade union congress in 1927, leader of the Labor Party Oscar Torp called for "an organized illegal activity against strike-breakers."

For something to be considered civil disobedience according to Rawls' definition, the action must be based on a perception of justice and aim to convince the majority of this. For an action to be normatively justified so that the state is obliged to take it into account, certain additional conditions must be met. Suggestions of such are put forward by the American legal philosopher Ronald Dworkin.

Dworkin believed that when someone challenges a law for being morally reprehensible the authorities should show special regard for his action and, under the circumstances, tolerate it, unless there are strong reasons for sanctioning the offence (Dworkin 1977, p. 260). The starting point for Dworkin's discussion was a case in which prominent Americans were punished for encouraging young men to refuse military service in the Vietnam War. An important distinction for the authorities in assessing whether to pursue an act of civil disobedience is, according to Dworkin, whether it violates the rights of others. If someone denies a black girl access to school to protest affirmative action laws, then this violates the girl's moral right to attend the school to which she is legally assigned. The authorities must protect her from that. On the other hand, refusing to serve in a war you consider immoral does not infringe on anyone else's rights. As Dworkin sees it, it is difficult to defend civil disobedience that violates the freedom or property of others or that uses violence.

The distinction between actions that violate someone's rights and other actions can be difficult to draw. Doesn't someone who has been given a public permit to build a wind farm have the right to do so, and wouldn't preventing him be a violation of his rights? What about the person who cannot get to work or an important meeting because the road is blocked by climate activists? Or what about the person who is called up for military service because someone who was called up before him refuses to show up? If the distinction is to provide clarity, it requires that we build on Dworkin's concept of rights. In Dworkin's view, civil disobedience can only be justified in defense of rights and not in the defense of principles. Dworkin also distinguishes between right in the sense of having an individual claim and being justified in the sense that one cannot be criticized for doing something, but without being protected against interventions that prevent the behavior.

The actions against the penitentiary laws were protests in the defense of the workers' rights. The requirement of non-violation of rights must be fulfilled in order for these protests to be justifiable according to Dworkin. The fundraising in support of the construction workers had no sign of violence. Nor did they violate anyone's rights. This action thus clearly fulfills Dworkin's criteria.

The actions against strikebreakers are more complicated, both when it comes to the issue of violation of rights and the issue of violence. Section 222 II of the Criminal Code was justified by the need to protect the freedom of work and the right to work. Initially, one could therefore believe that actions aimed at preventing or encouraging people to give up their work during a conflict violated their rights. But the right to work was not designed as an individual right. No one had a legal claim to work. However, a distinction must be made between unorganized workers who were employed before the conflict broke out, and workers who joined afterwards. When it comes to the latter, it must be obvious that no one had any legal claim to take or get work. Actions directed against them could therefore not be said to violate their rights in Dworkin's sense. It also turned out that many of the actions were simply legal, as the courts interpreted them, even though the campaigners probably thought they were breaking the law and intended to do so. But what about those who were already employed, had they not a right to have their employment protected? This also has a side against the freedom of association, which also has a negative side, namely the right not to participate in an organization. There are arguments for that actions aimed at the unorganized workers in the company and their right to continue working violated their rights.

On the other hand, there is always someone who benefits from the law, it always protects someone's interests. If the fact that their interests are affected or prevented should prevent civil disobedience from being justified, hardly any action will be legitimate. The starting point for the discussion is that we are faced with a law that clearly violates or sets aside basic principles of justice. Interests protected through such a law cannot be as worthy of protection as those protected by the laws in general. It is nevertheless possible that Dworkin would have objected to some of the actions against the penitentiary laws on this basis, and that it is a factor we must take into account when assessing the normative legitimacy of the actions.

The same ambiguity applies to the demand for non-violence. The case law provides good illustrations here. The different actions that we have described differed from each other along this dimension. Some demonstrations were restrained and calm, others were more violent and threatening. Although there were episodes of violence, one can hardly say on this basis that the actions were generally not legitimate civil disobedience actions according to the criteria in normative political theory outlined above. But some of the actions, or at least aspects of them, were hardly justified according to Dworkin's criteria for a legitimate civil disobedience action.

None of the leading philosophical approaches to civil disobedience argue that breaking the law should be immediately recognized as *legal* when it occurs as part of civil disobedience. The attitude of the law to civil disobedience in liberal societies is what Kimberley Brownlee has characterized as "checkered". "Sometimes they are treated well by police, praised in court, and acquitted. Sometimes charges against them are dropped. Other times, they are treated like ordinary offenders. And other times they are demonized as threats to social order. This checkered experience reflects the strong disagreement amongst judges (and juries) about the seriousness of civil disobedience (Brownlee 2012, p. 155)".

What moral theory argues for is that the state should be tolerant towards such offenses by not prosecuting civil disobedient in the criminal justice system or by taking the moral and political nature into account in sentencing. Rawls says that the authorities must consider that an offense occurs as part of civil disobedience and refers to Dworkin for a more detailed argument. Dworkin's position is that the authorities have an obligation to protect the activist and to moderate the reactions to the offence. It does not mean giving the plaintiff immunity from prosecution, but to abstain from prosecuting the offense unless there are strong reasons to pursue it (Dworkin 1977, p. 260). For this reason, the moral-philosophical discussion about when civil disobedience is justified and about the beneficial effects such actions have for democracy is important—they also constitute demands on the state authorities not to treat activists who practice civil disobedience as common lawbreakers. To what extent did the authorities follow up on such demands towards those who campaigned against the penitentiary laws?

7.5 The Reaction of the Authorities

There were voices demanding harsh measures against the activists. "Thousands of Labor Party members are breaking the law. A startling turn in the illegal action", wrote the conservative newspaper Tidens Tegn on the front page on 5 June 1928, and demanded action from the authorities. This attitude is always found in escalated conflicts, something we also recognize from civil disobedience actions in our time, whether it is about Sami activists demonstrating against windmills or Extinction Rebellion demonstrating in favor of the climate.

Police and prosecutors initially showed little tolerance towards activists against the penitentiary laws. The Attorney General announced harsh measures against the call to support the construction workers already the same day that it was published. The number of criminal cases for violation of Section 222 of the Penal Code rose dramatically, even though the number of conflicts decreased. This was particularly the case in the first years after Section 222 II was adopted.

The courts followed up on the cases against the fund raisers against the Arbitration Act and imposed severe fines on the initiators. The Supreme Court did not give instructions that the nature of the offense should trigger tolerance on the part of the authorities, on the contrary. In the case against the initiators of the action, the Supreme Court argued that the disobedience warranted a stricter reaction than otherwise would have been the case, due to the nature of the offence. The court emphasized that the law in question was given to protect important societal interests and that the accused action had been practiced in direct defiance of or open war against the law. The fact that several of the perpetrators were legislators was an aggregating circumstance.[2]

In the case against two newspaper editors 2 days later, the Supreme Court set the sentence to 30 days in prison. As justification, Supreme Court judge Paulsen, with the agreement of the other six judges, stated:

[2]Rt. 1928 p. 859, p. 860.

> Newspaper editors are in a special position when it comes to actions of the kind that are at issue in the present cases. A call in the newspapers to put themselves above the laws and seek to deprive them of their meaning has quite different consequences than where individuals act against the laws. I therefore believe that if the threats of punishment set by the Labor Disputes Act and the Arbitration Act are to be effective against newspaper editors, one cannot avoid using prison sentences, particularly when the newspaper articles have such a challenging content as in the present case.[3]

Here, too, the attitude of the Supreme Court was that organized disobedience must be met with a strict reaction. In other words, the attitude of the Supreme Court was that a case of civil disobedience called for a stricter assessment of the offence, not a milder one. The courts' approach to the action contrasts with that of the Storting. When the conflict was over, the majority of the Storting granted amnesty to all those who had been punished in connection with it. In the debate about the law, both those who believed that disobedience to the laws had to be severely punished and those who believed that the political motivation of the offense warranted tolerance on the part of the authorities were represented. It was the latter view that prevailed, despite the warning from the opponents that amnesty could have unfortunate consequences for future situations.

The approach of the courts to prosecutions for violation of Section 222 II of the Criminal Code was far more moderate. The lay judges, especially in jury trails, became the target of severe criticism in parts of the press, with accusations that they set the law aside in their verdicts. Closer studies show that many of the acquittals were the result of legal assessments that led to a restrictive interpretation of the provision. The leading criminal law professor Jon Skeie could therefore conclude that the new law did not represent any expansion of criminality compared to what applied before the provision was adopted. In addition, the courts were often moderate in their sentencing where the defendant was found guilty, although this was not without exception.

7.6 The Weapon Bearers—The movement's Lawyers

Lawyers are often considered a conservative profession. If members of the legal profession engage in politics, they do so for the classic liberal ideals such as equality before the law and political freedoms (Feeley and Langford 2023, p. 17). In Norway, too, the legal profession was predominantly conservative, although there were some radical exceptions in opposition to the civil servant state in the nineteenth century (Espeli et al. 2008, pp. 128–129). One, who actively got involved in the fight for universal suffrage in the 1880s, was lawyer at the Supreme Court Ludvig Meyer. At the same time, Meyer became a permanent employee of the labor movement's main newspaper, Social-Demokraten, and helped finance the newspaper with income he

[3] Rt. 1928 p. 862.

received from land speculation. From 1897 he was chairman of the Labor Party (Espeli et al. 2008, p. 141).

In the 1920s and 30s, there was a segment of the legal profession in Norway, which included both lawyers and judges, who committed themselves to fundamental liberal and professional rights. They developed through the 1930s into what the legal historian Harald Rinde has called "a new generation of socialist legal politicians" (Espeli et al. 2008, p. 139). Where did they come from and who were they?

In Norway at the turn of the century, there was fertile ground for political radicalism among students in Norway. This is where we must seek the answer to the question of how this period gave birth to a generation of socialist lawyers.

At the end of the nineteenth century the young radical Kyrre Grepp, communist and chairman of the Labor Party 1918–1922, gathered around him a circle of academics, who were all active socialists and communists (Bull 1955, p. 43). Several of these were lawyers: Adam Hjorth, Michael Puntervold, Carl Bonnevie, Cornelius Holmboe, Emil Stang. Other radical lawyers were part of the group *Mot Dag*, which emerged from the radical student environment after the First World War. Besides Viggo Hansteen, who was close to the founder Erling Falk, there were Dagfinn Bech, Teodor Broch, Arnljot Eng, Toralf Evje, the later right-wing politician and Prime Minister John Lyng, Aake Ording and Fredrik Schreiner. The lawyers were a numerically dominant group in Mot Dag, although they did not dominate Erling Falk's inner circle.

Particularly the lawyers Trygve Lie, Emil Stang, Viggo Hansteen, Michael Puntervold and Cornelius Holmboe, and the judges Dahl and Bonnevie were active in connection with the penitentiary laws. All of them held active political positions in the labor movement, and most eventually took up prominent positions in Norwegian society.

Trygve Lie was at the forefront of developing the trade union strategy against the Penitentiary Laws. In contrast to many of the other radical jurists, he was not of patrician lineage, but from more modest circumstances. He drafted and defended the policy of the trade union secretariat at the 1927 annual meeting of the Confederation of Trade Unions (LO), and as legal secretary he ligated many of the cases of the unions and their members before the courts. Together with LO chairman Halvard Olsen, in 1931 he wrote the book "The anti-workers laws and the struggle against them" (Olsen and Lie 1931).

In 1935 he was appointed Minister of Justice in the coalition government between the Labor Party and the Farmers Party, led by Labor politician Johan Nygaardsvold. This was the start of a new career as politician. He had the opportunity of both putting forward the bill that led to the repeal of Section 222 II of the Criminal Code and of appointing his comrade-in-arms Emil Stang to the Supreme Court. During the war he accompanied the exile government to London as trade minister and later foreign minister. On 1 February 1946, he was elected the first Secretary-General of the United Nations. When he returned home, he became county commissioner in Oslo and Akershus before becoming minister of industry and trade in 1963.

Today, LO's legal department is a large law firm with 50 employees, of whom 30 are lawyers. It is the country's largest legal professional environment in employment and labor law. When Trygve Lie was employed in 1922, it was as legal consultant and sole lawyer. Before that, a small number of lawyers had brought cases before the Labor Court and before the ordinary courts. The development into a full-fledged law office reflects a development of how society has increasingly interfered into the relation between employers and employees. As we saw in the first chapter, the first real start of this was the 1915 Labor Disputes Act.

Lie's main task when he was employed was to build up LO's legal service to serve the trade unions. He quickly got his hands full. In the first 10 years, he had an average of 100 cases a year, cases before the Labor Court, cases about real estate and criminal cases following legal and illegal labor disputes (Zakariassen 1969, p. 12). During this time, a second legal consultant was also employed in LO, Dagfinn Bech.

Emil Stang was the son of the conservative politician and nineteenth century prime minister Emil Stang and brother of law professor Fredrik Stang. He was thus one of society's absolute elite, but he did not follow in his conservative father's footsteps. Instead, he became a communist and a radical socialist. In the twenties and thirties, Emil Stang litigated most of LO's cases before the Supreme Court. He was deputy chairman of the Labor Party from 1918. He broke with the Labor Party in 1923 to help form Norway's Communist Party when the Labor Party broke with the *Comintern* (Bjørgum 2022). He expressed his attitude to the laws of capitalist society in several writings. In one pamphlet he cited the following quote: "The representatives of the working class in the municipal councils must without limits support the working class, the small-scale people interests against bourgeois society, even if thereby they come into conflict with state power and the current bourgeois laws." He wrote that this statement was "absolutely correct" (Stang 1927, p. 5).

In April 1936, he was appointed to the Supreme Court. Although he was appointed by a Labor Party government with his comrade in arms Trygve Lie as Minister of Justice, no one questioned the appointment. He was consistently recognized as a very sharp jurist and well qualified for the post of judge. From 1946 he was chief justice of the Supreme Court.

In the summer of 1936, Stang had Leon Trotsky staying at his country house outside Lillesand.[4] Trotsky was one of the communist leaders of the Russian Revolution who had fallen out with Stalin and was on the run from Stalin's murderous attacks on all competitors. He spent a short time in Norway. Because of his communist past, Stang was arrested by the Nazis in 1940 and spent the last year of the war in German captivity in Sachsenhausen and Neuengamme.

Viggo Hansteen took over the position as legal secretary in LO in 1936 after Lie became Minister of Justice. According to the historian Harald Berntsen, Viggo was born with a silver spoon in his mouth (Berntsen 1995, p. 29). His father was a doctor, son of the executive director of Røros Copper Works and later Kongsberg Silver Mines. Both his mother and father had a radical political attitude. He was a brilliant student.

[4] See Tiden, Saturday 8 August 1936.

Hansteen became member of the Labor Party in 1918 and quickly entered the circle around Erling Falk, the radical intellectual who formed the socialist society *Mot Dag*. He was later excluded from the Labor Party and joined the Communist Party, with which he broke in 1939 over the Soviet attack on Finland.

In 1923, he passed the legal civil service examination with honors. He would certainly have reached far in his legal career had he not been executed by the Germans after a summary judgment in 1941 together with union boss Rolf Wickstrøm. The reason was that the trade union at Aker's mechanical workshop in Oslo spontaneously went on strike due to a lack of delivery of milk to the workers. The judgment was a pure miscarriage of justice, there was no evidence tying Wickstrøm and Hansteen to the strike. The German Nazi judges, however, with their adherence to the *Fuhrer* principle, could not imagine that a local trade union could go into action without the approval of the superior trade union bosses (Graver 2019, p. 284).

His expressed his view of law as an instrument of class oppression clearly and publicly, for instance in an article in *Rjukan Arbeiderblad* on Saturday 12 June 1924, under the heading "Class justice". Here he wrote: "The laws are determined by time and place (. . .) and have nothing to do with divinity or justice. (. . .) It is therefore a matter of course that the legislation under whose dominion we live at the moment is a class legislation, just as the society for whose preservation and protection the laws serve is a class society. (. . .) The judges who enforce the laws of the bourgeoisie tend to boast that they are impartial and neutral, and that they do not in any way take sides in the class struggle that is going on in the country." But, he says, "No civil servant, whether he is a judge or an officer, has the right to be impartial or neutral in his activities. (. . .) Every judge is by profession biased and partisan when it comes to the part of the population that stands in opposition to the class society, whose tool he is."

At this time, he had several defense assignments for defendants in connection with illegal and legal actions. When the penitentiary laws were passed, he strongly opposed them. In 1927 he received a grant to study law abroad. From 1927–1929 he stayed mainly in the Soviet Union. He resumed legal practice after his return and was, among other things, a defense attorney together with Trygve Lie in the cases after the Menstad conflict in 1931. The head of the state police sought to have him removed because he was a communist, but Hansteen was allowed to keep the assignment following a decision in the Supreme Court's appeals committee (Berntsen 1995, p. 131).

Michael Puntervold was a lawyer and skilled at the bar.[5] Among his clients was the famous explorer Roald Amundsen. He was known as an ardent socialist agitator both in writing and in speech, especially in the period up to 1920, and became deputy chairman when Norway's Social Democratic Workers' Party was founded in 1921. In 1919, he traveled together with Emil Stang to Petrograd and Moscow for to study conditions in Soviet Russia. After the merger of the social democrats with the Labor

[5] A short biography is printed in Fri Fagbevegelse 1955 no. 3 p. 66.

Party in 1927, he stepped more into the background and devoted himself to his work as a lawyer.

Before Trygve Lie was employed as a permanent legal consultant of the LO, Puntervold was one of the permanent lawyers for the organization. He also later took on cases for the trade unions. Puntervold defended the accused workers in the Grytåen case before the Supreme Court. When the construction workers' dispute was brought before the Labor Court, he was a lawyer for the trade unions together with Trygve Lie and Emil Stang. He was also a defense attorney for defendants after the Menstad conflict and a lawyer for Leon Trotsky during his detention in Norway in 1935–1936 (Høidal 2009, p. 184 ff).

Cornelius Holmboe was a practicing lawyer in Tromsø from 1909 to 1937 when he became a magistrate in Nordre Hedmark (Larsen 1952, pp. 72–77). Holmboe was born in Tromsø in 1881. His ancestors on his father's side were civil servants and doctors, on his mother's side, merchants. Before establishing himself as a lawyer in Tromsø, he was for a while the editor of the newspaper 1. Mai in Stavanger, where he helped found the Stavanger Labor Party in 1908. Holmboe was Minister of Justice in the short-lived labor government in February 1928. When he was appointed, he was described as politically nondescript. He was defense attorney together with Viggo Hansteen and Adam Hjort in the great military strike case in 1924.

In 1925, he spoke publicly for the amnesty law that the Labor Party had proposed. He linked amnesty to the opportunity principle in criminal justice and the jury system. "A public prosecutor can refrain from bringing charges for obvious crimes if he deems it opportune. That can be the case when you are dealing with honest public prosecutors. But when right-wing public prosecutors deal with political opponents, then justice is in danger." He continued, "The jury – the great monument of the Liberal Party – is presently under strong attack. It is the recent acquittal of the Oslo Court of Appeal that is the reason for the strong attacks. It is people's legal conciousness that is reflected in these judgments. The jury must force the state to abolish barbaric laws. I think society is safer the more alert the jury is."[6] After the speech, the meeting adopted a resolution in support of the Labor Party's proposal for an amnesty law. Holmboe became a magistrate in Nordre Hedmark in 1937, where he sat until 1947. He was arrested by the Gestapo in December 1944 on suspicion of being part of the military resistance movement and was imprisoned until liberation.

Karl Frimann Dahl was at times central as a newpaper editor and politician for the Liberal Party. At the same time, he was a judge, first in the district court, later in the Supreme Court. Dahl, together with Paal Berg, as clear left-wing figures, constituted a radical counterweight in an otherwise conservative Supreme Court (Sandmo 2005, p. 38). Dahl was a member of the Liberal Party and active in municipal politics in both Bergen and Oslo. Later he switched to the Labor Party and was deputy to the Storting 1934–1936. The newspaper Norges Fremtid, which was linked to *Fedrelandslaget*, a right-wing, anti-communist political organization

[6]Nordlys Saturday 6 December 1924.

in the interwar period, characterized him in 1934 as "one of the most ardent revolutionary agitators in Norway".[7]

Carl Bonnevie took his civil service exam in 1904 and became a Supreme Court lawyer 7 years later. He represented the Labor Party in the Storting from 1912–1915 and from 1934–1936. The newspaper Norges Fremtid, a characterized him as "one of the moderate social democrats who, due to a misunderstanding and empty party coffers, have been forced into the Labor Party."[8]After he retired from the Storting, he became a judge first in Agder Court of Appeals and then in the old Eidsivating Court of Appeals.

After retirement he became involved in the cause of peace and worked for an international legal order based on peace between nations. He broke with the Labor Party over the party's rearmament policy and switched to the breakout Socialist People's Party. Unlike other radicals, he kept his dark red color into his old age, the newspaper *Hadeland* wrote at his death.[9] The tough party secretary in the Labor Party during the first years of the Cold War, Håkon Lie, was less positive in his characterization, describing him as probably "the most gullible politician our country has fostered" (Lie 1975, p. 81). "It's a foul bird that shits in its own nest," said Torjus, my grandfather, when he had read Håkon's book. He knew Håkon well from many years.

Credible or not, he bravely voiced his opinions and stood by his principles. Bonnevie was one of the very few judges who were dismissed by the Nazis during the war. The reason for the dismissal was that he had made offensive statements about the Nationalist Party and Quisling in a letter to the Ministry of Justice (Graver 2019, p. 60). The overwhelming majority of judges kept a low profile so as not to provoke.

Both Dahl and Bonnevie were mentioned as possible Minister of Justice when Hornsrud formed his Labor Party government in January 1928.[10] However, the choice fell on Cornelius Holmboe.

Were there any notable jurists on the other side? The laws were primarily driven forward by conservative politicians. The Arbitration Act and the amendments to the Labor Disputes Act were drawn up in the ministry by anonymous bureaucrats. Section 222 II of the Criminal Code was, as we have seen, primarily the result of the work of politicians. But the first draft was drawn up by Attorney General Bernhard Getz at the behest of the prime minister and law professor, and his relative and close friend Francis Hagerup. According to C.J.Hambro, one of the most prominent politicians of the Conservative Party in the twentieth century, Bernhard Getz was the only one who was close to Hagerup, and he was a man Hagerup "listened to, almost with veneration (Hambro 1960, p. 145). If one were to single out a couple of jurists who stood permanently and markedly on the side of the

[7]Norges Fremtid, Thursday 13 February 1934.

[8]Norges Fremtid Saturday 15 September 1928.

[9]Hadeland, Saturday 30 September 1972.

[10]See Aftenposten on Wednesday 24 January 1928.

penitentiary laws in the 1920s, one could mention state attorney and parliamentary representative Olav Fjalstad and state attorney, later judge Jørgen Christian Andreas Grøner.

Olav Fjalstad was a parliamentary representative for the Conservative Party from 1928. He studied law in 1911 and was state attorney in Troms and Finnmark from 1921. In 1931 he was appointed magistrate in Nedenes. The reason for mentioning Fjalstad in this context is that he was a member of the justice committee in the Storting and spokesman for the Conservative Party in all the debates on the penitentiary laws, from their adoption in 1927 to the repeal of Section 222 II of the Criminal Code in 1935. As a spokesperson, he was a sharp and principled supporter of punishing support for illegal actions and attempts to get strikebreakers to stop work.

As spokesman for the Conservative Party, he was keen to uphold the principles, regardless of whether it would lead to an escalation of the conflict. He was nevertheless mostly matter-of-fact and subdued in form. However, in the debate on amnesty for those who had violated the Arbitration Act, he was harsh. "To the best of my knowledge, it is a very dubious step to initiate some amnesty practices on the part of the Storting," he said during the debate.[11] He was not of the mind to show lenience because an offense had been committed as civil disobedience and not as a regular criminal act. He also argued against repealing Section 222 II of the Penal Code in 1935. He stated that "I, for my part, will not participate in relaxing the requirement for effective legal protection of the individual's freedom and right to self-determination."[12] The argument that the provision only protected the right to work during a conflict and not otherwise, did not impress him.

Jørgen Christian Andreas Grøner was born in 1882 in Gjerstad and passed his law degree in 1904. He was a lawyer and later a military attorney and state attorney from 1918–1930. In 1929 he was appointed as magistrate in Sør-Østerdal. 1915–1930 he taught criminal law at the University of Oslo. Grøner served on several occasions as an extraordinary judge in the Supreme Court.

As a public prosecutor, Grøner was notorious for his hard line against members of the labor movement, including as a prosecutor in the big military strike case in 1924. For this he was rewarded with the poem "*Lovedderkoppen*" (Law Spider) by the poet Rudolf Nilsen. "You're a spider, Mr. Lawyer." "But if there is chance of prey, you are happy! Then you hoist yourself down your thread with a cheerful mind - because you have said that law is law. At least for the little ones!" And the poem ends with: "And even if it is high treason to put the lawyers' law for hate - we say coldly and openly: It is we who are harboring plans to overthrow your state." Grøner presided over a number of the cases under the Penitentiary Act in connection with the logging conflicts in Østerdalen, and he was one of the judges who used the harshest punishments in such cases.

[11] Stortingstidende, forhandlinger i Odelstinget 10 June 1929 p. 494.

[12] Stortingstidende, forhandlinger i Odelstinget 13 June 1935 p. 517.

One of the prominent Labor Party politicians at the time, mayor, and parliamentary representative Olav Sæter from Elverum and Grøner carried on a vendetta against each other. In a case against a forest owner who refused to pay tax before he could see the municipality's arrears lists, Grøner came with accusations against Sæter and four other municipal politicians. He accused Sæter of having abused his authority as mayor and parliamentary representative to have a tax debt cancelled. Sæter and the other four sued Grøner for libel.

Grøner was upset about even having to stand on the dock. "He bears his teeth and looks madly at the five plaintiffs," Hamar Arbeiderblad reported.[13] The case went on for several years, as the case was stayed for an investigation into the tax affairs of the plaintiffs. When the verdict was finally handed down on 5 March 1935, the court pronounced Grøner's statement "dead and ineffective".

Elverum municipality was one of the few municipalities where the Labor Party used its majority to elect exclusively Labor Party members as lay judges and jury members. Sæter stated that the Labor Party fought a guerrilla war against Grøner because of the way he dealt with workers under the Penitentiary Laws. Grøner, on the other hand, was an outspoken opponent of lay judges in the administration of justice. He compared it to a surgeon at the operating table being forced to have a municipally elected trustee as an equal.[14] In this, he had the opinion of many prominent lawyers against him. The jury system was not just one of the favorite issues of the Liberal Party, it had solid support from many judges.

7.7 The Legal Complex

The Arbitration Act was effectively killed by civil disobedience, where also prominent lawyers publicly supported the demonstrators. The final death thrust to it was given by President of the Labor Court Paal Berg. From an examination of the cases brought against workers under section 222 II we saw that that courts did not particularly follow up the intentions behind the law. The provision quietly became "the object of mild torture on the part of the judges", its content was "rewritten" by the courts and, in some rare cases, was openly sabotaged.

How can we explain the approach of the judicial system to the Penitentiary Laws and to Section 222 II of the Criminal Code? The courts in general were loyal to the Arbitration Law, but this changed with section 222 II. There may be several explanations. One factor may be that the first case dealt with by the Supreme Court, which became a guideline for lower court practice, the case of the action in Grytåa, came up for consideration in January 1929, that is after the demise and the amnesty granted to the campaigners against the Arbitration Act. The Storting thus signaled that the workers' actions should be met with tolerance and not with harsh

[13] Hamar Arbeiderblad Wednesday 10 May 1933.

[14] Dagbladet Saturday 13 April 1935.

punishments. The president of the labor Court, Paal Berg, who at the same time was president of the Supreme Court, had also shown lenience in his dealing with the construction worker conflict and had demonstrated that even illegal action could be rewarded with a new and more beneficial collective agreement. Thus, restraint was the message when it came to an important part of the penitentiary laws. Of course, this was not a legal argument in the question of how to deal with violations of the criminal code, but it set the tone for how to approach the other parts of the laws. One cannot ignore the fact that this may have influenced at least some of the judges in the Grytåa case.

Nor can we ignore the skepticism that many within the legal profession expressed directly or indirectly towards the laws that were passed in 1927. Firstly, we had the radical jurists who, both in public opinion and in the courts, worked to delegitimize and take the sting out of the legislation. The lawyers associated with LO were quick to take advantage of the openings that the Supreme Court judgment in the Grytåen case gave to argue in favor of acquitting workers who campaigned against strike-breakers. Several of these lawyers were brilliant lawyers with respect far beyond the ranks of the labor movement. The lawyers were also publicly active in pamphlets and newspaper articles.

Such activity was not limited to the bar. Supreme Court judge Karl Frimann Dahl wrote several newspaper articles in which he criticized the Arbitration Act, calling it slavery and unconstitutional. The then district court judge Carl Bonnevie characterized the Arbitration Act as contrary to general principles of justice and in conflict with general legal awareness. In an article that looks like an echo of the argument of John Rawls and Ronald Dworkin, which of course it was not since it was written over 40 years before Rawls and Dworkin, he called for tolerance and leniency in sentencing the activists.[15] In this they legitimized the sharp criticism of the penitentiary laws as illegitimate laws.

Such misgivings extended far beyond the circles of the radical jurists. Well-known and respectable professors such as Ragnar Knoph and John Skeie expressed their skepticism. Professor of labor law Kristen Andersen did the same later. Paal Berg's intervention in the conflict in the form of the settlement in the construction workers' dispute in the Labor Court must also be seen in this light. In effect, Berg overturned the arbitration court's judgment, as he failed to follow what was the obvious order of the law, namely, to establish that a strike against the arbitration award was illegal. Berg had also previously shown his skepticism by as minister of justice stopping the process of adopting the Penitentiary Act in 1924. This was one of the first things he got involved in when he became Minister of Justice (Hem 2012, p. 313).

The skepticism was not limited to obvious authorities such as Knoph, Skeie, and Berg. Several observers have pointed out that state prosecutors and judges disliked to apply Section 222 II of the Criminal Code. There were examples of judges who let their criticism of the law shine through in their instructions to the jury.

[15] In Arbeiderbladet on Tuesday 3 July 1928.

What happened was the mobilization of a segment of the "legal complex"; a cluster of actors who related to each other through common interests and a multitude of different processes Karpik and Halliday 2011, p. 220). Interests, connections, and actions unite members of the legal profession in something that can be called a legal complex. A legal complex gathers around common interests in being able to act as an autonomous profession in the legal institutions. The legal complex is a concept aimed at explaining the dynamics of legal mobilization across occupational boundaries.

The concept of the legal complex recognizes that lawyers' politics and collective action are intertwined with other legally trained members of other occupations, such as the judiciary and the civil service. With the historian Francis Sejersted, one can say that it is the "resistance element" of the law that comes into play, linked to the liberal ideology of the rule of law (Sejersted 1993, p. 264). Therefore, the legal complex often defends liberal values such as freedom of speech and association, freedom of business, property rights and the independence of the courts. Since the legal profession is often entrusted with the protection of such interests, one might say that the interests that the legal complex mobilizes to protect to some degree, are the self-interests of the legal professions. In the penitentiary laws, both the freedom of association and the freedom of speech was at stake. At the time, the laws were perceived as undermining the basic legal fundament of equality before the law.

The theory of the legal complex is based on the work of the French sociologist Lucien Karpik and the American legal sociologists Terence C. Halliday and Malcolm M. Feeley. Through studies of many countries at different times, they have shown how members of the legal profession in different positions within the legal order, the administration and the private sector mobilize as a legal complex in favor of political freedoms (See most recently Feeley and Langford 2023). As Liu and Halliday write in their book on defense lawyers in China:

> Over the last four hundred years and across the world, individual and collective action by lawyers, and often a wider range of legally trained occupations such as judges or legal academics, to transform illiberal politics into an open and liberal political society can repeatedly be observed. In this new political society, institutions and practices are both transformed and maintained such that the structures of society press insistently, even if unevenly and episodically, towards basic legal freedoms, vibrant civil societies, and moderate states. (Liu and Halliday 2016, p. xi)

The studies of legal complexes show how members of the legal profession regularly organize themselves as a pressure group in situations that are critical in the struggle for political freedom. This is something that consistently happens in the name of the law and with some support both from the bar, judges, public lawyers, and legal scholars, often in collaboration with civil society organizations. Members from different parts of the legal profession come together in temporary clusters as segments of the legal complex. The connect through professional or personal networks, temporal alliances over profiles cases, in formal or informal communities and many other ways.

According to the theory, lawyers have notable advantages in political mobilization because they are often uniquely able to exercise moral authority in the name of technical competence. Liu and Halliday forward the following theoretical propositions that characterize the mobilization of the legal complex (Liu and Halliday 2016, pp. 3–11):

- In light of authoritarian policy there will be segments of the practicing bar that strive to institutionalize basic legal freedoms.
- Lawyers who strive for basic legal freedoms often insist that this is only possible if state power itself is fractured, most importantly through some independence or autonomy of the judiciary.
- While lawyers play a role in constituting the justice system of a state, and hence might be thought of as officers of the court or servants of the state, historically they have also fought to position themselves as actors in civil society.
- Lawyers have the capacity to check arbitrary state power, pursue legal proceduralism, and call for judicial independence. Concomitantly, they can mobilize and form alliances with the media and other sectors of civil society to protect the basic legal rights of citizens.

Such mobilization is not inevitable, and it does not involve the whole profession. It is often met with counter-mobilization or with a large part of the profession being passive or indifferent. When a legal complex mobilizes it is not for social justice but for restricted liberal freedoms, which are important for the rule of law and also the autonomy of the profession. The theory of legal complexes labels this political liberalism which has three principal components: basic legal freedoms, the moderate state, and civil society.

The enactment of the penitentiary laws with the reactions this provoked was such a critical situation which mobilized the legal complex. The laws went a long way in limiting freedom of association by depriving workers of the opportunity to form effective organizations that could support them in their struggle, and by taking away the effect of their most important means of action, namely the strike weapon. They handed over one party in a basic social conflict, unarmed, to the arbitrariness of the other party and thus violated the basic principle of equality before the law. It was not just about the usual effect of the law affecting different groups differently, such as the ban on begging, which of course affected the poor and the rich in different ways. Here the inequality was deeper as the laws in their intention and effect directly took sides. By criminalizing support for illegal actions, they also went a long way in limiting freedom of expression.

Of course, not all members of the legal profession supported the labor movement, probably even most were on the bourgeois side. But there were many enough who reacted to the one-sidedness of the penitentiary laws and who mobilized against them. The laws attacked the autonomy of the law and made the law a tool for one party in a harrowing social conflict. It was this that triggered the lawyers' resistance, and it is reasonable to assume that the effect of this was shown in the courts' approach in the cases of infringement of the Penal Code Section 222 II.

The dynamic forces are explained by the theory as the "push" factor of political liberalism and the "pull factor of the actor's embeddedness in the societal order. The political liberals are the vanguards of action for political liberalism, but as underlined by Liu and Halliday, their sense of justice, fairness, or professionalism may still press not-liberal embedded and non-embedded practitioners "to demand in their everyday work exactly the kinds of protections for their clients and themselves that are integral to politically liberal regimes (Liu and Halliday 2016, p. 172)." Utilizing these variables, we can categorize the main legal actors in the following way:

	Liberal	Not liberal
Embedded	Progressive elites Emil Stang (attorney, judge) Karl Frimann Dahl (SC judge) Carl Bonnevie (judge) Paal Berg (SC judge) Ragnar Knoph (law professor)	Pragmatic brokers Jon Skeie (law professor) Erling Broch (SC judge) Paul Ivar Paulsen (SC judge)
Not embedded	Political activists Trygve Lie (attorney) Viggo Hansteen (attorney) Michael Puntervold (attorney) Cornelius Holmboe (attorney, MoJ)	Routine practitioners

The persons identified here were connected through different networks. One obvious network was the labor movement with the Labor Party and the Communist Party. Stang, Dahl, Bonnevie, Lie, Hansteen, Puntervold, and Holmboe were all engaged in this movement. Both Holmboe and Lie served as Ministers of Justice for the labor Party and Berg as Minister for a liberal government. Bonnevie, Dahl and Berg were members of Stortinget, Bonnevie and Dahl for the labor Party and Berg for the Liberal Party. Another network was the labor law litigant lawyers, comprising Stang, Lie, Hansteen, Puntervold, and Holmboe. Berg, Dahl, Broch and Paulsen were Supreme Court judges. Knoph and Skeie were law professors. Stang was also connected to them through his brother Fredrik Stang, another law professor. The Stang brothers were sons of a former prime minister of the conservative party, and Emil Stang later was appointed to the Supreme Court where he ended up as its president, successor of Paal Berg.

The pivotal case on section 222 II was the case against the demonstrating timber workers at Grytåen, which was decided by the Supreme Court in early 1929. In this case, 5 of the 7 judges voted for the acquittal of the demonstrators of the charges brought under section 222 II. One of the 5 was the progressive judge Karl Frimann Dahl. Two of the others were the judges Erling Broch and Paul Ivar Paulsen, none of whom had engaged themselves in the political cause for the workers' movement in any way. Paulsen was one of the judges calling for harsh measures in the case against the newspaper editors who had published articles in support of the illegal action of the construction workers. The remaining two where judges from lower courts with temporary assignments to the Supreme Court.

The laws actualized a dilemma that judges can face when there is a strong conflict between, on the one hand, positive law and, on the other hand, a fundamental feature of the Western legal tradition, such as equality before the law (Graver 2018). Tradition expects judges to loyally enforce the law. On the other hand, tradition also expects judges to protect the fundamental ideals of the rule of law. Sometimes these come into conflict. The quotations above from Knoph and Berg show that leading legal thinkers at the time openly acknowledged that judges could come into such a normative conflict between positive law and the demands of the legal tradition. Judges can avoid this conflict by interpreting the law restrictively or by setting the law aside as part of the judicial review of the legislation. "A law whose content is opposed by the legal consciousness will thus, first of all, quietly become the subject of mild torture on the part of the judges", wrote Ragnar Knoph. "Perhaps completely unconsciously, the 'servants of the law' will tug at it to bring its content into harmony with their sense of justice, and under this meek but firm pressure, the edges that the sense of justice disapproved of are often polished off (Knoph 1923, p. 24)." He continues: "And if the law nevertheless hardens and refuses to comply with the demands of legal awareness, its content is quietly and imperceptibly rewritten in the dark recesses of legal awareness, until one day it is ascertained that it is not the law's own thought content, but something quite different that is living right in the people."

A restrictive interpretation, such as the Supreme Court and many of the lower courts made of Section 222 II of the Criminal Code, is not uncommon. In this case, there was an active movement in the legal complex to do this. At the same time, the amnesty for those convicted after the action against the arbitration law showed that there was no clear determination among the legislators or in the government to force the legislation through in its strictest form.

The many acquittals nevertheless provoked strong reactions from parts of the civil society. The conservative press referred to acquittals as "class justice", with accusations that lower courts set aside the law based on political considerations. The Labor Party was accused of abuse of power in the election of lay judgers and jury members. The investigations of the elections in 1928 and 1931 show that this was consistently incorrect. Moreover, it was not the working class that the judges protected in their approach to Penal Code Section 222 II, it was law's autonomy and its authority as an independent conflict resolver. The legal complex sided with the rule of law, not with the working class.

7.8 Could the Protests Have Led to Higher Levels of Confrontation?

The official view on civil disobedience in Norway is that it represents a disrespect of democratic procedures and of the authority of the law. This has been a consistent view in Norwegian politics and law up towards our time. In a comment on the disobedience against the development of the Alta-Kautokeino waterway the then president of the Storting Guttorm Hansen (Labor Party) wrote that civil disobedience represents a "danger" to government by the people (Hansen 1981, p. 143).

Should a civil disobedience campaign succeed, he wrote, the effect "would be that many lost confidence in the Storting's ability to govern, they would soon ask for the strong man who can govern without bothering with such soft compliance." Also, "for the individual elected representatives, a frustration would obviously develop which could either lead to a general decision-making crisis in controversial matters, or an aggressive attitude which would reject all objections in matters of this nature." Should an action not succeed, the risk would be for it to develop into "constant confrontations between campaigners and the police, between campaigners and construction workers and between campaigners and counter-campaigners." This would be equally detrimental to the social fabric.

The controversies over the Alta development were deep and large in Norway. This explains such strong words from a leading politician from the labor party. But his views are nevertheless representative of views widely held even today, and most probably in the 1920s.

Still, it is strange that a Labor Party representative born in 1920 could see disruption of the social fabric as a decisive argument against civil disobedience, given the importance of such action to the labor movement at the time of his youth. Admittedly, Guttorm Hansen opens for civil disobedience "where absolutely fundamental rights are violated by authorities who no longer want to stick to the rules of democracy." He also makes an exception for refusal to do military service or labor disputes that are illegal in the "labor law sense." Such actions are not civil disobedience by his definition.

It does not make much sense not to count the mass violations of the Labor Disputes Act's prohibition against supporting illegal strikes or the systematic refusal to bow to Section 222 II of the Criminal Code as civil disobedience. In both cases, the action was directed against the legislation, and not just against a recalcitrant employer. The aim was to get the legislators to change what were perceived as illegitimate laws, and the means were disregarding the laws.

Regardless of whether Guttorm Hansen would count the actions against the penitentiary laws as civil disobedience or not, he presented a principled argument against civil disobedience that there is reason to take seriously. The main arguments against civil disobedience are that it undermines the rule of law, that it undermines the democratic process and that it can lead to increase in violence.

Thus, Civil disobedience, in the view of its critics, undermines respect for the authorities, can lead to rebellion and destabilize society's institutions. This is the hypothesis the authorities often start from when they crack down with a heavy hand on civil disobedience as mass crime. This reaction is often supported by the courts. "Those who resort to illegal means to push their views through do not follow the rules of the legal order," says the Supreme Court in one of the cases following the actions against the development of the Alta watercourse in 1981.[16] "Should such confrontations become commonplace, it could have serious consequences for society and the democratic form of government. The protesters had to understand all this,

[16] Rt. 1981 p. 21.

and when sentencing it must weigh heavily that they did not remove themselves after the chief of police had given his order," says the court in another case from the same conflict.[17] The words of the President of the Storting and the Supreme Court express the attitude of the establishment towards civil disobedience in Norwegian society.

A classic argument against civil disobedience is that it undermines respect for the authorities and entails a danger that this could spread. Transferred to the history of the Penitentiary Act, this would imply a hypothesis that it was the authorities' restraint that led to the decline in the level of conflict beyond the 1930s and that the protests had no role in this.

If we look at how the conflict over the penitentiary laws unfolded, this is obviously not correct. The respect for the authorities was weakened even before the actions took place. One can of course argue that this was due to illegal actions in the years before 1927, so that this confirms the theory. But the follow-up was that the authorities first tried harsh measures, first with the police and courts against the fund raisers and then with the police against the demonstrating timber floaters and other workers in conflict. But the hard line was soon given up, both with the amnesty in 1928 and with the courts' restrictive interpretation of Section 222 II of the Penal Code. According to the theory, this should have led to less respect for the authorities and an increasing number of actions. This did not happen. On the contrary, in any case, the courts gained increased respect in the labor movement, and the Labor Party mostly protected a non-political appointment of the lay judges. The dispute over the Penitentiary Act thus does not support a hypothesis that it is necessary for the authorities to crack down on civil disobedience in order to prevent the authorities' authority from disintegrating and respect for the laws from weakening. These events also do not lend support to Guttorm Hansen's concern that people will lose confidence in the Storting's ability to govern if the decisions are not implemented.

Another objection to tolerating civil disobedience is that it can undermine democracy. Democracy's decisions are not implemented, and actions can promote the interests and opinions of those who are good at getting their point of view through. In an argument against Brownlee's theory on civil disobedience, Daniel Weinstock spells out this objection (Weinstock 2016). Weinstock claims that Brownlee's argument on democracy is that the democratic process, with all of its deficiencies, is disadvantaged in reaching better decisions than those closer to the problem and vulnerable to the force of lobbying. Allowing for civil disobedience may therefore allow for corrections of deficiencies in the democratic process.

According to Weinstock, this represents a too simplified view of the democratic process. Democracy is not only about deliberations in parliament. Political parties have elaborate processes developing their political platforms, that include consultations with citizens and stakeholders, experts and research, and many other elements. These platforms are presented to the population and debated in public, reviewed and criticized by political commentators and form part of election campaigns. There is no

[17] Rt. 1981 p. 887.

reason to assume that this is an inferior way of reaching good solutions to the conscientious reflection of the individual or groups of individuals.

Building on arguments of Jeremy Waldron, Weinstock also underlines that democracy in any case is not about finding the "right" solution or to put an end to disagreement, but about agreeing to live with the outcome of the democratic processes despite disagreeing with the specific outcomes. The civil disobedient does not have a claim to put his or her disagreement above the disagreement of others, in the face of a democratic compromise.

These are strong arguments against tolerating civil disobedience as a regular part om democratic politics. But Weinstock agrees, however, that civil disobedience has a place where values relevant to a policy debate are simply not being considered, even after attempts at introducing the value in question, or when groups are being effectively disenfranchised. Also, when the mechanism of public engagement break down, for instance through the imposition of unreasonable conditions on demonstrations and strikes, can civil disobedience be justified according to Weinstock.

But even under such conditions there are arguments against civil disobedience. The Norwegian professor of criminal law Anders Bratholm wrote the following in an editorial on the development of the Alta river and civil disobedience (Bratholm 1980):

"If they are at the same time strong, and skilled at marketing their view, they will have good opportunities to have their "description of reality" accepted by public opinion as correct, or at least to have their view forced through. A weak group will have far less chances of winning, even if it has a significantly better case. Added to this is the fact that the disadvantages of illegal actions in practice will easily hit the weak groups particularly hard, because the strong also show strength in such cases, whether it is a question of scarcity of vital goods due to illegal strike, or unemployment or lack of energy because hydro-power development is hindered. In a rule of law and welfare state, the law is not least the protection of the weak."

Added to this is the fact that groups who see themselves benefited from defying the law will easily consider that the conditions for civil disobedience are met precisely in their case. And should society accept civil disobedience regardless of the cause that is pursued? If not, how does one distinguish between the "good" cause for which civil disobedience is acceptable and the bas for which it is not? The Supreme Court underlines this in one of the cases about the actions of Extinction Rebellion where it says that "the determination of reaction should not depend on whether the court agrees or disagrees with the political message linked to the action".[18]

This objection is on a slightly different track than the objection based on democracy. The objection here is that civil disobedience should be dissuaded for the sake of justice and the protection of the weak. Rawls and Dworkin have an answer to this. In their view, it is possible to distinguish between different acts of disobedience. Dworkin believes that even if all forms of actions are illegal, the legal

[18] HR-2022-981-A.

apparatus need not be morally blind in dealing with them. It is not whether the court "agrees or disagrees in the political message" of the actions that is decisive, but whether there are morally relevant differences between the actions that should dictate different treatment of them.

Again, the conflict over the penitentiary laws supports the theory presented by Rawls and Dworkin. It was not so much the judges' support of the workers' political struggle as their reaction to legislation perceived as fundamentally unjust that motivated their lenient treatment of the activists. As we have seen, there were skilled lawyers who sympathized with the labor movement and who promoted its policies. But they alone would not have been able to influence the judicial system's treatment. It was only when they became part of a legal complex with a larger group of actors that tolerance towards the illegal actions gained traction. If one subjects civil disobedience actions to an assessment based on ethical theory, one need not fear that the authorities' tolerance leads to the rights of the strong at the expense of the weak.

What about the Alta action, where the authorities did not give in to the protests and got the development completed. It is true that the authorities won the battle, but there are many indications that they came out of it weakened. A later report concluded that based on "certain incidents in connection with the development of the Kautokeino-Alta watercourse", the government agreed to speed up the work on the constitutionalizing of the Sami's rights and the establishment of a separate Sami parliament.[19] Such concessions would hardly have been given if it were not for the actions against the development of the Alta river.

References

Aubert V (1989) Continuity and development in law and society. Norwegian University Press, Oslo

Bals J (2022) Streik! En historie om strid, samhold og solidaritet. Res Publica, Oslo

Berg P (1930) Arbeidsrett (labor law). Olaf Norlis forlag, Oslo

Berg P (1947) Dommerkallet (the call of a judge) a speech given in 1937 at a film recording for the Statens Filmarkiv, printed in Paal Berg. For godvilje og rett, Gyldendal Oslo

Berntsen H (1995) To liv - en skjebne (Two lives—one destiny). Aschehoug, Oslo

Bjørgum J (2022) Emil Stang, Store norske leksikon https://nbl.snl.no/Emil_Stang_-_1882–1964

Bratholm A (1980) Sivil ulydighet. Lov og Rett

Brownlee K (2012) Conscience and conviction: the case for civil disobedience. Oxford Legal Philosophy, Oxford

Bull T (1955) Mot Dag og Erling Falk (Mot Dag and Erling Falk). Cappelen, Oslo

Dahl KF (1928) Voldgiftslovens sammenbrudd (Collapse of the Arbitration Act), Kongsvinger Arbeiderblad Saturday 4 August 1928

Dworkin R (1977) Taking rights seriously. Duckworth, London

Espeli H, Eivind Næss H, Rinde H (2008) Våpendrager og veiviser. Advokatenes historie i Norge, (The history of lawyers in Norway). Universitetsforlaget, Oslo

[19]NOU 1984:18 p. 54.

Feeley MM, Langford M (2023) Nordic exceptionalism and the legal complex. In: Feeley MM, Langford M (eds) The limits of the legal complex Nordic lawyers and political liberalism. Oxford University Press, Oxford
Feinberg J (2003) Natural law: the dilemmas of judges who must interpret immoral laws in Joel Feinberg, problems at the roots of law: essays in legal and political theory. Oxford University Press, Oxford
Furre B (1992) Norsk historie 1905–1900. Det Norske Samlaget, Oslo
Graver HP (2019) Der Krieg der Richter Die Deutsche Besatzung 1940–1945 und der norwegische Rechtsstaat. Nomos, Baden-Baden
Graver HP (2018) Judicial Independence under authoritarian rule: an institutional approach to the legal tradition of the west. Hague J Rule Law 10:317–339. https://doi.org/10.1007/s40803-018-0071-8
Graver HP (2024) Valiant judges and iniquitous law. Routledge, Oxon
Habermas J (1985) Civil disobedience: litmus test for the democratic constitutional state. Berkeley J Sociol 30:95–116
Hagtvedt B (ed) (1981) Den vanskelige lydigheten (the difficult obedience). Pax, Oslo
Hambro CJ (1960) Francis Hagerup 1853–1921, in Konservative menn i Norges nyere historie: 15 politiske essays: Tilegnet C.J. Hambro i anledning av hans 75 års dag 5. januar 1960, Oslo
Hansen G (1981) Sivil ulydighet—en fare for folkestyret? (Civil disobedience – a danger to the people's government?) In: Hagtvedt (ed.) Den vanskelige lydigheten (The difficult obedience). Pax, Oslo
Hansteen V (1927) Tukthuslovene Fagorganisasjonen under offentlig administrasjon (the penitentiary law, the trade unions under public administration). Andelsforlaget Ny Tid, Oslo
Hem P (2012) Megleren Paal Berg 1873–1968, (The Mediator: Paal Berg 1973–1968). Aschehoug, Oslo
Høidal O (2009) Trotskij i Norge: et sår som aldri gror (Trotsky in Norway: a wound that never heals). Spartacus, Oslo
Karpik L, Halliday TC (2011) The legal complex. Annual Rev Law Soc Sci 7:217–236
Knoph R (1923a) Rett og rettsbevissthet, (law and legal awareness). Olaf Norlis forlag, Kristiania
Knoph R (1923b) Rett og rettsbevissthet (law and legal conciousness). Olaf Norlis forlag, Kristiania
Larsen E (1952) Det store gjennombruddet 1902–1952 (the great breakthrough 1902–1952). Nord Troms Arbeiderparti, Narvik
Lie H (1975) Som jeg ser det, bd. 1 (As I see it. Vol. 1). Tiden, Oslo 1975
Liu S, Halliday TC (2016) Criminal defense in China: the politics of lawyers at work. Cambridge Studies in Law and Society. Cambridge: Cambridge University Press, https://doi.org/10.1017/9781316677230
Lysaker O (2022) Civil disobedience in the age of the eco-crisis. Norwegian Philosop J 57(3–4): 208–218. https://doi.org/10.18261/nft.57.3-4.10
Maurseth P (1999) History and politics articles through fifty years, no. 56 writing series for history and classical subjects, Trondheim 2009
Nykänen T, Lehtola V-P, Vinkka B (2022) Civil disobedience and artistic protests the Áltá and Deatnu disputes and the development of Sámi resistance in Nykänen, Tapio, Tiina Seppälä, and Petri Koikkalainen. Civil disobedience from Nepal to Norway: traditions, extensions, and civility. Ethics, human rights and global political thought. Routledge, Taylor & Francis Group, London
Olsen H, Lie T (1931) De arbeiderfiendtlige lover og Kampen mot dem, (the anti-worker laws and the fight against them). Arbeidernes faglige Landsorganisasjon, Oslo
Ousland G (1975) Fagorganisasjonen i Norge 2 De store kamp-åra 1921–1931 (the trade union in Norway 2 the great fighting years 1921–1931). Tiden, Oslo
Rawls J (1972) A theory and justice. Oxford University Press, Oxford
Ross A (1953) Ret og retfærdighed, (On law and justice) Nyt nordisk forlag, Copenhagen
Sandmo E (2005) Siste Ord Høyesterett i norsk historie 1905–1965 (last word supreme court in Norwegian history 1905–1965). Cappelen, Oslo

Scheuerman WE (2021) Introduction: why, once again, civil disobedience? In: Scheuerman WE (ed) The Cambridge companion to civil disobedience. Cambridge University Press, Cambridge https://doi.org/10.1017/9781108775748
Schock K (2021) Consequences of civil disobedience. In: Scheuerman WE (ed) The Cambridge companion to civil disobedience. Cambridge University Press, Cambridge
Sejersted F (1993) Demokratisk kapitalisme (Democratic capitalism). Universitetsforlaget, Oslo
Sharp G (1973) The politics of nonviolent action, part two: the methods. Extending Horizon Books, Boston
Stang E (1927) Arbeiderklassens kommunepolitikk. Andelsforlaget Ny Tid, Oslo
Weinstock D (2016) How democratic is civil disobedience? Crim Law Philos 10(4):707–720
Zakariassen A (1969) Trygve Lie, egen publikasjon, Oslo

Chapter 8
All's Well That Ends Well

8.1 The Battle Was Fought in Court, Not Outside of the Law

The penitentiary laws and the subsequent political struggle in the courtrooms, in municipal councils and in the Storting (the Norwegian Parliament), led to a development that threatened the autonomy of law. In order for the law to function normally, the population must accept laws as binding and the courts as neutral and independent enforcers of the laws. Regarding the penitentiary laws, the labor movement and large sections of the population considered them illegitimate. They refused to bow to the laws and openly challenged them, with thousands in open defiance of the Arbitration Act. The authorities reacted with police, fines and criminal proceedings, with little effect. Sections of the working class had long seen the courts as biased class courts. Now the opinion that the courts were politicized, spread further into the population.

This situation could have escalated. Many have claimed that the democratic system itself was at stake in the interwar period, and that the fight between labor and capital could have ended much worse (Olstad 2014, p. 150). In many countries these conflicts ended in fascism. This did not happen in Norway. Instead, the construction workers' conflict has been highlighted as a turning point in a development from class struggle to class cooperation (Olstad 2009, p. 332). Is what happened around the penitentiary laws a confirmation of the claim by John Rawls that civil disobedience can be stabilizing for democracy? In my view, the effects of the popular resistance against the penitentiary law, the action of the courts to modify the repression, and the government's reaction with acceptance, not further repression, have been overlooked as important factors.

The legislature passed laws that many saw as an illegitimate abuse of legislative power. This led to a mass mobilization against the laws. The authorities reacted with police actions and fines to no avail. The authorities could have stepped up the oppression to force the people into obedience. The courts were reluctant to apply

H. P. Graver, *Democracy and Lawlessness*,
https://doi.org/10.1007/978-3-031-69055-6_8

the law in the strictest sense and the conservatives and the Farmers' Party wanted to change the law to ensure better control over the courts, particularly the rules on election of lay judges and jurors. This could have brought the courts more clearly into the social conflicts, which could have weakened the perception of their legitimacy, and thus the rule of law itself. Instead, the courts challenges the law. It is not a given that those in power respect the independence of the courts when the judges resist the authority of the state. In an escalation of conflict between the courts and the other state powers, the courts usually lose and become obedient enforcers of repressive legislation (Graver 2015, p. 53). It is not certain, however, that a toughening of the reactions and coercive measures would have led to the workers' movement giving up. It could have become more militant in its protests, and thus have provoked even stronger reactions from the authorities and led the development into a negative spiral for democracy.

The criminalization of measures against strikebreakers and the liability rule with the reverse burden of proof for the unions were seen as depriving the workers of their only means of power against the employers, as taking away their weapons in the struggle for their very existence. The right for the workers to act collectively in defense of their interests was at stake. This was no neutral framework, within which the conflict between labor and capital could play out. It was a one-sided support to the employers in order to protect them from the effects of strikes by being able to substitute the striking workers from the masses of unemployed. It was the ideal setting for Ricardo's iron law of wages: the employers could push wages down to the lowest level of subsistence.

Although the law was based on the principle of the freedom of work, it did not provide any security for the freedom of workers who opposed the employers. They could freely be blacklisted and excluded from work. It also did not give anyone the right to work. It was a protection of the employers' right to dismiss and employ anyone they chose, and not a protection of the right of the individual worker. The law therefore interfered with fundamental freedoms in a discriminatory manner. In the era of mass unemployment, there were plenty of unemployed people willing to work for lower wages. The use of punishment against striking workers in such conditions was perceived as intolerable and raised demands to take control of the appointment of lay judges if the courts started to enforce such laws.

The hardliners on the conservative side tried to kick up the storm, with demands to take hard action against those who would not respect the laws. The Conservative Party and the Farmers' Party were in favor of harsher punishments and against amnesty after the construction workers' conflict. Moreover, they strove to deprive the municipal councils of the power to decide who should be able to act as lay judges and jurors. In the shadows lurked the fascists.

The changes to the law in 1927 were a clear escalation in the use of the legal system to combat the growing labor movement. One could even say that the relation between the law and labor conflicts was fundamentally changed. Previously, the legislature had brought law into the conflict by adopting the Labor Disputes Act. Now the conflict was brought into the law, depriving it of its role as a neutral umpire. The conflict culminated with the great lockout and the Battle at Menstad in 1931, when state police and soldiers were deployed against protesting workers. The legal basis was Section 222 II of the Penal Code with its criminalization of measures against strikebreakers. But when the Battle of Menstad took place, most of the sting had already been taken out of the penitentiary laws. 1931 was the last year in a series with tens of thousands of workers in conflict. From 1932, the level of conflict dropped significantly. There were still many conflicts, but they were small and only involved just over 6,000 workers a year, compared to almost 60,000 in 1931.[1] 1927 could have been the starting point for a conflict over industrial relations which could have had far more damaging effects on Norwegian society and the rule of law. Instead, it was the peak of a wave that subsided rather quickly. The main agreement between LO and the Norwegian Employers' Association in 1935 finally marked a clear transition to a new era of cooperation, and a recognition by the establishment of the workers' trade unions as a responsible party.

There are many explanations why things went as they did, and why the struggle over the right to strike did not escalate from 1927 onwards. One explanation could be that the major conflict between the parties in 1931 ended in a draw and created a balance of power where neither the workers nor the employers had the resources to continue. This is a common explanation in the literature. Considering the economic crisis and the mass unemployment, it was important for both parties to find solutions (Olstad 2009, pp. 344–345).

Another explanation could be that in Norway, fascist movements lost the battle with the socialists to win support from the masses of unemployed (Bjørgum 1983). The similar development in the USA is explained by the fact that the economic crisis from 1929 mobilized the electorate and discredited business interests (Wisman 2022, p. 339). This development strengthened the moderate forces on both wings. However, the example of Germany shows that crises can strengthen the radical extremes.

The Norwegian historians Øystein Sørensen and Nik. Brandal talk about a Norwegian political culture, characterized by peaceful solutions and compromises, which goes back to 1814 and which goes through the shattering events of Norwegian history of 1884 and 1905 (Sørensen and Brandal 2018, p. 52). It would lead too far to embark on a complete analysis of this in this context. Here we shall content ourselves with pointing out certain developments in the development of legal policy, the struggle over the law and how the courts should apply it, which can contribute to the explanation.

It is important that the struggle was brought into the courts. There was no consistent strategy on the part of the labor movement to disregard the law and the courts as "class laws" or pure means of oppression by the bourgeoisie as the communists saw it. The law was not written off by the labor party or by the influential circles in the labor movement. Even the illegal actions against strike breakers were mostly restrained and disciplined. Moreover, the actions were not carried out as actions against the system as such, but against individual laws, which were perceived as a breach of basic justice, fundamentally out of step with the

[1] Statistical yearbook 1935, table 163 Labor conflicts p. 144.

general concept of law in society. The demand was not revolution, but justice in legislation. Here the movement's lawyers played a role. Trygve Lie moderated LO's reaction and contributed to the conflict not escalating into a battle over the courts in the municipal councils.

For their part, the authorities largely adhered to the law in combating illegal actions. Although the authorities went so far as to legalize the near fascist private civil defense as reserve police and military personnel were called in for some conflicts, the authorities refrained from using means of terror against insurgent tendencies.

In this connection, it is interesting to look closer at the legal processes.

8.2 The Courts and the Arbitration Act

The first sign of de-escalation was when the construction workers' dispute was resolved by settlement brought about by Paal Berg in the Labor Court. The employers brought the illegal action before the Court. A victory here would give the employers access to implement a lockout, and an opportunity for a significant escalation of the conflict. The stage was set for a judicial confirmation that the conflict was illegal. This in itself was something everyone knew, but such a judgment would be an important underlining of the law's authority, and an important weapon in the hands of the employers.

After the negotiations had been completed and the case taken to court, Paal Berg contributed to an amicable solution. This was, according to trade union historian Gunnar Ousland, "a step quite outside of all ordinary legal practice (Ousland 1975, p. 361)." The fact that Berg announced a settlement in this way was perceived at the time as putting "an end to all prosecution and all talk of illegal action."[2] In other words, the president of the Supreme Court Paal Berg and the Labor Court refused to act as an extended arm for the employers and the authorities. If the labor court had contented itself with ruling that the conflict was illegal, this could undoubtedly have led to an expansion and sharpening of the conflict. Now it was muted instead.

The government also faced opposition in the Storting when the Arbitration Act was to be extended. The Labor Party was of course against it. Now the employers' association was also against it, they had regained their traditional opposition to state interference in wage setting. Both LO and the employers' association were determined to resolve the construction worker conflict through conciliation, and this contributed to the solution in the labor court. The Arbitration Act had not prevented the strike by outlawing it, and the result was a negotiated solution anyway, not the decision by the arbitration court. The employers influenced the Conservative Party, which together with the Labor Party voted against the extension of the law in the

[2] Østfold Arbeiderblad, cited after Hem p. 316.

Storting. Thus, an important part of the potential for conflict brought about by the changes in the law in 1927 was already gone after 1 year.

The fundraisers were punished for their support of the construction workers' strike. The Supreme Court underlined that no account should be taken of the political and ideal motives of those who defied the law. However, the wounds were healed by the amnesty act which was passed in 1929. This exempted from criminal prosecution and punishment "persons who, on the occasion of the 1928 strike in the construction trades and the graphic trades, have been charged, prosecuted or convicted for violating Act no. 2 of 5 May 1927." Rolf Thommessen, editor of Tidens Tegn and representative of the liberal party, explained why he voted for the amnesty law as follows:

> It may be unavoidable that this country splits into two irreconcilable camps, and should that happen, each of us will have to do what the position requires. But I have no doubt that it would be the greatest calamity that could befall our country and the future of the people if we were to get there. I therefore think that perhaps for that reason it could be worth showing that, in any case, on the side of the non-socialist parties, class struggle and all that is connected with it is not regarded as a completely inevitable development. I will therefore vote for the proposal for special amnesty.[3]

There was a broad settlement behind the amnesty law, which thus left the punishment for disobedience behind.

8.3 The Courts and the Criminal Code § 222 II

Penal Code section 222 II had a longer lifespan and a different history. While the Supreme Court and the ordinary courts applied the penal provisions in the Labor Disputes Act according to the intention during the conflict over the Arbitration Act, they helped to moderate the provision which was supposed to protect those willing to work during conflict.

The provision raised many questions of interpretation and can thus be said to have been poorly prepared. The opinion of those who were in favor of the provision was to expand the use of criminal law to suppress conflict. The ministry said in the proposal that it was necessary to strengthen the protection of those willing to work, and that it was necessary to criminalize "a number of acts of a more or less serious nature that the criminal law does not cover at all." As an example, the ministry mentioned "demonstrative stalking the person willing to work, gathering about him, publication of the name of the person willing to work, as well as many cases of threats," and "even a threat of a behavior which in and of itself is not unlawful can, however, exert equally strong and undue pressure."[4] The ministry also held that the penalty framework should be changed since it had proven difficult to get the courts to

[3] Stortingstidende, forhandlinger i Odelstinget 10 June 1929 p. 504.

[4] Ot. prp. No. 54 (1924) pp. 2–3.

apply prison sentences according to the rules that applied. However, the courts did not follow this up in their application of the law, therefore nothing much was changed.

Thus there were several conciliatory actions which helped reduce the level of conflict which the adoption of the penitentiary laws created. The effect of the Arbitration Act was curtailed by the labor court and Berg allowing settlements, instead of branding the conflict as illegal and giving the employers the opportunity for further escalation. The Storting did not extend the Arbitration Act, and those who had been punished in connection with it were granted amnesty. The Supreme Court narrowed down Section 222 II of the Criminal Code so that it in practice lost its effect. Workers who gathered in large demonstrations against strikebreakers were not punished, and even when there were episodes of the use of force and violence, the leaders could not be punished unless they themselves had been directly involved. Together, this accomplished that the rift created with the passage of the penitentiary laws did not develop into a devastating battle over the courts.

8.4 The Repeal of § 222 II

On Friday 8 June 1934, 50,000 people gathered for a demonstration outside the parliament building in Oslo. They demonstrated against the Penitentiary Law and the "gag laws". People stopped working all over the city. The reason was that Stortinget was to deal with new rules on voting in connection with salary negotiations. These rules were set aside by the main agreement of 1935, where the parties themselves decided how voting on proposals for a collective agreement should take place. The slogan for the demonstration was "Away with all penal laws, full freedom for the workers to fight for their dearest interests."[5] People also gathered for demonstrations in Trondheim, Bergen and other cities.

The labor agitator Martin Tranmæl stated in his speech: "Laws that lack any legal basis (. . .) are a violation of the people's legal awareness. You cannot demand that they be respected. It is every worker's moral right and duty to break them. (Violent and prolonged applause.) And if now those on the other side of the barricade pass the law, they should know that the fight will be intensified, not only against this law, but against all other reactionary policies."

In 1935, three weeks after it was appointed, the coalition government between the Labor Party and the Farmers' Party put forward a proposal to repeal Section 222 II of the Criminal Code.[6] The proposal was put forward by Trygve Lie, now Minister of Justice. In its justification, the ministry showed that the Criminal Code Committee and Professor Jon Skeie had argued for a repeal of the provision. In the Storting, the Conservative Party voted against. They agreed that the provision had received an

[5] Arbeiderbladet Saturday 9 June 1934.

[6] Ot.prp. No. 35 1935 On changes in § 222 of the Criminal Code.

unfortunate design from a legal technical point of view, but would not repeal it without conducting a review of the other provisions of the Criminal Code which could be applied in the event of coercion and threats, in order to ensure effective legal protection for those willing to work. For the majority, it was crucial that one should not maintain a provision that an entire class felt was aimed at them. The new era, with greater understanding between social classes, was also highlighted. The former opponents, the Labor Party and the Farmers' Party, were now together in a government coalition. With this, the most controversial part of the penitentiary laws was removed from the legislation. The last part, the penalty provision for breach of the duty of peace in the Labor Disputes Act, disappeared from the law only in 1956. But there it had led a dormant existence for 20 years.

The history of the penitentiary laws shows the law's limitations and about how its autonomy is threatened when it is used as a means of combat in the battle between strong social groups. The Arbitration Act and the other changes to the rules on industrial action were clearly biased and favored the employers at the expense of the employees. The government and the authorities tried to take a hard line to push the law through. This line was nevertheless quickly given up after the conflict with the construction workers had ended in a settlement. The investigation shows that this cannot be explained solely by the labor movement forcing the conservative majority to its knees through its actions. The development can hardly be understood without considering how the penitentiary laws violated fundamental principles of justice and how this affected the general perception of the laws in large sections of the population. The laws also triggered the formation of a legal complex that opposed them, and which gathered support in central parts of the legal apparatus.

The events could have resulted with not only the law, but also the legal order as such losing legitimacy and being perceived as biased and political. Instead, the story stands as an example of how civil disobedience against unjust laws can stabilize and strengthen the system. The government had the wisdom to realize this, and to withdraw the repressive measures. The courts contributed to moderation by interpreting the law restrictively. Thus, the conflict contributed to a strengthening the rule of law and to the strong position that it has in our country today.

References

Bjørgum J (1983) Arbeidsløshet og fascisme. Et perspektiv på Quisling og Nasjonal Samlings politikk i begynnelsen av 1930-årene (Unemployment and fascism A perspective on Quisling and Nasjonal Samling's policy in the early 1930s). Tidsskrift for arbeiderbevegelsens historie 1983(1):107–153

Graver HP (2015) Judges against justice on judges when the rule of law is under attack. Springer, Berlin-Heidelberg

Olstad F (2009) LOs historie. Med knyttet neve, bd. 1, (The history of the federation of trade unions With clenched fist) 1899–1935. Pax Forlag, Oslo

Olstad F (2014) Det farlige demokratiet Om folkestyrets vilkår i Norge gjennom to hundre år (The dangerous democracy On the conditions of the people's government in Norway over two hundred years). Aschehoug, Oslo

Ousland G (1975) Fagorganisasjonen i Norge 2 De store kamp-åra 1921-1931 (The trade union in Norway 2 The great fighting years 1921–1931). Tiden, Oslo

Sørensen Ø, Brandal N (2018) Det norske demokratiet og dets fiender 1918–2018 (The Norwegian democracy and its enemies 1918–2018). Dreyers Forlag, Oslo

Wisman JD (2022) The origins and dynamics of inequality: sex, politics, and ideology. Oxford University Press, Oxford

Chapter 9
Epilogue

9.1 The Small White Farm

I sit at my desk and look at the picture of the farm where my grandfather grew up, my family roots. A stone fence marks the bottom of the picture. It has a wide opening, and the dust road leads straight onto a barn bridge and into a red barn. To the left are two storage cages, one white and one red. The small, white farmhouse has a cornice with a sheet over it. Under the ark is an open porch. The trees that grow towards the yard are fir trees. Behind the small field slopes, and behind that again rolling hills, green-brown in front and bluish behind. No other buildings are visible in the picture. The farms were small, few, and far apart. The land did not provide income for many, the people did not live in abundance, but they managed. They were independent, and they were literate. They were small-scale people, just like the many who fought against the Penitentiary Act in town and country. They were fighting for better conditions, but they were also fighting because the authorities suddenly turned the law and the legal system against them. Then even law-abiding people could break the law. As I look at the picture I wonder, does the history of the Penitentiary Laws have any significance for us today?

Grandfather was a man of peace, but he was from Telemark and often amused himself by quoting the seventeenth century clergyman and historian Peder Claussøn Friis that the inhabitants of Telemark "are evil, wicked, hard, wild and rebellious people, of whom all who live in this country had their greatest desire in old time to kill bishops and priests, bailiffs and commanders (Friis 1632, p. 46)."[1] One should not accept all kinds of suppression from the authorities.

We have no great battle between classes in today's Norway, we have no fight over the rule of law. But we do not have to go far to find such conflicts and battles. A country many regard as a beacon of liberty and democracy, the USA, is characterized

[1] Peder Claussøn Friis, Norriges and surrounding islands truthful description, Kiøbenhavn 1632 p. 46.

H. P. Graver, *Democracy and Lawlessness*,
https://doi.org/10.1007/978-3-031-69055-6_9

by a deep crevasse splitting both people and politicians who mostly do not talk to each other. President Trump himself attacked the courts, and both parties are doing what they can to install their people as judges. This is how the Republicans managed to remove the right to free abortion as a right in the constitution. Although policy is often decided in other forums, the battle for control over the law, when politics is played out in the courts, can have a great impact on people's well-being. As I write this, the New York Times is reporting that Democrats are doing what they can to delegitimize the Supreme Court, which they believe has been hijacked by Republicans. The population's trust in the court has halved in a few years.[2]

9.2 Democracy Under Attack

Democracy is under attack in many places. The research project V-Dem writes in its report for 2024 that the level of democracy enjoyed by the average person in the world in 2023 is down to 1985-levels; by country-based averages, it is back to 1998.[3] The years of progress for democracy since the fall of the iron curtain have been erased. The judiciary, especially the courts, are at the center of the attacks. Several researchers use "rule of law backsliding", the downsizing of the rule of law, synonymous with decline in democracy (Pech and Scheppele 2017). Autocratic rulers of our time shun institutions that can hold them to account, such as the press, academia and the judiciary, and direct their actions against them.

The Hungarian professor and former judge of the Human Rights Court András Sajó has studied how those in power in many countries maintain a semblance of legality while in reality they dismantle democracy. In countries such as Venezuela, Turkey, Hungary and Poland, this follows a familiar pattern (Sajó 2022, pp. 66–84). First, the authorities attack constitutional courts, as we have seen in Poland. The aim is to put them out of the game, and later turn them into supporters to ensure the legitimacy of those in power. The judges can be put out of business by lowering the retirement age so that they can be replaced, by fabricating allegations of corruption or other wrongdoing, and by ensuring political control over the appointment of new judges. In Poland, the authorities refused to announce the judgments of the Constitutional Court while the dispute was ongoing, and therefore did not comply with them either. As soon as the constitutional courts are put out of action, much has been achieved for those in power. Reforms, that in themselves can be masked as necessary reforms of a malfunctioning system, are systematically used in bad faith to dismantle legal controls on power. Sajó calls this cheating as a form of government.

We saw how the courts quickly became targets in connection with the penitentiary laws. Many in the labor movement believed that they had to take control of the

---

[2] Supreme Court Criticism - The New York Times 22 May 2023, https://www.nytimes.com/2023/05/22/briefing/supreme-court-criticism.html accessed 05/22/2023.

[3] https://www.v-dem.net/documents/43/v-dem_dr2024_lowres.pdf p. 6.

judges to prevent the application of what they saw as illegitimate legislation. The conservatives, for their part, attacked the courts, and the juries in particular, for not practicing the law as they intended it to, and sought to change the very system of judicial appointments. Controversies surrounding the content of the legislation quickly shifted to become controversies surrounding the courts and their operation. Thus, the conflict followed a pattern that we see repeating in our time.

Several countries introduce disciplinary measures against recalcitrant judges. Authorities in Poland banned judges from refusing to recognize pro-regime "neo" judges, ordering them to cooperate with them. They refused judges to refer cases to the European Court of Justice "untimely" and made it an offense for judges to publicly speak out against government policy (Bojarski 2024). Some of the measures that the authorities in Poland have taken against the judges go further than the measures taken against Norwegian judges during the Nazi Occupation.

9.3 Targeting the Courts

What makes the courts the main target for those in power in the so-called "illiberal democracies"? One reason may be that the courts' control of political decisions has increased in recent decades because of international judicialization. Thirty to forty years ago, only few countries in Europe had some legal control over legislation. The development of international human rights protection and legal integration through the EU has changed this.

Increased judicial control of political decisions is partly a consequence of conscious political choices, such as in Norway in 2014 when a bill of rights was written into the Constitution. But it is also a consequence of a separate logic in the application of law in courts, which interpret rights catalogs dynamically and which must decide on increasingly complex questions about the demarcation of rights against each other. Finding the balance between the interests of plot owners and plot holders was previously a purely political issue. Now it is a question of a legal boundary between the right to property and the right to housing.[4]

The legalization has given rights vis a vis the authorities, but aspects of it have led to criticism in many countries. In England, the government recently presented a bill that would remove the influence of the Court of Human Rights over British courts and authorities. Legalization increases the need for autocratic leaders to clip the wings of the courts, while the discussion also in solid democracies that respect the rule of law gives them an opportunity to justify such a policy.

A further explanation for the policy targeting independent courts can be found in the history of many of the countries where democracy is under attack. The notion of independent courts was introduced in these countries quite recently, partly under

[4] See case before the European Court of Human Rights, EMD-2008-13221, Case of Lindheim and others v. Norway.

pressure from outside, for some countries in connection with the negotiations on EU membership. The relationship between the state powers and the functioning of the judicial apparatus follows long historical lines and can take a long time to change, even in the case of quite fundamental changes (Graver 2018).

Historically, the courts in countries such as Hungary and Poland have long been under political management and control. This has created roles and attitudes that change slowly (Fleck 2021, p. 1315). The position of court leader was a key position for political influence during the communist era. The presiding judge's influence over the court has persisted into the democratic era and has made it easy for the authorities to exert influence on the courts by securing loyal presiding officers.

The traditional role of a judge and legal education do little to encourage independence and critical thinking. This makes the judges vulnerable to measures by the authorities that aim to control them. It also contributes to politicians' expectations of obedient judges and lowers the threshold for intervening if they experience criticism or opposition. In Hungary, the authorities have reinforced this by writing into the Constitution that the judges must interpret the laws as the politicians have intended them (Gyöngyi 2020, p. 205). If our authorities had attempted this in 1927, it would have been much more difficult for the courts to interpret Section 222 II of the Penal Code as they did. On the other hand, it had set the stage for a confrontation between the authorities and the Supreme Court over the courts' interpretative autonomy.

At the same time, all was not well in the legal system in countries such as Hungary and Poland before the autocratic parties came to power. After the transition from the communist era, few of the countries carried out any comprehensive reform of the communist legacy. Trust in the courts is consistently low among the population, and there is a need to carry out reforms both to improve the quality of the judicial system, to overcome corruption and obedience and to increase people's trust in the judiciary. This is different with us.

Perhaps that is also part of the explanation for the fact that the battle did not develop in a destructive direction in Norway in the 1930s. We have a longer tradition of independent courts and judicial autonomy than the countries of Central Europe. The debate on the structural reforms of the courts in Norway shows how any court reform easily gets overtones of discussions about the rule of law. A similar structural reform carried out in Hungary or Poland would perhaps not be innocent. In order to distinguish between measures that are reforms of the judiciary and measures that are attacks, a holistic approach must be taken (Čuroš and Graver 2020). Reforms that are unlikely to threaten the rule of law here are dangerous in countries with different experiences and traditions.

Both the Court of Human Rights and the European Court of Justice have dealt with several cases about the measures in Hungary and Poland. Both courts have emphasized that a contextual approach must be taken, where one must look both at the legislator's purpose and compare with international standards for the independence of the courts. But most importantly, the measures must be seen from the perspective of the image they create of the judges' independence and political interference in the courts. With such a perspective, there is no doubt that what the authorities in Poland have been doing is attacking the courts, not reforming them.

How the legalization of conflicts with great contradictions turns the courts into targets is a parallel between the battle over the penitentiary laws in Norway in the 1920s and 30s and the battle against the rule of law in countries such as Poland and Hungary today. Judges sometimes have the courage to respond to legislation that violates elementary principles of the rule of law or fundamental principles of justice. The penitentiary laws challenged justice in that the law was not perceived as neutral. A judge characterized Section 222 II of the Criminal Code as a "panic measure with significant technical deficiencies".

9.4 Weaknesses Revealed by the Pandemic

Does this mean that all is well with us and that our rule of law is protected from authorities that set aside elementary guarantees of the rule of law? The answer to this question depends on the specific circumstances in which the problem arises. The context is decisive. The studies by Halliday, Karpic and Feeley of the functioning of legal complexes under different conditions and in different countries show that the courts and jurists are not active in the defense of liberal values where the security of the state is threatened and in situations of a state of emergency Halliday et al. 2007, p. 25). The Covid-19 pandemic showed how even Norwegian authorities can resort to legal rules and measures that deviate from normal principles of the rule of law if the situation is perceived as serious enough.

On 12 March 2020, the Prime Minister announced "the most invasive measures the Norwegian population has experienced in peacetime."[5] The population was presented with two resolutions: Resolution pursuant to Act on Protection against Infectious Diseases Section 4-1 second paragraph on prohibition of meetings and closure of business, Established by the Directorate of Health on 12 March 2020 based on Act 5 August 1994 No. 55 on Protection against Infectious Diseases diseases § 4-1 second paragraph, cf. first paragraph letters a and b and Resolution pursuant to the Act on Protection against Infectious Diseases § 4-1 second paragraph on quarantine (isolation) after travel outside the Nordic region Established by the Directorate of Health on 12 March 2020 with authority in Act 5 August 1994 No. 55 on protection against infectious diseases § 4-1 second paragraph. The country was closed down and isolated from the outside world.

The following week, another bomb exploded. An extensive mandate for the government to issue laws (the corona law) was prepared in secret and discussed with the largest parties in the Storting outside the usual rules for presenting legislative proposals. When this was announced in the afternoon before the matter was to go to the Cabinet, everyone thought that the law would be hammered through in the Storting within a few days without discussion. At the same time, the Prime Minister

[5] Aftenposten 12 March 2020, https://www.aftenposten.no/norge/i/mR4pRL/regjeringen-setter-inn-de-sterkeste-tiltakene-vi-har-hatt-i-fredstid.

and several of the country's mayors threatened with civil defense and home guards to chase people home from their cabins when a ban on staying on leisure property outside their own municipality was introduced. This was a winter weekend, when traditionally many Norwegians leave their homes in the cities for the snowy mountains.

The extensive measures were gradually eased out over the spring, and the government did not get the powers it wanted in the Corona Act. The bill met with public criticism, and the Storting unanimously agreed on a less extensive and better controlled mandate for the government to issue laws to remedy the pandemic's harmful effects.[6]

When the infection rose again in the autumn of 2020, the restrictions were reintroduced, and new restrictions were added. Among the most controversial were restrictions on the number of visitors allowed in private homes. In some municipalities the limit was two people. When, in January 2021, the government submitted for consultation a proposal authorizing the government to introduce a curfew, the result was a storm of protests. This led to the proposal being dropped. Many also protested against the introduction of corona passports for domestic use. This resulted in that such passports were not introduced domestically in the same way as in many other countries.

Some of the measures eventually ended up in the courts. Despite the fact that these measures were very intrusive and restricted fundamental rights, the courts failed to subject the assessments of the authorities to particularly intensive scrutiny.[7] In the cases it heard about the infection prevention measures, the Supreme Court ruled that, even though the courts in principle have the possibility of a full review, the courts must be careful in reviewing the purely medical assessments that are linked to the terms "clear medical justification" and "necessary for reasons of infection control". In on case, the Supreme Court gave the term "medical justification" a very broad understanding and let it also include assessments of risk for non-compliance with the restrictions.[8] Assessments of the extent to which people comply with rules or adjust their behavior lie not within a traditional competence of the discipline of medicine. If such assessments are to be decided by discipline, they belong more in the sociology of law than in the medical field. Such assessments are made by the courts in many contexts, whether it is a question of assessments of prevention in criminal law or tort law, or of deciding which interpretation of a rule best fulfills the purpose of a law. When the Supreme Court leaves the assessment of such matters to the authorities, it gives the authorities leeway than cannot be justified by the authorities having better insight and knowledge than the courts.

The Supreme Court also said that the courts must be reticent to review proportionality assessments that contain "broad societal considerations". In effect, this means that the authorities can intervene and limit human rights in an exceptional

---

[6] See Prp. 204 L (2019–2020).

[7] See HR-2022-2171-a and HR-2022-2172-a.

[8] HR-2022-718-A.

situation without an effective judicial review, as long as they claim to take rights into account in their assessments.

Other controversial measures were related to entry restrictions. Norway had among the strictest entry rules in Europe, with practically closed borders to anyone who not living in Norway except to perform socially necessary work. Many of those who were allowed to enter had to quarantine in special hotels. This was an extensive restriction of liberty and freedom of movement, and the way in which the quarantine hotel system was also practiced in some cases, must be considered a deprivation of liberty according to the way this is interpreted by the ECHR.[9]

It was also problematic in terms of legal certainty that the rules gradually became very complex, were changed frequently and were issued at both state and municipal level, with partly contradictory content. The communication of the rules was often unclear, with difficult distinctions between requirements, orders, recommendations, and advice. The result was that it was almost impossible to familiarize oneself with the legal situation, which was shown, among other things, by the Prime Minister herself having to endure a fine for breaking the rules.

The effects of the restrictions were often uncertain. Currently, there was little research into the effects of the authorities' regulations. This means that an assumption that the infection control measures were necessary appeared as a pure hypothesis.

The government set up a commission early on "*to get a thorough and comprehensive review and evaluation of the authorities' handling of the pandemic*". In its first interim report, NOU 2021:6, the commission dealt with the first months of the pandemic. From a rule of law perspective, it is worth noting that the commission says that "For the commission, it appears clear that neither the government, central administrative bodies nor the municipalities paid particularly much attention to the overarching principles surrounding the rule of law in the initial phase of handling the pandemic." The commission notes that the Constitution was breached when society was shut down without a decision in the cabinet, something which the constitution requires "in cases of significant importance". The commission also criticized that "even though the measures were described as the most invasive in Norway in peacetime, the decision does not contain any assessments of whether the measures are compatible with constitutional and human rights and obligations."[10]

In its final report, NOU 2022:5, the commission says that the authorities' handling of the pandemic worked well. At the same time, the commission has several critical remarks about the infection control measures, such as requirements for

[9]In case LH-2022-126731, the Hålogaland Court of Appeal rejected the defendant's objections to the legality of the quarantine hotel scheme. The judgment does not go into the objections that were raised in the Ministry of Justice. It is also linked to the rules after they were changed so that everyone who came from countries with a high infection rate had to be quarantined. Originally, only those who had been on so-called "unnecessary journeys" had to be quarantined, regardless of the infection rate in the country they had been in. Originally, moreover, you could not test your way out of quarantine.

[10]NOU 2021:6 p. 304.

isolation and quarantine, entry restrictions and the closure of businesses and social functions. Neither the infection control rationale nor the relationship to human rights were sufficiently researched, which led to the decisions being ineffective, having unintended consequences and being difficult to implement. Overall, the government's basis for deciding on infection control measures was in many cases inadequate, according to the commission.[11]

What have we learned from a legal and rule of law perspective? We have seen how easily our central authorities set aside clear rules in the Constitution and basic legal principles when society is gripped by panic. We have also seen that the population largely accepts this. Nor do the courts seem willing to intervene and defend the rule of law by subjecting the authorities' assessments to any extensive control. The does not only apply to the assessments under the Infection Control Act, but also to the assessment of whether restrictions of rights in the Constitution and the ECHR are proportionate.

Under normal circumstances, the administration has a certain leeway to exercise professional and political discretion. Trust in the administration is high in Norway. At the same time, the administration is monitored by the parliament and a critical press. Judicial control is not the only instrument to keep the administration in check under normal conditions.

Under the pandemic this was different. The administration operated under broad delegated powers without the transparency and public consultation that is required under normal circumstances. Nevertheless, the Supreme Court dealt with the issue of judicial review as if conditions were normal. But during the pandemic, we did not face a normal situation. The pandemic brought society and the authorities into an extraordinary situation, a national emergency. In such a situation, the authorities go further than usual within the framework of authorizations that have been designed with more ordinary situations in mind, and they can deviate from normal rules for the processing of cases such as investigation, hearing and justification. Neither parliamentary control nor civil society control functions as normal. In such a case there is a special need for effective legal control mechanisms, to ensure that the authorities respect basic rights and legal principles. The rulings of the Supreme Court contain no traces of this.

The Corona Commission wrote in its first report: "When you are in the middle of a serious crisis, many will be able to claim that it is understandable that the authorities concentrated on solving all the specific problems that arose along the way and did not make the comprehensive assessments that are made under normal circumstances. But the democratic principles, the Constitution and human rights frame what the authorities can do also in a crisis. And it is precisely in such situations that the Constitution and human rights become particularly important. It is in such situations that the risk is greatest that the Constitution and human rights will be violated, and that citizens' rights may be violated. The reflex of the authorities should therefore have been to make sure that the handling of the pandemic took

[11] NOU 2022:5 p. 450.

place within the framework set by the Constitution and human rights. That obviously did not happen at the beginning of the pandemic, when neither central nor local authorities assessed the infection control measures against constitutional and human rights standards.[12]

And I would add: It did not happen during the continuation of the pandemic either. The Corona Commission's second report shows how the objections of the lawyers in the Ministry of Justice were overruled when the boarder control measures, and quarantine hotel scheme were introduced.[13]

As an emergency, the pandemic was special in that there was no major political disagreement that society was facing a crisis and that extraordinary measures were necessary. But the guidelines drawn up by the Supreme Court for the judicial review will easily become guidelines for a new crisis where the government uses exceptional powers. It is not certain that this will be a situation equally free of political controversies.

There were some events during the pandemic that could have led to larger conflicts. The first was in connection with the demonstrations and rallies in support of George Floyd at the beginning of June 2020. Despite the authorities refusing to waive the infection control rules and their warning people against demonstrating, thousands took to the streets in Oslo, Bergen and Trondheim. The online newspaper Vårt Oslo claimed that the George Floyd marking was the largest demonstration in front of the Storting ever and wrote that there were between 12,000 and 15,000 people in Eidsvoll Square.[14] Although three times as many demonstrated against the Penitentiary Act in the same place in 1934, this was still a considerable crowd, especially in light of the fact that the infection prevention rules prohibited gatherings of more than 50 people outdoors and required people to keep distance from each other. Had the authorities followed a hard line, this could have led to confrontations with undermining effects for the trust in the authorities. Here, the police showed great wisdom by problematizing the relationship between freedom of expression and the infection control regulation, allowing freedom of expression to take precedence.

The authorities also showed restraint by not introducing the most far-reaching measures that were proposed, curfews and vaccination passes. This contributed to us not having an escalating conflict about the corona regulation.

---

[12] NOU 2021:6 p. 304.

[13] NOU 2022:5 p. 196.

[14] Our Oslo Friday 5 June 2020 https://vartoslo.no/african-students-association-arise-bydel-sentrum/george-floyd-markeringen-den-storste-demonstrationsjonen-foran-stortinget-noensinne/241349.

9.5 Managing Exceptions

Extraordinary events put society's institutions under pressure. At the same time, they are a test of the stability of the institutions, and how suitable they are to handle large and unexpected challenges. Society rarely emerges unchanged from such events. In the best case, the institutions come out better equipped to handle new challenges. In other cases, the institutions are weakened, if not completely collapsed. In still other cases, society puts a parenthesis around the events and continues as before. The use of exception powers can help to generalize governance through exceptions. Most regimes, even the most authoritarian, see a need to legitimize their rule against legal principles. Invoking exceptions is both a common and effective way of doing this.

The most dangerous are the exceptional situations which have been brought about by the authorities themselves, as the Nazis in Germany used the opportunity when the Reichstag burned down in 1933 to claim that the communists were starting a violent uprising. Situations that provoke a political overreaction are also dangerous, such as the attacks on the USA on 11 September 2001 that led to the war on terror in Afghanistan and later Iraq. Pure natural disasters, such as the pandemic we faced, need not be a threat to the stability of society. But it can lay the foundation for abuse of exceptional situations in later cases, if the authorities do not have the necessary legislation in place, so that they must resort to exceptional powers.

The corona situation showed how easily the authorities deviate from normal procedures and requirements for legal certainty, and with what ease they interfere with basic rights, even in countries where we believe that the rule of law is strong. In the next crisis, we cannot be sure that the crisis will be equally uncontested and the entire population equally obedient. Harsh measures on the part of the authorities can arouse counter-reactions in the population, which in turn will lead to demands for stricter and more consistent enforcement. One must hope that in such a case the courts will seek guidance in the approach that the courts chose to the penitentiary laws rather than the approach that the Supreme Court chose to the corona legislation.

The conflict surrounding the penitentiary laws subsided after a series of wise choices by the authorities and the courts. The driving force was nevertheless the great popular opposition to the legislation, which was shown, among other things, by the fact that thousands defied the penalty orders in protesting the Arbitration Act and in the mass demonstration against the anti-worker laws in front of the Storting in 1934. I think grandfather had reason to be proud he got fined. This was his diploma for participation in the struggle to fight back the penitentiary laws and thus for a more stable democracy.

References

Bojarski L (2024) Resistance against the rule of law backsliding — judges and citizens — the case of Poland, PhD Thesis. University of Oslo. https://www.duo.uio.no/handle/10852/105831

Čuroš P, Hans Petter Graver (2020) Dissimilar Similarities: Structural Reforms of the Courts in Norway and Slovakia, VerfBlog, 2020/11/26, https://verfassungsblog.de/dissimilar-similarities/ . https://doi.org/10.17176/20201126-123123-0

Fleck Z (2021) Changes of the political and legal systems: judicial autonomy. German Law J 22: 1298–1315. https://doi.org/10.1017/glj.2021.64

Friis PC (1632) Norriges oc omliggende Øers sandfærdige Bescriffuelse, (The true description of Norway and its surrounding islands) Kiøbenhavn

Graver HP (2018) Judicial Independence under authoritarian rule: an institutional approach to the legal tradition of the west. Hague J Rule Law 10:317–339

Gyöngyi P (2020) The obligation of judges to uphold rules of positive law and possibly conflicting ethical values in context. Neth J Legal Philos 2:196–217

Halliday TC, Karpik L, Feeley MM (2007) Introduction—the legal complex in struggles for political liberalism. In: Halliday TC, Karpik L, Feeley M (eds) Fighting for political freedom: comparative studies of the legal complex and political liberalism. Hart, Onati

Pech I, Scheppele K (2017) Illiberalism within: rule of law backsliding in the EU. Cambridge Yearb Eur Legal Stud 19:3–47. https://doi.org/10.1017/cel.2017.9

Sajó A (2022) Ruling by cheating governance in illiberal democracy. Cambridge University Press, Cambridge

SPRINGER NATURE

GPSR Compliance

The European Union's (EU) General Product Safety Regulation (GPSR) is a set of rules that requires consumer products to be safe and our obligations to ensure this.

If you have any concerns about our products, you can contact us on ProductSafety@springernature.com

In case Publisher is established outside the EU, the EU authorized representative is:

Springer Nature Customer Service Center GmbH
Europaplatz 3
69115 Heidelberg, Germany

The manufacturer's authorised representative in the EU is Springer Nature Customer Service Centre GmbH, Europaplatz 3, 69115 Heidelberg, Germany. If you have any concerns regarding our products, please contact ProductSafety@springernature.com

Printed and bound by CPI Group (UK) Ltd, Croydon, CR0 4YY
28/09/2026
02224070-0017